English Dramatic Form, 1660–1760

ENGLISH DRAMATIC FORM, 1660–1760

An Essay in Generic History

LAURA BROWN

New Haven and London

Yale University Press

Designed by Nancy Ovedovitz
and set in Century Medium type.
Printed in the United States of America by
Edwards Brothers, Inc., Ann Arbor, Mich.

Library of Congress Cataloging in Publication Data

Brown, Laura, 1949–
    English dramatic form, 1660-1760.

    Includes bibliographical references and index.
    1. English drama—Restoration, 1660-1700—History and criticism.
2. English drama—18th century—History and criticism. I. Title.
PR691.B7   822'.4'09   80-25702
ISBN 0-300-02585-8

10 9 8 7 6 5 4 3 2 1

For Walter Cohen

CONTENTS

ACKNOWLEDGMENTS —————————————

I am grateful to The Johns Hopkins University Press for permission to reprint in chapter 2 portions of my discussion of intrigue form, which originally appeared in "The Divided Plot: Tragicomic Form in the Restoration," *ELH* 47 (1980): 67–79, and to *Genre* for permission to reprint, especially in chapter 6, parts of "Drama and Novel in Eighteenth-Century England," 13 (1980). I must also thank the Committee on Research of the University of California at Riverside for consistent support in the form of various grants toward the completion and revision of the manuscript.

The present study owes an enduring debt to Ralph W. Rader, whose initial influence has shaped my understanding of literary form and whose criticisms of my work have sharpened its conceptual clarity. My differences from him are my most eloquent tribute to his intellectual generosity. I am further grateful to Eugene M. Waith for his reading of the manuscript and apt suggestions for its improvement, to Eric Rothstein for instructive disagreement and advice, to Jonas A. Barish, Norman Rabkin, and Alvin Eustis for early encouragement, and to Harry E. Shaw for a careful and invaluable critique. My greatest debt is to Walter Cohen, to whom this book is dedicated.

INTRODUCTION

The history of English drama in the century following the restoration of the monarchy is in some respects a simple tale. Despite the emphasis placed by recent critics upon its diverseness, the dramatic production of this period lacks the prolific variety that characterizes the Renaissance theater. And despite the complexities that modern readers have discovered in the best Restoration plays, they generally do not raise the vexing questions that pervade the drama of Shakespeare and his contemporaries. But this disarming simplicity conceals the presence of interpretive problems as significant as any that the study of generic evolution can pose. Most fundamental is the issue of generic history itself: how its process is to be discerned and documented, and how its trajectory is to be explained. A history such as this one can address these theoretical questions only at the local level, but it can nevertheless contribute a significant particular answer to the largest general problems posed by generic change.

More specific is the matter of the "decline" of the drama in the latter part of the century, and the coincidence of that decline with the rise of the novel. The first challenge in this case is to define "decline" in such a way that it designates particular formal facts rather than an unspecified evaluative judgment. The second is to explain the relationship between these formal facts and the emergence and success of a new genre. The ultimate test of this dramatic history, then, is in the extrageneric evidence of the rise of the novel. But the most specific questions of genre studies are always those presented by individual works, since they are the concrete embodiment of literary history. The task here is the difficult one of joining the most specific with the most general—of reconciling the details of individual texts with the processes of literary evolution.

These are the kinds of problems this book addresses. They are historical and conceptual problems, and as a result the argument that follows is a historical and conceptual argument. In both of these respects it differs from much of the recent criticism of this drama. Modern studies have characteristically confined themselves either to the Restoration or to the eighteenth-century stage, and often even within those periods to either comedy or tragedy. Furthermore, specialists in the theater have seldom referred to the other major genres of the time, notably neglecting the contemporary rise of the novel. This fragmentation has enforced an ahistoricism in drama studies. And it has led to a related alienation of literary modes or periods from one another, contributing, for example, to the contention that the comedy of manners and the heroic drama are irreconcilable products of a "schizophrenic" age, or to the tendency on the part of critics of Restoration plays to dismiss "sentimental" eighteenth-century drama out of hand.[1] From the initial revival of interest in this theater in the early years of the twentieth century, critics in the field, following the lead of the dominant theoretical trends in the English-speaking world, have produced studies emphasizing authorial biography, character psychology, theme, language, irony, ambiguity, and self-consciousness. Inevitably, few attempts have been made to address the issue of generic history.

Literary and theatrical historians have produced some of the broadest and most useful studies of the drama by describing its relationship to the political history of the period, to the survival of classical and Renaissance themes and motifs, or to the intellectual background of the age. But though these approaches are historical, their aim is typically not to explain the evolution of the genre, but rather to locate the plays in some larger context. The most recent critical histories—*The Development of English Drama in the Late Seventeenth Century*, by Robert D. Hume, and A. H. Scouten's section on "Plays and Playwrights" in *The Revels History of Drama in English*[2]—attempt to combine survey and interpretation, and their success is in their convenient admixture of intelligent particular explication with a seriatim description of the plays. These studies do not claim to be generic histories in any conceptual sense. They deliberately ask no questions of the drama, and thus, in principle, they see no direction in its development and no shape in its history.[3]

My essay finds both shape and direction. It addresses major questions that cannot even be asked in the context of the predominant assumptions of contemporary criticism in the field. This history does not seek to imitate the extensive theatrical and repertorial studies of Restoration and eighteenth-century drama that have been made available in recent years. It does not document debt or influence. It is a history neither of the theater, of the repertory, nor of dramatic taste. It is an essay in generic history, narrowly defined by the evolution of dramatic form.[4] Though its purpose distinguishes it from recent criticism, my study is perhaps even more heavily indebted to previous scholarship than most revisionist histories. Where my analysis is derived from or corroborated by earlier work, I have been able to assume and build upon an established critical heritage. I have profited almost equally, however, in those cases where I disagree, or where prior discussions reveal a significant interpretive crux. There I have sought to use the dispute itself as a means of illuminating the nature of the problem that caused it. In this respect my critical debts are genuinely catholic, and I tend to cite as evidence both supporting and opposing views.

This enterprise depends first upon the assumption that it is not only possible but essential to find a means of organizing and classifying the drama of the Restoration and early eighteenth century. Several recent critics have taken the opposite position, arguing that any codification is irrelevant, unwise, and even misleading; that the drama's uniqueness places it beyond classification; that is is too diverse to tolerate the definition of workable categories; or that the categories that have been applied are unclear, overly broad, or insufficiently inclusive.[5] In one sense, such admonitions are a welcome antidote to ahistorical generalizations, especially those made about the nature or spirit of the comedy of manners, and the field has profited from these critics' insistence upon the diversity and specificity of the plays. In effect, however, the argument that denies the possibility of classification and explanation merely represents a new kind of ahistoricism, one that simply perpetuates the limitations of the old in a different form. Such a position has serious implications for students of the drama, or of any discipline: in denying the validity of categorization, it denies in principle the possibility of knowledge, since our means of knowing is based on our perception of similarities and differences among the objects of our experience. Aside from the explication of individual texts, the drama is theoretically beyond explanation for critics of this persuasion. In fact, though, surveys of this sort are inevitably forced to fall back upon an approximation of the traditional categories.

But despite the inadequacy of their solution, the problem formulated by these critics remains a serious one: how to deal responsibly with the large volume of data presented by a well-documented genre. Fortunately, Restoration and early eighteenth-century drama is not the hardest case in this regard. The English novel of the nineteenth and twentieth centuries is considerably more diverse and experimental, and Spanish Renaissance drama offers the unhappy historian more than three hundred different extant works by a single playwright. As critics of these periods have shown, and as our own experience of perception may perhaps suggest, there is no necessary conflict between wealth of detail and the possibility of generalization. On the contrary, detail can serve to strengthen generalization, to give it greater breadth by sharpening its explanatory power. Previous attempts to provide a conceptual order to this drama have been unsatisfactory not because of the nature of the material, but because of the means used to organize it. The solution is not a rejection of order, but a new effort using a superior analytical tool.[6]

The second central assumption of this book is closely related to the matter of classification: the priority of major works in the study of literary history. Those critics who reject categorization necessarily also reject an emphasis upon representative plays, however they are defined. Indeed, a history that claims only to describe the literary events of a period must reject selectivity of any kind in order to fulfill its purpose. For critics who seek to organize and conceptualize literary history, however, the problem of selectivity is more delicate. In all but the most voluminous catalogues, some choice is unavoidable; and in this essay, as in any other, the choice of works reveals the fundamental premises of the method. A sample of the repertory from 1660 to 1760 would be essential to a history of the theater or of dramatic taste. But it is less important in a history of dramatic form, because, while repertorial favorites may influence original composition, they do not determine the direction of generic evolution. Shakespeare has held a prominent position in the English theatrical repertory since the end of the sixteenth century, but English drama of the past three hundred and fifty years cannot be reduced to a Shakespearean model. In the Restoration and eighteenth century, for example, playwrights from Dryden to Lillo produced imitations of Shakespearean tragedy, and yet we can easily distinguish between *All for Love* and *Fatal Curiosity*, or between either of these works and the Shakespearean plays that inspired them. In fact, as Nahum Tate's adaptations reveal, the interpretation of Shakespeare at any particular time in the history of the drama actually seems to accord more closely with the original composition of the age than contemporary imitations do with their Renaissance model.

The decision of whether to select "major" or "average" works from that body of original productions is more problematic. The best works of a period are those of most enduring interest, the works that survive the passage of time. An attention to plays like these has at least the advantage of avoiding antiquarianism and of addressing literature of recognized significance and merit. The obvious danger is that such a perspective may simply project present concerns into the past and thus impede our understanding of the age. The simple solution in this case is to read the major plays against the context of the minor works, using the latter as a constant test of the argument derived from the former. This, in part, is the method employed here. But my argument implies an even greater priority for the major literature. It suggests that the best works are more representative of their genre and of their period than minor or average works, because they come closer to fulfilling the potential of their form. They grasp the realities of their age more fully, and they embody its concerns and contradictions more completely. This in fact is the source of their aesthetic merit and the reason for their survival.[7] *The Conquest of Granada*, for instance, completely realizes the implications of heroic form in its incorporation and co-optation of the most radical possible challenge to the royalist status quo. *The Country Wife*, likewise, represents the fullest expression of the satiric potential of social comedy. In this sense, the lesser works of a period may be read against the context of the major works, as closer or more distant approximations of the deepest formal and ideological forces of their age.

The theoretical assumption behind this methodology is that of the intimate connection between literature and social history. This essay depends upon a definition of literary form that includes ideology: form is the meaningful aesthetic shape that men and women of a particular historical time and place give to their understanding of reality. It is not a simple reflection of social history. In fact, the connection between literature and society may be invisible, complex, or indirect. But literary form is ultimately imprinted with the ideology of the age.[8] In practice, the historical forces to which this argument refers are broad and undisputed social trends of general acceptance, they appear only at the periphery of my discussion, and they are greatly overshadowed by the more strictly literary emphasis of my analysis. In principle, however, they are essential to my thesis. They constitute the ultimate reference of my formal categories, the basis of my explanation of the parallels between the evolutions of serious and comic drama, and the source of my conceptualization of the whole trajectory of this generic history.

In the Restoration and early eighteenth century, the form of the drama can be most generally described as a coherent fiction. It is distinguished from forms that do not seek to tell a story, or that tell stories that depend not upon the controlled process of fiction, but upon some determinate connection with fact. More specifically, these plays are actions, constructed from the unfolding conflicts and relationships among characters whom we understand according to our evaluation of them in the terms of their represented fictional world. This evaluation is the basis of our comprehension of the plot and thus of our engagement in the story, since it directs our expectations about the characters' fates in relation to our immediate assessment of their merits.[9] Actions can differ, then, in regard to the terms of evaluation they represent, the kinds of characters and conflicts they depict, and the nature and dynamism of the relationship between their characters' deserts and fates.

The argument that follows begins with a designation of formal categories based upon the local definition of individual actions, and it ultimately uses the relationships among these categories as a means of assessing the nature and explaining the direction of dramatic evolution. The early forms of this century—heroic action and dramatic social satire—are parallel in the sense that their actions are both shaped by a social standard of assessment, enacted either in the niceties of the Platonic honor code or in the witty decorums of contemporary aristocratic

manners. By the end of the century, however, dramatic form is governed by an entirely different sort of structure, one that defines merit
in terms of inner moral worth and assumes a direct identification between audience and protagonist. This moral action is dominant in both
the drama and novel of the age,[10] and it is the antithesis of the social
forms of the Restoration. Though the moral action is coincident with
major technical innovation in narrative fiction, it is only imperfectly
realized in the drama. In fact, its emergence coincides with the repeated
occurrence of a series of similar structural difficulties that defy the
best efforts of the age's most talented playwrights. The example of the
novel, then, serves as a gauge of the drama's development. The formal
antithesis between the beginning and the end of this history is the conceptual basis for my explanation of that development. But the conclusion of the story must defer to its beginnings, of which it is a product,
and to the plays, ends in themselves, which give it substance and meaning.

PART I
SOCIAL FORMS, 1660–1677

ONE
Heroic Action

Heroic drama and comedy of manners are the familiar labels given to the major serious and comic plays of the Restoration English theater. In most criticism of the period, these descriptive terms are used to refer either to theme, to verse form, to the presence of certain kinds of characters, or to a particular artificial, sophisticated, and witty tone. Traditional categories of such duration and currency deserve respectful treatment, and they do provide an intuitively accurate and generally useful means of perceiving the large resemblances and distinctions among the plays of this period. But the imprecision of their definition and the diffuseness of their application have made it difficult to see any coherence either between the major and minor drama of the early Restoration, or between the traditionally irreconcilable serious and comic forms of the age.

If we accept the largest contours of these categories, however, and attempt not to transform them but to refine and clarify them—to provide them with precise and explicit definitions that extend beyond the narrow questions of theme, character, or language to the shape and significance of the whole drama—we can produce a set of formal concepts that remains true to the collective assessment of generations of audiences and readers and yet can also serve as a sharper critical tool. The broad notions of heroic drama and comedy of manners have an important but limited explanatory power; the technical formal concepts of heroic action and dramatic social satire, however, can provide the basis for a discussion not only of individual plays and of the relationship between similar plays, but also of the links among dissimilar plays, the decisive influence of Restoration forms upon the subsequent evolution of the genre, and the determining connection between dramatic form and the social context of the period.

The heroic action is shaped and governed by a system of precise epic, chivalric, or Platonic standards, which express the ideology of a self-consciously exclusive social class and which are justified aesthetically by neoclassical epic and dramatic theory. Alfred Harbage describes the heroic ideal as a "conception of virtue [that] was purely aristocratic, limiting the quality to the traits of epic heroes: physical courage, prowess in arms, magnanimity, and fidelity to a code of personal

honor."[1] The conflicts in these plays are defined, represented, and
resolved entirely in terms of this aristocratic code. The protagonists are
static emblems of Platonic or epic virtue, and their actions typically
consist of a series of episodes in which that virtue is enacted and reen-
acted. As a rule, characterization is simple rather than complex, character development is minimal or absent, and depth or interiority are rare.
The setting of this drama, like its language, is distanced and remote.
In fact, the stichomythic debates that are so typical of the heroic action
perfectly embody its most prominent and congruent formal attributes:
a remote, elevated style and a precise and invariable social code. This is
to say that the heroic plays of the period share a social form that reflects the historical context of an aristocratic, coterie theater and, more
specifically, the particular situation of the aristocracy shortly after
the monarchy's return.

     Within the general confines of this category, the heroic action evolves
from a rigid, straightforward, aesthetically simple, and ideologically
sanguine version of the form to an increasingly problematic and complex one. In early heroic plays, like those of Davenant and Orrery,
the governing aristocratic code is explicit and unambiguous. Character
and conflict are shaped directly by a clear evaluative hierarchy that
is rigidly and unvaryingly enacted in every episode of the plot. These
plays automatically reproduce a social ideal whose primary political
premise is royalist and whose central aesthetic quality is the elaboration
of a self-consciously elevated, elitist, or baroque manner. In Dryden's
mature heroic action, the form is complicated either by a fragmentation
of the aristocratic code itself or by the challenge of a radical protagonist who eludes the orderly assumptions of that code. When the complexity outweighs the efficacy of the standards, and the evaluative hierarchy
becomes arbitrary or meaningless, as in Lee's marginal heroic actions,
the form has reached the end of the period of its generic priority. Heroic
plays, like neoclassical epics, continue to be written in the late Restoration and early eighteenth century, but such works are historical anachro-
nisms, no longer central participants in the development of their genre.

I

The most important early example of the heroic action is William Davenant's *Siege of Rhodes* (Pt. I: 1656, Pts. I and II, revised: 1661).
Davenant is a significant figure for historians of the theater because of
his association with the dramatic efforts of Henrietta Maria's court,
his interregnum compositions, his own attempt at a heroic poem, and
his later role as patentee of the Duke's company. *The Siege of Rhodes*
is generally described as the first heroic play, and Dryden, the primary theorist of heroic drama, credits Davenant as well as Orrery with

substantial influence on the form.[2] More significant in the context
of this argument, however, is *The Siege of Rhodes*'s illustration of the
aesthetic and ideological simplicity of the early versions of the heroic
action. The play's ideal is the perfect conjunction of the Platonic standards of honor and love. The conflicts that sustain its episodic action
arise directly from the failure of this conjunction: each of the main characters comes perilously close to dying of dishonor, Alphonso because
he suspects Ianthe's virtue and Ianthe because she resents Alphonso's
jealousy.[3] The conflict is resolved and the action ended when love and
honor are joined—when Ianthe has conquered Solyman with her honor
and virtue and consequently saved Rhodes and her love. The last lines
of the play, spoken by Solyman to Ianthe, represent the conclusive and
concluding expression of this heroic ideal:

> And still, to Natures Darling, Love
> (That all the World may happy prove)
> Let Giant-Virtue be the watchfull Guard,
> Honour, the cautious Guide, and sure reward:
> Honour, adorn'd in such a Poets Song
> As may prescribe to Fame
> What loyal Lovers name
> Shall farr be spread, and shall continue long. [*Exeunt omnes*]
> [Pt. II, V.vi.216-23]

Literary historians commonly attribute the extreme artificiality and
stylization of this play to its original interregnum presentation in recita-
tive verse and to the strong influence of masque and opera upon Davenant's drama.[4] The significance of such factors is incontestable, but they
do not completely explain the internal logic or the external origins of
the drama. Davenant chose to write dramatic opera after the Restoration,[5] and his earlier nonoperatic *Love and Honour* (1634) aspires, in
its main plot, to the same kind of esoteric and artificial tone and incident
that is the hallmark of Restoration heroics. *The Siege of Rhodes* need
not have been sung, or even produced on the narrow stage at Rutland
House. The play's form in itself prescribes that distance, elevation, and
stasis. The rigid evaluative hierarchy that governs the form is by definition a remote standard, the property of an elite class, uncommon and
unrealistic. The enactment of such a standard is inevitably episodic
and static, a series of emblematic scenes that display rather than involve.
Proximity might make Alphonso's jealousy seem justified. Naturalness
would certainly render the protagonists' symmetrical near-deaths ridiculous. And realism would contradict and invalidate all the assumptions
of the form. In short, the details of the drama's manner—its style, tone,
and language—are not merely local consequences of its theatrical context. They are integral characteristics of its form. In the context of a

formal history, qualities like Davenant's extreme artificiality must first
be defined formally, even though a full account of *The Siege of Rhodes*
would ultimately return to the context of the play—and to the social,
economic, and political as well as the intellectual, cultural, and theatrical history that determines its form.

The heroic actions of Roger Boyle, Earl of Orrery, present the narrow heroic standards of conduct with even more simplicity and precision
than Davenant's drama. Orrery's plays appear particularly rigid and
hierarchical partly because he scarcely varies his dramatic formula from
one work to the next, but mainly because his actions are simple and
the terms that govern them are expressed in the form of repeated and
explicit maxims. In *Mustapha* (1665), for instance, Zanger and Mustapha illustrate one of the most basic laws of Orrerian drama. Both are
in love with the Hungarian queen, and they are required by honor to
urge each other's suit:

> *Mustapha.* True Friendship, Madam, cannot yield to this;
>   If you reject my Love, accept of his. . . .
> *Zanger.* I am amaz'd at what you seem to do;
>   Let me not bear Loves wounds and Friendships too.
> *Mustapha.* Only those Lovers should be counted true
>   Who Beauties int'rest, not their own pursue. . . .
> *Zanger.* Madam, I thus would expiate my crime;
>   That which he beg'd for me I beg for him. [6]

In *Henry the Fifth* (1664) Tudor and King Henry engage in a similar
exchange. Each pleads the other's suit, but, as Tudor explains, their
social relationship alters the rule:

> All, Sir, that in my cause is said by you
> At once is for me, and against me too.
> Howe're I'le rather speak than quite despair;
> Since she is just and you my Rival are:
> Yet, Sir, this diff'rence to my case is due,
> You speak for me, but I resign for you. [V.iv.325-30]

Honor demands that the aristocrat relinquish his love in favor of the
monarch. *The Black Prince* (1667) provides perhaps the best example
of this Platonic scrupulousness. The mistress of the king, Alizia, who
lies dying of his unfaithfulness to her, gratefully receives the proof of
his utter renunciation of her rival, but still determines to die:

> *King.* If you forgive me, yet your Death pursue,
>   You will at once Forgive and Kill me too:
>   Loves Pow'r you wrong while at this rate you grieve,
>   For Love should heal worse Wounds, than it can give.
> *Alizia.* I can, alas, Sir, but too truely say
>   'Tis only Love which makes me disobey,

> For I should not deserve the Love you give,
> If after you recall'd it, I could Live. [V.iii.231-38]

The king convinces her that she should recover, but only by noting that her death would unjustly cause his own. All of these passages illustrate at once the means by which Orrery communicates the controlling values of the drama as well as the stylistic elevation and detachment that are formally contingent on those means.

Orrery's kind of heroic action amounts to a rather simple contest, in which the audience is presented with a cast of dramatis personae vying for merit by the standards of heroic honor provided, usually as maxims, at crises in the action throughout the play. The rules for the contest are so explicit that they constitute a catalogue of prescriptions for exemplary behavior. In *Tryphon* (1668), a representative play, the prescriptions, transcribed chronologically, make up a simple list that accurately records the essential structure of the action:

1. Honor obliges a daughter to regard filial allegiance over true love (II.iii).
2. Honor obliges a friend to reveal all secrets to her friend (II.iii).
3. Honor obliges a subject to hold allegiance to his king over allegiance to his friend (II.iv).
4. Honor demands that a woman value her word over her love, since without honor she would be unworthy of love (III.i).
5. A woman is bound by honor to conceal her love until her lover speaks (III.i).
6. Honor obliges a friend to help his friend, but only if that does not involve betrayal of another friend (III.ii).
7. When love and honor are at odds, a lover must choose to lose his love to honor (thus continuing to merit love) rather than to possess love without meriting it (III.iv).
8. A friend who betrays his friend is unworthy of love (IV.i).
9. Honor forbids a woman to accept her true love after being rejected by another (IV.ii).
10. Honor obliges a friend to die before fighting his friend (IV.ii).
11. Love and honor demand that a lover who cannot have his love must die (IV.ii).
12. Honor forbids a lover to seek revenge on his rival, since that makes him unworthy of love (V.ii).
13. Honor forbids any doubt about the suicide threats of a lover (V.ii).
14. Guilt and dishonor make one unworthy of love and turn it to hate (V.iii).
15. Neither love nor honor can be bought or sold, and love and honor forbid such an attempt (V.iii).

16. Love and honor oblige a lover to trust his love completely (V.iii).
17. Honor obliges a lover to give up his interest in his love if he has offended against love by injuring honor (V.iv).
18. Honor always obliges a lover to give up his love to his king (V.iv).

The ideology of the play is equally direct and explicit. Orrery is, of course, a royalist and nationalist, and those positions are frequently presented as detached *sententiae*, like King Henry's assertion:

> That Prince, whose Flags are bow'd to on the Seas,
> Of all Kings shores keeps in his hand the Keys:
> No King can him, he may all Kings invade;
> And on his Will depends their Peace and Trade.   [*Henry the Fifth*, V.i.57-60]

But more characteristically, Orrery's ideology simply informs the list of heroic maxims that shapes the play and that discriminates the deserving from the less deserving. This incorporation of ideology into the central judgmental hierarchy of the heroic action is typical of Orrery's nationalistic English history plays as well as of his largely fictional heroic drama. The historical context of *Henry the Fifth*, for instance, serves exactly the same end as the largely fictional context of *Tryphon*. The nationalistic details and royalist setting of the earlier play merely make the ideological content of the form more explicit. The rule that requires Tudor's relinquishment of his love in favor of Henry in *Henry the Fifth* (V.iv) or Seleucis's in favor of the new king, Aretus, in *Tryphon* (V.iv) is an obvious instance. The mere fact of monarchy determines the outcome of these love contests, and Orrery is careful to avoid any suggestion of a contradiction with the other Platonic law that the most impeccably honorable character deserves the woman by making both Tudor and Seleucis slightly defective in honor. Thus Tudor apparently fails to merit his love by too eagerly relinquishing it for honor in conceding to Henry, and Seleucis by attempting to win his love actively rather than honorably losing and thus truly meriting it.

Mustapha, Orrery's most popular play, provides the significant example of a heroic action with a tragic conclusion. It is symptomatic of the form that this tragedy does not differ fundamentally from plays like *Henry the Fifth*, *The Black Prince*, or *Tryphon*, all of which end happily. Mustapha and Zanger, two sons of Solyman the Magnificent, swear loyalty to each other, fall in love with the captive Hungarian queen, and honorably compete for her favors in exactly the same manner, with exactly the same rhetoric, and by exactly the same standards as Orrery's other heroic protagonists. Like Henry and Tudor in *Henry the Fifth* (V.iv), they urge each other's suits before their love. They swear eternal loyalty, despite their love rivalry, as do the prince and King John of France in *The Black Prince* (IV.i). And they express an eagerness to die for love and honor as do Demetrius and Aretus in *Tryphon* (IV.ii). The only difference is that Orrery takes them up on their interest in death.

The assumptions and effect of the play, obviously, are not like those of classical or Shakespearean tragedy. There are no tragic flaws. Zanger and Mustapha are as perfect as the protagonists who are permitted to live happily ever after in Orrery's other plays. In fact, the form of the heroic action is such that a fortunate or unfortunate conclusion requires no fundamental change in the structure of the drama. The heroic action is predicated on a series of clearly defined and absolutely rigid social principles, and not on any evolving or problematical relationship between those principles and the characters' eventual fates. We know that the ending is tragic when the characters do not get what Orrery's standards say they deserve, but we do not necessarily expect either a tragic or a fortunate conclusion to a heroic action. Instead, we expect and receive a clear judgmental hierarchy, and the particular pleasure provided by the form (for those who can appreciate it) consists in the systematic application of that hierarchy to the individual characters who, because they are static, in turn serve to diminish our anticipation of their fates: we are concerned mainly about how well they live up to their standards of honor, and only minimally with the likelihood of their living happily ever after. Thus, traditionally, the heroic action, like relatively few other forms, includes plays that end tragically as well as plays that end fortunately, without necessitating any major discriminations between the two. This important formal peculiarity need not be inferred solely from the varying endings of Orrery's plays or of Restoration heroic actions in general. It is also subject to internal, textual verification: *The Vestal Virgin* (1665), by Robert Howard, was written and printed with alternative tragic and comic conclusions. [7]

The episodic nature of the heroic action is both contributor and corollary to this aspect of its form, since the isolation of individual scenes serves to increase the static and emblematic representation of the characters and to diminish any anticipation of their fates as well as any depth or complexity in their portrayal. But the tendency toward episode is itself another consequence of the stern judgmental hierarchy of this form, which subordinates character development and process to the static enactment of a social code. The heroic dramatists, in their use of episodic structure, are deliberately imitating epic and heroic romance as these were understood in Renaissance epic theory. [8] But here again the integrity of the heroic action obviously accounts in itself for the phenomena that can be explained extrinsically by reference to literary or theoretical sources.

II

With John Dryden's major drama we can begin to see portentous alterations in the shape of the heroic action. Dryden's most important contribution to the form, as Eugene Waith has shown, is the Herculean
hero.[9] Davenant and Orrery have no protagonists of the make of Montezuma, Maximin, or Almanzor. Furthermore, as the catalogue of *Tryphon*'s heroic virtues illustrates, they tend to see love and honor ideally
in some kind of cooperative interaction, where one produces or guarantees the other. But Dryden frequently emphasizes choice, at the expense of congruence, and his characters are less likely than Orrery's
to discover and verbalize any necessary relationship between the two.[10]
Consequently, and most important, Dryden's heroic action is formally more complex, historically more transitional, and ideologically more
self-conscious and daring than Davenant's or Orrery's. Where Orrery's
royalism is supplied by maxim in a simplistic heroic hierarchy, Dryden's
is rescued from the peril of political chaos by a form that deliberately
risks and then completely undercuts the Herculean hero's challenge to
society.

Within Dryden's own heroic career we can perceive two parallel and
corollary evolutions: the development of a kind of heroic action that
includes the erratic and godlike hero, and the subtle softening of the
neat Orrerian hierarchy. The turn, in *Aureng-Zebe* (1675) and the much
later *Don Sebastian* (1689) and *Love Triumphant* (1694), toward an
adjustment of heroic form to the incorporation of pathetic effect is
ultimately a consequence of these related earlier changes. In general,
then, Dryden's heroic action represents the most sophisticated version
of the form. Seen in the larger continuum from Davenant to Lee,
Dryden's heroic drama, because of its choice of the Herculean hero and
its fragmentation of the previously integrated love and honor code,
stands somewhere between Orrery's rigid evaluative hierarchy and Lee's
meaningless one. And finally, from a still broader perspective, it also
anticipates the major formal shift to affective tragedy.

As an initial example of Dryden's heroic propensities, *The Indian
Queen* (1664) can be seen as a pale early version of *The Conquest of
Granada*. Its formal proximity to that later play gives additional credence to the argument, already well substantiated, for Dryden's virtually
sole authorship.[11] In fact, *The Indian Queen* contains material typical
of many of Dryden's later works. Just as *The Indian Emperor* dramatizes
Almeria's stylized attempt to kill Cortez, *The Indian Queen* contains
a scene in which two captive lovers are threatened in the prison by their
infatuated captors, who approach, retreat, and change sides in the same
emblematic pattern. Montezuma fights with and captures his lover's
father, like Alphonso in *Love Triumphant*, only to have her reject him

to join her father in captivity. Like Almanzor in *The Conquest of Granada*, he is a hero of unknown origin who, in the last act, is discovered to be the long-lost son of the king. And again like Almanzor, Montezuma is a turncoat: he first fights and conquers for the Ynca, then after quarreling with him goes over to the Mexicans, who consequently win the war.

But despite Montezuma's numerous resemblances to Almanzor, his presence in the play is less strongly felt, his language less bombastic; and *The Indian Queen* in general is less vehement and heroically violent than *The Conquest of Granada*. The play is shorter and simpler than Dryden's later heroic drama. Its action consists of mechanical and instantaneous decisions to change sides, to fall in love, to fight, or to die. Formally, then, though Montezuma's erratic heroism has a significant effect on the terms of judgment presented by the play, the simple love and honor choices made by the decidedly unerratic Acacis and Orazia dominate the action. There is less rant because these characters, like Orrery's, are merely required to act out the precise standards of the Platonic hierarchy.

The play is characterized by deeds like those in *Tryphon*. When Montezuma offers to free the captured Mexican prince, Acacis, the prince refuses to accept a dishonorable liberty[12]—but he is obliged in turn to help his captor escape to the Mexicans (I.i.122–23). Later, when Montezuma is captured by the Mexicans, Acacis, still bound by honor but now also his rival in love, frees and arms him, then challenges him to a duel. In the same scene Orazia, their beloved, who was also freed by Acacis, insists upon returning to prison, accompanied by Montezuma, to die with her father. Acacis, who has been wounded in the duel, consequently resolves not to die, since he is required by honor to live and free Montezuma from prison again. When Acacis discovers that Montezuma and Orazia are to be executed, he vows to die with them and eventually kills himself, though the rest are saved by a timely interruption.

The rigid Platonic code and the impeccable behavior of the characters in scenes like these make the play seem much closer to the drama of Davenant and Orrery than to *The Conquest of Granada*. But Montezuma is not always contained within the narrow bounds of the simple Orrerian categories. He deserves our admiration but, especially in the first half of the play, that admiration comes more from his advertised military prowess and his open defiance of the Ynca's royal authority than from any submission to nice standards of honor. Montezuma is an erratic, Herculean hero, though a restricted one, and his character and action are ordered on different terms from those of Acacis and Orazia.

In the first scene, for instance, Montezuma, enraged by the Ynca's refusal to reward his military victories with the hand of Orazia, thinks

first of killing the Ynca, then of joining the opposing army, even though
Acacis tells him such an act would be dishonorable:

> No, I must your Rage prevent,
> From doing what your Reason wou'd repent;
> Like the vast Seas, your Mind no limits knows,
> Like them lies open to each Wind that blows. [I.i.59-62]

Montezuma's willful shifting of sides and his invincible military prowess
are a visible threat to political stability. Dryden has introduced into
an otherwise straightforward heroic form a character who is defined not
by his simple compliance with the stated maxims of honor, but, at
least on occasion, by his erratic and passionate defiance of them. How
does a royalist dramatist reconcile this defiance with an aristocratic
status quo?

As a static character in an episodic action, Montezuma does not
evolve. Those critics who believe that he matures in the course of the
play[13] are responding to Dryden's concluding repudiation of Montezuma's radical individualism. But Dryden's formal incorporation of the
subversive Herculean hero, in this work as in *The Conquest of Granada*,
does not follow a simple formula of conversion and reward. Montezuma
is nowhere explicitly converted to civic responsibility; he is given no
scene of *anagnorisis.* In fact, the simplicity of his portrayal forbids the
kind of complexity that would make such a transformation probable.
Furthermore, if the play were merely a history of Montezuma's education in self-control, Dryden would certainly not have needed to exercise the formal sleight of hand with which he rescues *The Indian Queen*
from social anarchy. Dryden uses Montezuma's loyalty to the studiously virtuous Orazia and the fortunate discovery of Montezuma's royal
parentage, which legitimizes the hero's claims to her, to tame the Herculean demigod without quelling his subversive magnificence. The dangerous rebel turns out to be the rightful king of Mexico. Thus, despite
its resemblance to Orrery's simplistic heroic action, *The Indian Queen*
contains an element—Montezuma's character as represented by his
early, erratic behavior—that prefigures Dryden's complex and transitional version of the heroic action as it is embodied in its most fully
developed and integrated form in *The Conquest of Granada.*

The Indian Emperor (1665) contains no Herculean hero on the model
of Montezuma in *The Indian Queen* or Almanzor in *The Conquest of
Granada.* The Montezuma of this play is a different character from his
earlier namesake. Neither he nor Cortez is able to change sides and
carry victory with him, and neither is explicitly larger than life, as are
the heroes of the other plays. Though Cortez wins in the end and
carries off Cydaria, he presents no implicit challenge to society. He
behaves in general like an orderly and ethical hero, freeing his captive

and rival Orbellan after an honorable duel, releasing Montezuma from the tortures of the horrible Catholic priests, and allowing Guyomar and Alibech, after the conquest is over, to go "beyond the Mountains." In fact, he represents explicitly, by the end of the play, the beneficial coming of responsible Christendom to the heathen world, and he is artfully dissociated at every point from the brutal Catholic priests and the lustful Pizarro. Thus, in choosing to dramatize the last days of the Indian empire, Dryden was forced to eschew the Herculean hero, since Montezuma must be weak enough to provide the pathos and nostalgia with which the play treats his hopeless defense, and Cortez must be honorable and responsible enough to embody the forces of civilization that succeed him.

The Indian Emperor, then, displays a rather conventional series of love-and-honor choices in various static and stylized episodes. The novelty of the play resides in Dryden's definition of those choices. In *The Indian Queen* we are presented in effect with two standards of judgment: one applies to the erratic Montezuma because he is apparently a superman incomparable to the other characters in the play, and the other to Acacis and Orazia, who are not assessed as demigods but rather according to the Platonic categories of Orrerian love and honor. In *The Indian Emperor*, however, though only the second standard is functional, the terms of the relationship between love and honor are not so clear.

This play, in fact, provides the first example of Dryden's fragmentation of the love-and-honor code. Guyomar and Odmar, for instance, who seem equally admirable and responsible for at least the first half of the play, must choose in an initial battle between saving Montezuma, their father and king, and Alibech, the object of their love. At this point in the action Dryden makes no connection, as Orrery inevitably would have, between love and honor. Guyomar follows honor and saves Montezuma, but his choice does not seem to imply that he now merits and will automatically receive Alibech's love. Odmar follows love and rescues Alibech, but he does not immediately forfeit love because of his loss of honor. Both go on to perform equally honorable acts. Guyomar saves Cortez's life to repay a debt of honor. Odmar later saves Guyomar from Montezuma. Only quite late in the play does Alibech decide which lover she prefers, and only at the point when her choice is made does Odmar appear to have forfeited both love and honor.

Thus, while *The Indian Emperor* never openly challenges the relationship between love and honor, it is rather slow to affirm it. The choice throughout most of the play is one of opposite extremes, each of which necessarily excludes the other. This weakening of the neat heroic hierarchy emerges in the assessment of Montezuma as well. His infatuation with

Almeria never includes the "losing and meriting" act inevitable in an Orrerian play. It represents love with no reference to honor, depicted as an infatuation instead of being placed in a clearly defined love-and-honor hierarchy. This judgment, in its recognition of Montezuma's weakness, forms the basis of our nostalgic sense of the inescapable downfall of his ancient empire. In *The Indian Emperor*, then, Dryden is still experimenting with the heroic action, but by weakening and fragmenting the conventionally rigid standards of judgment rather than, as in *The Indian Queen*, by introducing a separate kind of hero with a separate kind of assessment.

In his next heroic play, *Tyrannic Love* (1669), Dryden comes much closer to the full development of his particular kind of Herculean hero. Maximin is a ranting protagonist like Almanzor, except for the significant fact that he is a villain. Maximin's extravagant tyranny and Catherine's equally defiant Christianity clearly dominate the action, despite the Orrerian love-and-honor conflicts of Valeria, Berenice, and Porphyrius. But Dryden avoids the socially subversive consequences of the positive demigod by making his protagonist a villain, and in addition by making Catherine, who also participates in the extravagance, a Christian martyr. In *Tyrannic Love*, as in the later *Aureng-Zebe*, the Herculean hero is split in two, so that one half can maintain the values of virtue and order and the other the erratic qualities of violence and passion.[14] Dryden's heroic action ceases to be socially problematic from a royalist point of view when the Herculean hero is such that he must be killed in the end and his death seen as just and desirable. Maximin, unlike Montezuma in *The Indian Queen*, need not be incorporated into a stable society. He is clearly evil, and his death in itself represents a victory for the forces of order and justice. This type of heroic action, in which subversive defiance is consigned to the part of the villain, is illustrated equally well by Elkanah Settle's *Cambyses* (1671) or Aphra Behn's *Abdelazer* (1676).

Almanzor in *The Conquest of Granada* I and II (December 1670 and January 1671) is not a villain, but a protagonist who maintains the audience's sympathy throughout. He is introduced as a superman, who must be judged not by the common standards of love and honor that define Ozmyn and Benzayda,[15] but by his own erratic and magnificent code of heroic assertion. We know this from the opening description of his incredible feats in the bullfight, from his own and other characters' statements, and from the apparent fact, borne out in each skirmish and battle of the play, that he is invincible. Like Montezuma of *The Indian Queen*, Almanzor is a kind of demigod whom we are called upon to admire unconditionally, and his actions are the translation of his magnificent passions and heroism into a dramatically visible form. But significantly, this later hero is a much stronger and formally much more dominant character than Montezuma. He performs acts of erratic and defiant heroism throughout the action, rather than merely at its beginning, and his verbal assertions, which set the tone of the play, are more frequent and vehement than Montezuma's. He explicitly challenges the social status quo, in speech and in deed. He can always justify his changes of side in the local war, but his response is based not upon any premises of royal control or civil order, but upon the assumption that "I alone am King of me."[16] He occasionally does behave rashly, and honorably admits his error (Pt. II: III.i.181–82), but this behavior itself is seen as a consequence of the admirable extravagance of his passion, and his admission is only further substantiation of the grandeur of his soul.

In short, Dryden designs Almanzor's career to represent a serious threat, not only to monarchy in general, but to the king of Granada in particular, and eventually to the invading Spanish army and the forces of European civilization and Christianity as embodied in Ferdinand and Isabella. In Part II, after all, he is only prevented from killing the duke of Arcos, and presumably from conquering all of the duke's forces, by a voice "from above" (Pt. II: V.iii.195), which informs him that the duke is his long-lost father.[17]

The play proceeds as a series of episodes in which Almanzor behaves admirably or passionately according to the Herculean standards applicable to demigods: the bullfight, his various battles, his passion for Almahide, his generous though reluctant decisions to fight for his rival. Though he acquires additional virtue from his contact with Almahide, our assessment of him does not evolve, but remains consistent with his initial grandeur and generosity. The heroic action, here as in *The Indian Emperor*, forbids a genuine development of character. Critics who see a change in Montezuma invariably find a similar transformation in Almanzor.[18] But again, this view confuses the reversal of the plot with the reformation of the protagonist. The virtuous acts that Almanzor performs at Almahide's behest, while they do represent a change in his style of heroism, do not negate any of the Herculean principles that define his magnificence from the beginning of the play. When he sacrifices his love for Almahide, he does so out of "exalted passion," claiming: "I dare be wretched not to make her so" (Pt. I: III.i.452–53). Dryden thus assigns the same motive to Almanzor's virtue as he does, from the first, to his protagonist's defiant heroism: "because I dare." Almahide's power over Almanzor is demonstrated by his growing self-control and willingness to follow her lead of virtue, but it does not transform him into an obedient Orrerian hero. When encouraging him to perform his last generous act of fighting for her husband Boabdelin, Almahide exhorts Almanzor to "be a god again" (Pt. II: V.iii.114). She too evidently sees his virtue as an expression of his superhuman extravagance.

   The career of this Herculean superman can be brought to a close only
by the arbitrary imposition of a fortuitous and fortunate conclusion
upon the static and episodic structure of his action.[19] The duke of Arcos
claims Almanzor as his son, the war ends, Almahide's troublesome
husband dies in the last battle, and Almanzor and Almahide are taken
in by the generous and kindly Ferdinand and Isabella of Spain. The
extravagant hero remains unchanged. His submission to Almahide at the
end of Part II simply repeats his similar submission to her at the end
of Part I; the only addition is the sudden and unexpected good fortune
by which the hero's situation is miraculously reversed. Thus Almanzor's fate is made to correspond with what we have felt he deserved
throughout the play: he wins Almahide and the war, though only because she suddenly becomes a widow and he turns out, by paternity,
to belong to the victorious army. Furthermore, the erratic hero, without
ever revoking his claim that "I alone am King of me," is made to accept
the power and royal authority of the Spanish monarchy. The combination
of Almanzor's fortuitous good fortune and Almahide's tested influence
serves to incorporate the Herculean hero into an orderly social hierarchy
at the conclusion of the play without qualifying his subversive magnificence.[20] *The Conquest of Granada* ends as a celebration of stable monarchy, pronounced by Almanzor himself:

> Our Banners to th' *Alhambra*'s turrets bear;
> Then, wave our Conqu'ring Crosses in the Aire;
> And Cry, with showts of Triumph, live and raign,
> Great *Ferdinand* and *Isabel* of *Spain*. [Pt. II: V.iii.345-48]

   This play, then, contains a more dangerous and problematic protagonist than either *The Indian Queen* or *Tyrannic Love*, but it also provides
a more explicit and emphatic royalist social message.[21] Unlike Montezuma's, Almanzor's challenge to civic order is vigorous and consistent.
Unlike Maximin, this later demigod is no villain, but a hero designed
to command our admiration and approval. And yet it is Almanzor himself who finally voices the play's conservative political and social ideology. The sophisticated heroic form of *The Conquest of Granada* consists
of this juxtaposition of radical challenge and royalist resolution. The
play reveals Dryden's ingenious efforts to bring these irreconcilable forces
into formal conjunction.
   The first means to this conjunction is the motivation of the plot.
Almanzor is the admirable hero, but not the agent of his action. He is
not only denied an active role in the arbitrary conclusion of the play,
he is excluded from responsibility for his misfortunes as well. He attributes the vicissitudes of his love to the "Gods" (Pt. II: III.iii.183). And
in his defiance of "fate," he provides a metaphysical definition of his
plight:

O Heav'n, how dark a Riddle's thy Decree,
Which bounds our Wills, yet seems to leave 'em free!
Since thy fore-knowledge cannot be in vain,
Our choice must be what thou didst first ordain:
Thus, like a Captive in an Isle confin'd,
Man walks at large, a Pris'ner of the Mind:
Wills all his Crimes, (while Heav'n th' Indictment draws;)
And, pleading guilty, justifies the Laws.— [Pt. II: IV.iii.143-50]

"Fate" is also made responsible for the problems and misfortunes of
the other characters, especially for the near-tragic difficulties of Ozmyn
and Benzayda. These standard Orrerian lovers, like Acacis and Orazia,
provide a model of strict aristocratic virtue that supports the royalist
message of the play's conclusion, but they enact that virtue in a world
of pervasive metaphysical reference.

"Fate" provides Dryden with an external means of motivating his
action and bringing about the final reversal without implicating the
erratic hero. The conservative conclusion of the play is thus easily dissociated from Almanzor's subversive character. This dissociation itself is only possible because of the inherent weakness of our concern
for the ending of a heroic action. As we observed in Orrery's *Mustapha*,
heroic drama is predicated on the static definition of the epic or Platonic virtues of the protagonist and not on any necessary relationship
between those virtues and his fortunate or unfortunate end. Hence,
the general nature of the form as well as Dryden's specific use of a pervasive metaphysical reference keeps radical and royalist scrupulously
apart. Almanzor, the primary impediment to political order, is given no
direct role in his action's conservative conclusion, and thus he is never
forced to repudiate his heroic magnificence.

More important, since "Fate" is explicitly apolitical, it enables Dryden to restrict Almanzor's action to the realm of private affairs. The
real subject of the "conquest of Granada" is frustrated love, and Almanzor acts throughout the play on purely private motives. Even when he
takes part in the great historical events that constitute the backdrop of
his story, he does so as "a private man" (Pt. I: IV.ii.474). If he were a
public hero, a Tamburlaine, for instance, Dryden would be unable to
provide a conclusion that incorporated him into the social status quo.
Only because his motivations are purely personal can Almanzor secure
his dual fortunate fate—marriage to Almahide and allegiance to the
king—without repudiating his heroic identity.

But *The Conquest of Granada* is designed to seem like a vehemently
political drama. A historical event provides the setting, and the action
represents the battles and intrigues attendant on that event. Many of the
minor characters are obsessively concerned with political power and
involved in political intrigue. And Almanzor himself is always seen as a

potentially public hero, a "Soul which Empires first began" (Pt. I: IV.ii.475). The political references in setting, characterization, and language set up a consistent formal analogy between public and private affairs, between politics and Almanzor's heroic passions.[22] This analogy transforms a private action into the vehicle for a public lesson, and it also makes possible the concluding equation of Almanzor's happy private fate with the conservative restoration of public order. It enables Dryden to have his subversive hero and his royalist message too.

The Conquest of Granada is a formal tour de force in which a contradiction is given dramatic substance. Its tone is even more elevated and exaggerated than that of Orrery's works or of Dryden's other heroic drama. In effect, Almanzor must indulge in more bombast, and the bombast itself must be violent enough for an audience accustomed to the heroic action to distinguish the special erratic and subversive nature of this particular protagonist. D. W. Jefferson, Bruce King, and other critics who discover absurdity, irony, or even satire in this drama testify to the greater degree of stylization and distance demanded by Dryden's mature heroic action.[23] The exaggeration essential to the depiction of the subversive Herculean protagonist is easily mistaken for irony, though Dryden gives no sign, either in the plays or in his comments on them, of such an intention.

As we have seen, Dryden is able to sustain the contradiction between royalist and radical only because the heroic action itself requires the dissociation of character and conclusion, the separation of merit and fate. In a sense, then, this sophisticated version of the form represents a fulfillment of the inherent potential of the heroic action: to assimilate everything, even the most radical challenge, to the static assertion of aristocratic ideology.[24] Significantly, the royalist position of *The Conquest of Granada* is asserted, not won, and asserted arbitrarily in the face of challenges that threaten society with chaos. The social stability of the conclusion does not represent the necessary consequence of the action, but rather an ideological incorporation, expressed formally, of the subversive hero that Dryden sought to portray. The arbitrariness of Dryden's restoration of civic order reproduces in dramatic form the instability that began to be felt in the political Restoration by the late 1660s and early 1670s with the impeachment of Clarendon, the decline of Cavalier control in the Commons, the weakening of the House of Lords, and the increasing power of merchant and agrarian capitalist interests in the nation.[25] In this sense, Dryden's most daring heroic action is an immediate product of its time, and its formal flirtation with and flight from social anarchy closely parallels the premises of the major dramatic social satire of the 1670s. Furthermore, Dryden's most sophisticated version of the form challenges the clarity and simplicity of the heroic hierarchy and thus anticipates the change to a new kind of serious drama that comes to express the full disaffection and disillusionment of a later decade.

In *Aureng-Zebe* (1675) Dryden avoids the confrontation he provokes in *The Conquest of Granada*. He divides the qualities of the Herculean hero between Aureng-Zebe and Morat, much as he divides heroic defiance in *Tyrannic Love* between Maximin and Catherine. Morat is a ranting, uncontrollable rebel, but he presents no ideological problem because, like Maximin, he is consistently seen as the villain and receives death, with our approval, for his defiance. Aureng-Zebe, on the other hand, an accomplished fighter, obeys, albeit with some difficulty, all the standards of love and honor. In this respect he is explicitly contrasted with Morat, who invariably ignores the Orrerian precepts that his counterpart upholds. Aureng-Zebe is so "excellently good"[26] that he can even forgive his father's unnatural rivalry for Indamora, among other crimes. In fact, the last lines of the play, in which the Emperor grants Aureng-Zebe the throne, are a direct pronouncement of his merit and its immediate consequence in his happy fate:

> *Giving him Indamora's hand.*
> The just rewards of love and honor wear.
> Receive the mistress you so long have served;
> Receive the crown your loyalty preserved.
> Take you the reins, while I from cares remove,
> And sleep within the chariot which I drove. [V.670–74]

In these respects, then, Aureng-Zebe resembles the characters in Dryden's earlier plays who embody the conventional, neatly integrated love-and-honor standard with none of the vagaries of the erratic hero: Acacis and Orazia in *The Indian Queen* and Ozmyn and Benzayda in *The Conquest of Granada*. *Aureng-Zebe* is somewhat like Orrery's kind of heroic action, with its primary emphasis on a discrimination of proper heroic behavior, defined not so much by maxim as by the repeated contrast between Aureng-Zebe and Morat. But the similarity, like many such resemblances in literary history, is deceptive. As several critics have noticed, Dryden uses the virtuous behavior of his characters in adversity to construct a deliberate appeal for pathos.[27] Where Orrery seeks our admiration, Dryden attempts to arouse our sympathy.

The repeated scene of misunderstanding between Aureng-Zebe and Indamora (Acts IV and V), in which Aureng-Zebe is induced to believe the innocent, pathetic Indamora false, anticipates the last misunderstanding in *All for Love*, which results in Antony's suicide. This kind of episode, which exploits the emotional potential of the painful confrontation between an innocent victim who, despite her pathetic pleading, cannot make herself understood or believed by her equally innocent but misled lover, is quite atypical of Orrery,[28] but common

in Lee.[29] In *Aureng-Zebe* the scene serves as the focus and emblem of
Dryden's formal intention. It epitomizes Dryden's definition of Indamora's pathetic innocence, and more generally, it conveys the import of
the action: that individual virtue seems to be the inevitable victim of
cruel circumstance.

The play consists of a series of episodes representing the assertion of
virtue on the part of Indamora, Aureng-Zebe, and the notable subsidiary character Melesinda, Morat's forsaken and loving wife. Female innocence and weakness are at a premium. Unlike Dryden's earlier stalwart
heroines, Melesinda weeps frequently, despairs, helplessly follows the
unresponsive Morat about the stage, and is obviously powerless to provoke even a nominal losing-and-meriting sacrifice. Indamora, too, fears
death and pathetically begs for her life (V.261–325), while Dryden's
earlier characters, like Orrery's, would have leapt at the chance of suicide. In the process of the action, the very innocence and virtue of
these characters result in a further worsening of their situation, until
the final reversal rights the balance. But even after all the material
obstacles to their happy fate are removed, Aureng-Zebe and Indamora
must play out the last scene of misunderstanding, in which Indamora
attempts to explain that her sympathy for the dying Morat, misinter-
preted by Aureng-Zebe, does not involve a betrayal. And Melesinda,
though fortunate ends are guaranteed for the other characters, goes off
mourning to perish on Morat's funeral pyre, as a reminder of life's in-
justices to the innocent.

Thus, while Dryden's heroic action in *Aureng-Zebe* is significantly
indebted to an Orrerian kind, to the extent that he varies that model he
represents the beginnings of the major formal shift from heroic drama
to affective tragedy. The fact that the Orrerian heroic action survived
into the eighteenth century, while the extravagant form of *The Conquest
of Granada* quickly became dated,[30] shows that the relatively passive
features of the earlier form are more readily adaptable to the affective
impetus in drama, even though the later one presents a more direct
challenge to the rigid judgmental standards of the heroic mode. The
growing importance of pathos and the corollary emphasis on innocence and weakness are typical of Otway and the later Lee, and of Dryden's *Don Sebastian, Cleomenes,* and *Love Triumphant.* But unlike
Otway and Lee, Dryden produces only one genuine affective tragedy,
All for Love. Aureng-Zebe remains a heroic action despite its con-
cessions to pathos. Its careful definitions of heroic standards, its episodic representation, its unexpected and formally disjunctive fortunate
conclusion, its stylized and distant tone and setting, and its subtle
royalist public-private analogy are all products and characteristics of
the heroic action. The play, in the end, is more like *The Indian Queen*
and *The Conquest of Granada* than like *All for Love* or Otway's and

Lee's pathetic plays, despite the particular similarities that, with the retrospective wisdom of literary history, we can discover in its attention to pathos and emotion.

Dryden's later serious drama is transitional in the sense that it contains this same distinct preference for pity over admiration. But Dryden continues to write heroic actions long after his younger contemporaries have turned irrevocably to affective tragedy. His concession to pathos and innocence never entails a lowering of the tone of his plays or of the status of his characters. [31] With the exception of *All for Love*, he consistently creates dramatic actions in which social standards are determinant. The later Lee, however, and Otway, Banks, Southerne, and others who represent the general formal shift to affective tragedy, demote the criterion of judgment altogether, presenting fictional worlds in which the action is based instead upon the pathetic situation of the characters. Dryden does not consistently go this far. But because duty is a process of obedience rather than an occasional assertion of magnificence, and because sympathy is an accession of fellow feeling rather than static admiration, his later heroic plays are less episodic, more coherent actions than *The Indian Queen* or *The Conquest of Granada*.

Don Sebastian (1689), like *Aureng-Zebe*, presents heroic virtue and endurance as the admired standard of aristocratic behavior, but the focus of its action is the tragic situation of the protagonists' incest. *Love Triumphant* (1694) represents what remains in the 1690s of Herculean extravagance; Alphonso, like Montezuma and Almanzor, advertises his willingness to accept total disruption of the state if he cannot secure his love. The fortuitous happy ending of this play, brought about by the sudden and rather arbitrary expression of mercy on the part of the tyrannical king, provides an explicit dramatic example of Dryden's tendency throughout his career to equate an asserted civil stability with the granting of royal mercy. Ferdinand and Isabella show such mercy to Almahide and Almanzor, as do David in *Absalom and Achitophel* and Albion in *Albion and Albanius*. In *Love Triumphant*, as in all these works, the spontaneous final act of mercy serves to add an even further degree of chance to the reinstatement of social order, since it makes that order depend explicitly on the arbitrary decision of an obviously fallible monarch.

As I have described them, the general characteristics of Dryden's heroic actions define his place in the local evolution from Orrery to Lee as well as his relation to the larger formal shift, which comprehends that local evolution, from the heroic action to affective tragedy. First, as we have seen in *The Indian Emperor* and *The Conquest of Granada*, Dryden deliberately disturbs rigid and simple judgments of merit, either by making honor and love apparently irreconcilable and thus eliminating the clear and obvious choice as it manifests itself in Davenant and

Orrery, or by introducing an erratic character who cannot be contained
by the standard categories and whose radical individualism actually
challenges the royalist status quo. Lee's early heroic actions represent
a further step in the undermining of simple Orrerian assessment in their
depiction of a world of judgmental anarchy, where merit is undeter-
mined or undeterminable. This in turn parallels the central feature of
the fully developed affective form, where the action is ordered not by
the status, but by the pathetic situation of the characters.

In addition, Dryden's career, as it develops after *The Conquest of
Granada* and the heyday of Restoration heroics, tends toward more
pathetic, innocent, and virtuous protagonists, and even toward an emphasis on defenseless women. This constitutes a strong thematic resemblance both to Lee's early, pathos-ridden heroic plays and to the
affective tragedy, which begins with Lee's *Rival Queens* and Dryden's
All for Love and dominates the serious drama of the next two decades.
In his use of pathos to augment the appeal of the heroic action, Dryden presents as a subsidiary means the formal factor that is the determining end of affective tragedy.

III

Nathaniel Lee's early heroic plays contain formal experiments with
the assessment of character that provide us with an unusually precise
definition of the limits of the heroic action and of the ideological
assumptions that it embodies and that Lee apparently did not consistently share. Because Lee is a transitional figure, I have included his
later, mature plays in my description of affective form, but in some
ways *The Rival Queens* and *Lucius Junius Brutus* resemble *Sophonisba* and *Gloriana* as much as they do Otway's affective tragedies, *Venice Preserved* and *The Orphan*. The distinction between Otway's early
heroic play, *Don Carlos*, and his later affective drama is similarly ambiguous. In these writers the transition from heroic to affective is almost
imperceptible, primarily because the substitution of pathetic situation
for social status as a formal determinant cannot absolutely divide the
two forms: a character who is admirable by heroic standards can also be
seen as a pathetic victim. To the extent that a play is fully an affective
tragedy, however, the judgments typical of heroic drama are systematically superseded or obliterated, and this formal ambiguity disappears.

Sophonisba; or Hannibal's Overthrow (1675), one of Lee's most popular plays, is generally representative of his early heroic drama. Like
Gloriana (1676), it contains most of the usual qualities of the heroic
action: stylized and episodic scenes, love-and-honor conflicts, extravagant defiance of the gods, and an emphasis on heroic glory, death,
suicide, and conquest. But Lee's episodes of heroism convey an air of

irrationality and randomness that is immediately attributable to his
implicit rebellion against the nice judgmental constraints of the heroic
action and to his related turn to pathetic effect at the expense of character consistency.

Sophonisba contains two nominally related plots. One, the material
of its subtitle, bears most of the burden of the play's allegiance to the
heroic action. It portrays the defiant Hannibal and his equally heroic
lover Rosalinda in the throes of their last battle against the Romans. The
other plot, which ends with the double suicide of Massinissa and his
lover Sophonisba, emphasizes pathetic defeat, inaction, failure, retreat,
and submission. While both plots produce an oppressive sense of des-
peration and doom, and both heroes are passionate victims of the powers
of love, the presence of Hannibal enables Lee to maintain the heroic
action while injecting as much emotion as possible into the form. Hannibal's heroism raises the pitch of the play, but Massinissa and Sophonisba's action gives it all of the material and some of the sensuous effect
of pathos. This vacillation between heroic and pathetic is typical of
the early plays of the "new writers" of the mid-1670s, most of whom
were to become full-fledged affective tragedians. *Lucius Junius Brutus*
(1680), *Don Carlos* (1676), and *The Rival Kings* (John Banks, 1677)
all provide clear examples of this phenomenon. *The Rival Kings*, like
Sophonisba, mixes two separate dramatic modes. One is heroic and
involves the boasts and vaunted bravery of Alexander and Oroondates,
the rival kings. The other tends toward the pathetic in its portrayal
of Alexander's and Ephestion's deaths.

But Lee's attempt to supply pathetic effect within the formal limits
of the heroic action produces another kind of consequence besides
that of the divided plot. Many of the main characters in *Sophonisba*
and *Gloriana* are inconsistent, or at least profoundly enigmatic. Sophonisba, for example, is introduced as a grand, Cleopatra-like figure,
whose main fear is that she will be forced to endure a Roman triumph.
Her first lines propose a defiant suicide at the approach of Massinissa's
forces:

> Though Massinissa has the King or'ethrown:
> And his Victorious Troops possess the Town.
> Yet Sophonisba is, and shall be free,
> Spight of the frighted Senators Decree.
> They blush to see this life so glorious shine;
> And fear their Eagle's eyes, should dazled be with mine. [III.iv.3–8]

Her maids counsel her, however, to try to win over Massinissa instead,
and in the ensuing confrontation Sophonisba does just as her maids
advise. She and Massinissa were avowed lovers before her forced marriage to another, and Massinissa proves to be highly vulnerable to her

charms, which she plies with such art as to pretend to resist, though
gently, his plan to save her from the Roman wrath by marrying her
himself. It is never clear whether this scene represents a defiant and desperate heroine's ambiguous use of her lover as an escape from an ignominious defeat, or a pathetic and moving reconciliation. From this point
on, however, Sophonsiba is no longer the glorious queen of her entrance,
but rather an innocent victim of fate and misunderstanding. In the intimate and pathetic suicide with which she and Massinissa end their story
and the play, Lee presents the pair as loyal and passionate lovers, entirely unconcerned with glory or defiance, who bid a moving farewell to
life and each other and follow their draught of poison with a parting
kiss.

The elusive portrayal of Sophonisba, as well as the inconsistency of
numerous other characters in these plays, [32] is an immediate consequence of Lee's emphasis on pathetic effect. In his attention to the
emotionalism of individual scenes, especially toward the conclusion
of the drama, he neglects the consistency of the characters involved.
Sophonisba's behavior is determined by her role in the intensification of
Massinissa's torturous dilemma: the choice between love and Rome.
This subordination betrays the hierarchy of Lee's formal predilections:
effect, at least at times, is obviously more important than the consistent portrayal of individual character.

But from a larger perspective, the collective inconsistencies of Lee's
characters produce a sense of judgmental incoherence and instability
that gives these plays their peculiarly disturbing tone. In this respect,
Lee's constitutional neglect of character consistency is only a local
manifestation of his more general attitude toward assessment. In most
cases, his inconsistent characters are used to pathetic advantage. In
all cases, however, they entail a subversion of judgment and evaluation.
And this subversion, in turn, generates Lee's inclination toward affective form, in which judgment is superseded by emotional response. Since
our understanding of these elusive or inconsistent characters is frequently and rudely undercut, our reliance on formal assessment in
general is seriously imperiled. The worlds of Lee's early plays are
largely impregnable to evaluation because we are never permitted to see
through the contradictory external behavior of the characters to ascertain the true state of their emotions or their souls. We never discover
whether Sophonisba is a manipulative queen or an injured lover, and the
random opacity of her characterization is presented as casually as if it
merely reflected an obvious state of affairs.

Sophonisba remains a heroic action, however. Massinissa's choices
are consistently phrased in the familiar love-and-honor terms and
consistently presented as formally meaningful, though it appears in the
end that he cannot have love with honor, as the earlier heroes invari-

ably could. Love and honor are in this play in conflict. Massinissa
chooses love, and his choice and consequent suicide provide a prime
example of the fragmentation of the Orrerian standard in late he-
oric drama. This is a significant, but not in itself a fundamental, change
in the heroic action. Despite its tampering with the coherence and
reliability of assessment, the play provides no substitute for the clear
and self-contained evaluative hierarchy of heroic form. It represents,
in the terms of our definition, only an experiment in the direction of
affective tragedy.

The unique form of *Sophonisba*, however, reflects an attitude toward experience that we will discover to be typical of the affective
tragedy's rejection of judgment and discrimination in favor of emotion
as an end in itself. Lee's early plays illustrate, incoherently, his refusal
to judge and his sense that discrimination is impossible, and this attitude
is echoed in his pessimistic version of the fragmented heroic standard.
In his later plays the indeterminacy of evaluation begins to be rational-
ized through its incorporation into a form that simply eliminates judgment altogether.

IV

This segment of formal history illustrates both the uniqueness of the
particular plays that I have used to define the heroic action and the
coherence and continuousness of the evolution of serious drama in the
period. The form typically contains simple, static, and flat characters
who are presented in repeated, stylized episodes according to an explicit,
self-enclosed, and socially defined standard that is necessarily restricted
to the narrow representation of a particular class. In this respect, the
heroic action from Davenant to Lee is relatively regular and consistent.
It embodies the royalist ideology of the reinstated aristocracy, and
the initial simplicity and evaluative clarity of its dramatic world reflect
the early, unqualified assertion of a class ideal at the time when that
ideal still seemed possible, or at least admirable. But as we have seen,
beneath the surface of that consistency, the heroic action has a short-
lived history of its own, moving from extremely rigid and explicit
evaluative categories to more arbitrary, exceptional, or subtle distinctions of virtue, until finally the formal efficacy of such assessments
is altogether subverted, along with the ideology which they had expressed and affirmed. If Davenant's and Orrery's simplistic plays reveal
the obliviousness of the illusory royalist self-confidence of the 1660s,
Dryden's best and most sophisticated heroic action voices the implicit
tensions that became evident in the political settlement by the end
of the first decade of the Restoration.

The development of the primary serious dramatic form of this period, then, is discernible as a series of slight alterations of orientation within the larger category of the heroic action. Our perception of the course of this generic history does not depend upon the documentation of influence or cooperation, though of course those relationships existed at various times among all these dramatists. It does not depend upon a survey of sources in heroic romance or epic theory, though the findings of such studies provide significant substantiation for our observations. It is not impeded by an awareness of the vagaries of minor playwrights and plays, nor does it exclude such works from consideration. Our understanding of this segment of dramatic history depends first upon our definition of its primary form. That definition comprehends the attributes that are common to heroic drama in general, but it also discriminates among individual writers and individual works. Thus the larger conception that permits us to document the aesthetic originality and uniqueness of a play like *The Conquest of Granada* also provides us with a description of the changes that take place between Orrery and Lee and enables us to anticipate the more essential changes in the shift to affective tragedy.

The perspective of the later forms will clarify the relationship between the increasing emphasis upon emotional effect and the weakening of evaluative assessment that we have observed in embryo in Dryden's and Lee's heroic actions. These two phenomena are reciprocal manifestations of the same incipient formal change, incomplete and sporadic in Dryden, more clearly recognizable in early Lee, but receiving full realization only in the true affective tragedy. As love and honor drift apart, dramatists can begin to describe pathetic, essentially honorless characters who choose only love. In general, the breakdown of the clear evaluative hierarchy in this highly artificial form produces an intensification of emotional effect as well as involvement. Conversely, the growing formal prominence of pity and sympathy begins to preclude any absolute and rigid standard of behavior: the turn to pathos itself forces a further fragmentation of the love-and-honor hierarchy. The disintegration of the heroic standard ultimately implies the substitution of some new kind of formal coherence that does not depend on judgmental categories at all.

The Conquest of Granada, as the keynote of this portion of my history, provides a more specific example of the parallel between the serious drama and the comedy of this period. The two forms are notably distinct from one another in material and manner—so distinct in fact that several critics have argued that they are fundamentally dissimilar, and that the period is "schizophrenic."[33] The differences between the forms are numerous and significant, but they are not deep. As we shall see, dramatic social satire also presents a protagonist who threatens the status quo, but, like Almanzor, that protagonist secures our approval, at one level, throughout his action. While his admirable characteristics are maintained, his challenge to society is defused formally, in a manner that can produce no true social reconciliation but that instead provides two judgments in satiric disjunction, in the same way that Dryden's best heroic play juxtaposes royalist and radical.

TWO————————————
Dramatic Social Satire

Like the heroic action, the dramatic social satire of the Restoration is
ordered by a set of aristocratic social determinants. In this respect,
it resembles the serious drama of its own period more than it does the
comedy of the eighteenth century. The form bases its characters, conflicts, incidents, and even its language upon the conduct of contemporary genteel society. The plots of the plays depict the process of social
interchange and their conclusions represent the workings of social justice.
The morality of a character like Sir Fopling Flutter in *The Man of
Mode*, for instance, is irrelevant. Sir Fopling is portrayed solely in terms
of his social performance, and it is his failure to achieve the grace and
wit necessary to social success that determines the significance of his
role. Similarly, the dramatic dynamics of *The Country Wife* produce, in
the last scene of the play, a moment of high comic tension in which
Horner's "ladies of honor" must silence the voluble Margery in order to
save their sexual trick from exposure. The anxiety Wycherley creates
for Horner's preservation is not based upon any indication that Horner is
"right," or morally deserving, but rather upon the established fact
that Horner is the wittiest and most adept member of his society.

A necessary implication of this kind of drama is the potential discrepancy between the social assumptions that are expressed explicitly
in the working out of the action and the dramatist's implicit moral
position. Such a form inevitably suggests, because of the very nature of
its fictional world, that the way things happen in society does not
necessarily correspond to what is "right." In this sense, then, the form
can be called satiric. The crucial consideration here is not the presence
of local satiric caricature, but the whole shape and meaning of the play.
Dramatic social satire depends upon the potential discrepancy between
social and moral assessment, or, on occasion, between social and "practical" or social and romantic, whenever those latter terms are viewed
as inherently "right" in contrast with the represented workings of society.

As our definition of the form emerges and develops in the course
of this chapter, we will discover that it contradicts, in at least three important respects, one of the most useful recent technical descriptions
of satire. Sheldon Sacks distinguishes absolutely between a satire and an
action, defining the former as "a work organized so that it ridicules

objects external to the fictional world created in it," and further noting
that such a work therefore advocates no positive moral alternative.[1]
These plays, however, usually are actions of the strongest sort, they do
not necessarily include specific recognizable external objects of satire,
and they also do not programmatically exclude the representation of a
positive alternative. But their characteristic formal disjunction is essentially identical to the structure of standard nondramatic satire. This disjunction is the essence of the form, and the definition of its extent and
nature will provide the basis of our understanding of this segment of
dramatic history.

In practice, the various kinds of dramatic social satire are defined by
the degree of discrepancy between the represented social context and
the dramatist's implicit moral judgment. The permutations are obvious:
the social world depicted in a play may seem to correspond fully to
the dramatist's sense of what is "right," as in Jonson's *Every Man in His
Humour*, where all the final rewards and punishments seem not only
socially appropriate but also morally just; the social world may correspond only partially to the implicit moral judgment, as in Jonson's
Epicene, where some defective characters are punished in the end, but
some are not; or the social context may completely contradict the
dramatist's moral assessment, as in *The Country Wife*. Obviously, the
greater the disjunction, the sharper the moral criticism of society implied by the comedy. Major Restoration social satire like that of Etherege and Wycherley occupies the wider range of possible discrepancy.[2]

This kind of drama typically requires a cast of stereotyped characters, since its premise is not the exploration of motive or the revelation
of psychological depth, but rather the representation of an identifi-
able social context. The characters are the primary substance of this
context, and as such they are portrayed solely in terms of their relationships with one another and with the norms of social behavior. The
action cannot easily contain a character whose portrayal transcends
such social norms—a character of any depth or complexity. The form,
then, seems to dictate the kind of characterization most common to
manners comedy, in keeping with the rules of decorum so frequently
cited in the Restoration.

During the period of formal uncertainty in the drama, immediately
following the reopening of the theaters, social satire is not yet fully
preeminent. The early years of the Restoration's first decade are dominated by revivals of Tudor and Stuart drama and by translations and
adaptations of French social comedy and the Spanish intrigue play imported by the Cavaliers from the Spanish Netherlands. As in any period
of little dramatic originality, the imitations produced in the early 1660s
are relatively devoid of serious meaning. Plays like Samuel Tuke's successful *The Adventures of Five Hours* (1663) and Dryden's derivative

The Rival Ladies (1664)[3] exist in a formal no-man's-land between
comedy and tragedy; they are intrigues.

Both plays depict a series of accidents, misunderstandings, coincidences, and mistaken identities that result in moments of apparent
peril for the protagonists and that are fortuitously resolved by a timely
revelation of the errors.[4] In *The Adventures of Five Hours* each of
two rather violent lovers is separated from his loved one by a series of
unfortunate mistakes that ultimately result in the contracting of the
wrong pair. The play ends abruptly with the opportune disclosure, in
the middle of a heroic duel, of the central mistaken identity, and the
characters are immediately and neatly married off. The action of *The
Rival Ladies* consists of a similar love conflict among three pairs of
lovers in various disguises, which is arbitrarily concluded by a convenient and surprising pairing of the least likely couples. The honor duels
and nighttime escapades of these plays serve only to increase the expectation of a solution to the intrigue; interest is consistently directed
toward the untangling of the trivial mistakes of the plot, at the expense
of characterization or theme.

Gonsalvo of *The Rival Ladies*, for instance, who has been violently
in love with Julia throughout the play, can cheerfully accept Honoria
instead without incurring any accusations of disloyalty or inconsistency.
Such judgments are irrelevant to the structure of an intrigue. Similarly,
both Dryden's Rhodorigo and Tuke's Henrique, who seem at first to be
excessively jealous and violent characters, are ultimately not distinguished from the others. Their jealousy has no wider implications and
carries no consequences. Characterization in these plays serves only
to increase the tangles of the plot and thus the pleasing effect of its
final ingenious unraveling, and not to delineate consistent individuals.
What we want for each character is limited to what we want for the
whole intrigue, and our sense of particular fates and deserts is subsumed
by our desire to see the trick of the plot ingeniously provide for all.

The reformation of the Robber in *The Rival Ladies*, who mends his
ways after generous treatment, represents that play's closest approach
to thematic meaningfulness, but it too is ultimately used only to the
end of the intrigue effect, becoming the basis of the final improbable
plot reversal and at that point losing most of its serious content. The
play concludes with the lesson that "Obligement keeps our Love"
(V.iii.280), in order to justify the unlikely pairings that round off the
action. But this sententia is far from an expression of Dryden's meaning, since it fails to account for two of the matches: Julia is not obliged
to Rhodorigo, nor Honoria to Gonsalvo. Like characterization, meaning is clearly secondary to the aesthetic effect of a neat and symmetrical
resolution.

The intrigue subordination of character and idea to plot device is

often as blatant as the vehement Gonsalvo's meek acceptance of a substitute mate in Act V of *The Rival Ladies*. But intrigue can on occasion
become difficult to disentangle from social satire, since both forms
exclude explicit moral judgment and emphasize the relationships among
flat or stereotyped characters. In fact, the intrigue form is like an empty
vessel which, once filled with meaning, changes its nature. When tainted
with the serious implications of social satire, whether through the inclusion of a strong social context or through the suggestion of an implicit
moral divergence from the social status quo, it takes on the most important qualitites of the meaningful form. Literary seriousness abhors a
vacuum.

Significantly, plays like *The Rival Ladies* and *The Adventures of Five
Hours* contain elements that are typical of the later social satire as well
as of the contemporary heroic action. Honor duels and love debates
make up some of the material of these early intrigues, but without determining the structure or the comprehensibility of their dramatic
worlds. The unique divided tragicomedy of the period is a testimony
to the peculiar emptiness of this form. The coexistence of serious
and comic in divided plays like Dryden's *Secret Love* (1667) or *Marriage A-la-Mode* (1671), *The Comical Revenge* (1664), by Etherege,
James Howard's *All Mistaken* (1665?),[5] or *The Mulberry Garden* (1668),
by Charles Sedley, is made possible by the compatibility of two intrigue actions, each with a different theme and set of conventions, but
both finally seeking to provide the same aesthetic pleasure—the simple
pleasure of formal unraveling typical of the single intrigue plot.[6] In the
early Restoration, then, intrigue is a kind of dramatic common denominator with which both social satire and the heroic action have affinities.
But its most direct and continuing relationship is with the comedy,
simply because the premise of pure entertainment is more compatible
with comic form. Intrigue is a constant resort of the minor comic
dramatists of this period, as well as of the major writers in their minor
plays. Because of their relationship to intrigue, the minor comedies
often do not seem like full social satires, but despite its typical intrigue
plot, *The Country Wife* does not seem like a formal intrigue.

I

The crucial development in the comic drama of the early Restoration
is the movement from the intrigue form—whether simple or, as in the
divided tragicomedy, compound—to the serious and sophisticated form
of the major dramatic social satire. This movement, however, is not
based upon any deep affinity between intrigue and satiric form. Several
recent critics have claimed such an affinity, finding in the tragicomedy
a raw version of the contradictions that later become the mainstay of

the comedy of manners.[7] But an attention to the details of this dramatic history reveals that, far from sharing the formal vacuity of the intrigue—with its indistinguishable characters, its collective symmetrical fates, and its aversion to conflict and meaning—the major social satire represents a generic rejection of the aesthetic premises of the earlier form and a turn instead toward clearly differentiated characters, toward conflict, and even toward unresolvable contradiction.

The course of John Dryden's comic career illustrates the general direction of formal evolution in the Restoration. Dryden's plays are often neglected in studies of the comedy of manners, perhaps because they are more diverse or less clearly assimilable to a common mode than those of Etherege or Wycherley. For this very reason, they provide us with a good test case for the usefulness of our formal categories. Even if we acknowledge Dryden's diversity, as well as his tendency to imitate, to pursue theatrical fads, and to cater to the passing tastes of his audience, a formal perspective reveals the general coherence of his comic corpus and its similarity to those of Etherege and Wycherley.

Dryden's first play, *The Wild Gallant* (1663), exemplifies the close relationship between intrigue and a kind of muted social satire in the early comedies of this period. Its action is based upon a series of tricks and disguises by which Loveby, the penniless Wild Gallant, is united with Constance, daughter of the wealthy Lord Nonsuch. The emphasis on empty stratagem is characteristic of intrigue, but a list of the tricks of the plot cannot fully account for the effect of this play. First of all, the final scheme is not complete or successful enough to provide the full pleasurable reversal that intrigue demands: Constance pretends to be pregnant but Loveby fails to heed his cue and take her off her father's hands. Furthermore, the machinations of the action emphasize Constance's wit and control instead of the ingenuity of the author. And the tricks directed against Loveby by Constance have a specific thematic meaning: all of them are predicated upon the importance of money in Restoration marital relationships. Cleverness and wit are, moreover, implicitly defined as the traditional property of the upper class through the constant commentary of the tailor, Bibber, who associates class and ingenuity so strongly as to be willing to give his poverty-stricken aristocratic tenant, Loveby, credit for a jest.[8] This consciousness of class at the center of the action creates a social context that transcends mere entertainment and places the play outside the category of intrigue.

To this extent, *The Wild Gallant* begins to approach social satire. Dryden briefly exploits the potentially satiric implications of the form by questioning, sketchily and tangentially, the "rightness" of the social status quo that he presents. Justice Trice, the play's epitome of juridical order, is a figure of comic ridicule who is shown rolling and tickling with Loveby's whores (IV.i). And Lord Nonsuch, the comedy's ranking aristocrat, is depicted as a ridiculous old fool (IV.ii). More important, while the clever aristocratic couple scheme and jest, their morality is criticized by Frances, the tailor's wife, who in some of her early scenes is portrayed with a reserved sensitivity incompatible with a sympathy for Loveby. She justly complains of her plight as a victim of the aristocratic prerogative of limitless credit (I.ii.47–50). And Dryden turns Loveby's response to her complaints into a momentary irony directed against aristocratic morality itself:

> *Frances.* I hope you intend to deale by my Husband like a Gentleman, as
> they say?
> *Loveby.* Then I should beat him most unmercifully, and not pay him neither.
> [I.ii.19-22]

While Bibber's role in the play reflects, in ridiculous caricature, the assumption that the upper class, with its unfailing wit, should live off the lower, Frances comments on the injustice of that relationship, without, of course, ever constituting a challenge to the status quo. The conclusion of the play is appropriate and satisfying according to the social standards invoked as the working premises of the action, but along the way we are treated to a hint that the triumph of aristocratic wit, though perhaps necessary or inevitable, may not invariably be completely "right."

In these respects *The Wild Gallant*, like the best Restoration comedies, is a kind of social satire. The disjunction between Dryden's depiction of the workings of the social world and his moral judgment upon that society is slight, but not insignificant. Though assuming the social standards of the upper class as the basis of his motivation of the action as well as his definition of the characters and his depiction of their fates, Dryden is able to point out both the faults of the aristocracy and those of the typically satirized citizen classes.[9] He provides a critical perspective upon libertine morality and aristocratic superiority, but that perspective does not affect the structure or the outcome of the action, which is social: the witty characters outwit the fools, achieve matrimony with money, and end their careers with a dance. It is roughly this shape, though in very different manifestations, that characterizes the best dramatic social satire of the Restoration.

Despite this first play's slight tendency toward social satire, the earlier half of Dryden's comic corpus is characterized by the deliberate avoidance of major conflict between the characters or of actual moral transgression on the part of the protagonists. Although the heroes are gay young rakes, their actions are usually irreproachably chaste. And even when they attempt a bit of rakish behavior, they are rarely allowed a consummation. In *The Wild Gallant* Loveby is loyal to Constance, in *Sir*

Martin Mar-all (1667) there are no illicit allusions, in *Marriage A-la-Mode* the two couples never succeed in committing adultery, and in *The Spanish Friar* (1680) the young libertine's sexual efforts are directed toward none other than his own sister. In short, Dryden consistently (though not invariably) attempts to keep the satiric disjunction slight by avoiding conflict altogether or by denying it in the last act. In a play that is already dominated by tricks and disguises, the negation of significant conflict gives the intrigue effect further prominence. This tendency brings much of Dryden's early drama close to intrigue, except that in a pure intrigue serious issues would not even initially be entertained. Both *Sir Martin Mar-all* and *An Evening's Love* (1668) portray vivid city settings and characters, and in this respect are more nearly social than *The Rival Ladies*, but both avoid even so muted a satiric effect as that in *The Wild Gallant*. These plays are typical of the kind of social satire that fails to exploit the potential disjunction of the form and instead encourages the audience, through its emphasis on entertainment rather than judgment, to assume that the action is "all in fun."

In attempting to classify *An Evening's Love*, some critics have emphasized its Spanish material and therefore its affinities with *The Adventures of Five Hours* and *The Rival Ladies* as "Spanish romance."[10] Maximillian Novak's legitimate objection is that such an approach is incapable of distinguishing tragicomedy, comedy, and farce.[11] In the context of my argument, the fact that *An Evening's Love* seeks to depict a recognizable social world, that its action emphasizes wit rather than arbitrary error, and that it ultimately omits the disjunction of full satire is more significant than its use of Spanish material. During the early part of this period, Spanish effects were pervasive in the intrigue, the divided tragicomedy, the early social satire, and the heroic action. Only by defining the formal use to which such effects are put can we make meaningful judgments about the significance of Spanish sources or about the evolution of the genre.

Dryden's later comedies, *The Assignation* (1672), and especially *Mr. Limberham* (1678) and *Amphitryon* (1690), are full social satires. Dryden himself describes *Mr. Limberham* as "an honest *Satyre* against our crying sin of *Keeping*,"[12] and the play provides an example of what I have termed "practical" disjunction. The implicit judgment that is passed on the keeper, Limberham, and, in a more complicated manner, on Woodall, the young rake, is nowhere enacted in the plot, which ends with a happy reconciliation of all the characters. But Limberham's experiences suggest that keepers become the dupes of their mistresses. And the accumulating anxiety surrounding Woodall's increasingly close escapes and the apparent inevitability of discovery force us to conclude, with Woodall, that his sexual exploits are dangerously impractical (V.i, p. 331).[13] Erratic and profligate sexual behavior is implicitly judged to

be self-destructive, though not necessarily immoral. This emphasis on
pragmatism over morality may be a consequence of the play's bourgeois
milieu: middle-class characters of this period are stereotypically (often
hypocritically) prudish and therefore less open to moral attack than the
self-consciously amoral libertines of the aristocracy, the more typical
subjects of social satire. Critics have attempted to account for the play
by suggesting that it might have been intended for a more bourgeois
audience than Dryden's earlier drama,[14] or by emphasizing Charles's
contribution.[15] In the context of this argument and of our understanding of dramatic history, *Mr. Limberham* provides an example of the
range of dramatic types that can still be said to share the same formal
structure.

   Amphitryon is set not in contemporary London, but in ancient
Thebes. Its dramatic world, however, is an obvious projection of Restoration English society. The pervasiveness of economic motives,
especially in the relationship between Mercury and Phaedra, represents
the contemporary materialism that so many of the best Restoration
comedies condemn. More important, Jupiter's divine cuckolding of Amphitryon is clearly seen as the equivalent of the contemporary aristocratic privilege with citizens' wives. From the play's critical perspective
upon that privilege, Jupiter's sonorous thunderclaps, juxtaposed with
the tawdriness of his mission, only increase his ludicrousness. The comedy ends with a moment of ambivalence in which this satire almost
becomes explicit, and Jupiter is indirectly called a "cully." In effect,
Dryden's use of classical material serves to distance the social issues
only enough to make it easier for him to discuss contemporary manners.
For that reason, *Amphitryon* is a more straightforward dramatic satire
than *The Wild Gallant.* But, again because of its distance, it is inevitably
less harsh and less vehement than those earlier works or than the major
social satire of the period.

   Dryden's adoption of a more consistent satiric form in the latter half
of his career entails a greater degree of comic seriousness which in turn
produces, I believe almost inevitably, better plays. The near-intrigue and
the "all in fun" social forms, with their acceptance of aristocratic ideology and of the status quo, are intrinsically trivial—as the socially conservative satires of Etherege and Wycherley are not—because they lack
the satiric disjunction that is the basis of comic seriousness in this drama.
The differing degrees of seriousness between intrigue and social satire
afford a precise and effective means of discrimination between the minor
comedies, or the immature plays of the major comic dramatists, and the
great comic works of the period. In addition, even within satiric form,
practical disjunction like that of *Mr. Limberham* is typical of those plays
that are somewhat less mature and serious than *The Man of Mode* and
The Country Wife. Amphitryon, one of Dryden's most successful comedies

and arguably his best, is closer in form to the comic masterpieces of this period in its implicit attention to moral discrepancies, although, because of its derivative nature, it is quite distinct from and incommensurable with them.

Thus, Dryden moves in his comic career from primarily intriguelike and "all in fun" drama to an increasingly satiric form which points in the direction of Etherege's and Wycherley's great plays without ever equaling their full effect. Though Dryden's comic corpus spans both the years of the dominance of social satire and part of the later period that I see as transitional in the evolution of the genre, Dryden, in his comedies as well as his serious plays, remains a dramatic conservative. He produces no transitional drama, and his strong allegiance to intriguelike and "all in fun" forms makes delight rather than instruction the main characteristic of his comic works. Perhaps the fact that Dryden is the only major Restoration dramatist who produces important comedy as well as serious drama explains his propensity for entertainment in the "lower" form. Etherege and Wycherley write only comedies, and both of them, in their short careers, work from forms like Dryden's toward more fully realized and moral social satire.

II

George Etherege's drama, like Dryden's, falls into two main periods, a single work, *The Man of Mode*, constituting the second. And again, those two periods exemplify the course of generic evolution that we have been tracing in this chapter. Etherege's first plays (*The Comical Revenge*, 1664, and *She Would If She Could*, 1668) contain the same intriguelike or "all in fun" qualities as Dryden's early comedies: a tendency to emphasize a clever resolution of the plot at the expense of serious content, and, as a corollary, a consistent attempt to defuse conflict and eliminate sexual impropriety. But even more than Dryden's, Etherege's career clearly evolves toward full social satire. For this reason, the distinction between Etherege's early comedies and his last, best play provides a good basis for a clear definition of the form and ideology of the major dramatic social satire of the mid-1670s.

Etherege's first play, *The Comical Revenge*, is a multiple-plot tragicomedy with the characteristic early Restoration intrigue structure. The high plot presents the love conflicts of aristocratic characters in lofty heroic verse. It portrays a duel and an attempted suicide, and ends with the convenient and appropriate pairing of the necessary couples. The low plot is a simple stage farce, including an echoing mock duel. The middle plot represents the libertine-protagonist Frederick's pursuit of the Widow and hers of him, their schemes to entrap each other into marriage or a declaration of love, and their inevitable coupling.

The play contains much of the material of social comedy, though little of the serious meaning of a satire like *The Man of Mode*. Its setting (London taverns, Covent Garden), dialogue (the language of London low life), and dramatis personae (widows, rakes, cullies, and tricksters) are vividly mimetic of familiar London scenes according to the conventions of city comedy. Its action, however, depends mainly upon the neatly propitious shuffling of partners in the serious plot and the fortuitous removal of the nonexistent obstacles in the comic middle plot that are the hallmarks of intrigue. The low plot, which is closest to Jonsonian social satire,[16] is the least formally intriguelike of the three, since its farcical action does differentiate one fool from another, and metes out separate fates to each. But it criticizes only the Puritans and the London lower classes rather than the aristocracy. Ironically, in the evolution of social satire in the early Restoration, those plays that imitate Jonsonian comedy, with its much broader class perspective, are formally more conservative and dramatically less significant than the narrowly aristocratic major comedy of manners. The Restoration's version of the form is only fully serious when, in the later and greater social satires, it turns from blind royalism and anti-Puritanism to libertine ideology.

The coexistence of serious and comic plots in *The Comical Revenge* demonstrates the significance of intrigue form in the early stages of this dramatic history. The juxtaposition is only possible because both plots are so close to intrigue that their characterization and their thematic implications are secondary to the pleasing neatness of their tricks and resolutions. Despite their radically different manner and matter, both plots are designed to furnish the same kind of aesthetic pleasure. Dramatic interest is primarily directed, as in an intrigue, by the expectation of a neat pairing off in the final scene, rather than by the clear and potentially contradictory judgments that genuine tragedy and comedy would demand.

In his early intriguelike plays, Etherege, like Dryden, carefully absolves his characters of actual sexual conflict or even impropriety. Frederick chooses a widow as the happy recipient of his sexual interest and is thus, according to the standards of the day, practically immune to moral reproach. But to make Frederick's innocence unmistakable, Etherege studiously denies him even the opportunity of sleeping with his widow. In fact, unlike *The Man of Mode*, the play portrays no illicit sexual relations, though the characters often seem on the verge of some tantalizingly indecent behavior. In the end, the whole brunt of the play's supposed sexual daring is borne, farcically, by Frederick's comical, poxy French valet, who is locked in a tub to publicize his contraction of a social disease.

The play's proximity to intrigue and avoidance of conflict places it in that part of the spectrum of social forms which exhibits the least degree of disjunction between social material and implicit moral judgment. The conservative social resolution, directed in part by Frederick himself, who personally gives the Puritan cully and the lower-class gamesters their just deserts, is accepted without qualification, as the unquestioning royalism of the context demands. In *The Man of Mode* neither royalism nor Dorimant has such a role, and the lower-class characters, drawn with even stronger city "realism," are shown to be far beyond this simple formal jurisdiction.

She Would If She Could does not contain the same radical variety of plots and characters as *The Comical Revenge*, and, as a corollary, it is less immediately related to intrigue and somewhat closer to the specific form of *The Man of Mode*. Significantly, Etherege does not make his second play a tragicomedy, despite the success of his first. From the changeable and diffuse action of *The Comical Revenge*, with its frequent moments of farce and stage complication, he turns to an essentially single plot dominated by two pairs of comic lovers who occupy lengthy stretches of stage time in stationary dialogue. For this reason, those critics who do not consider *The Comical Revenge* the first comedy of manners invariably select *She Would If She Could*. In fact, John Harrington Smith designates the appearance of the "gay couple" as the most important aspect of this play and also of the succeeding drama.[17] But in terms of the evolution of social satire in this period, the mere presence of these lovers and their debates is less significant than the formal developments of which they are only a sign. Smith's isolation of a specific kind of character allows him to document the presence of a particular dramatic formula, but it does not enable him to explain the diminished variety of episodes and dramatis personae, the decreased use of mechanical tricks, the lessening emphasis on comic reversal or symmetrical concluding marriages, the growth of conflict and contradiction—in short the transcendence of intrigue concurrent with the development of the major comedy of manners. In *She Would If She Could* the centrality of the witty lovers signifies a change in the formal importance of individual characterization and thus, inevitably, a turn away from the unspecified interest in a neat conclusion that dominates *The Comical Revenge* and reconciles its disparate actions. In effect, the increasing prominence of the gay couple in social satire is a sign of the evolution away from intrigue, since the love-game material reflects an interest in clearly defined character relationships rather than in the simple unraveling of the plot.

But despite its proximity to full social satire, *She Would If She Could* contains the studied evasion of sexual conflict that characterizes intrigue-like and "all in fun" social forms and that makes the play, in its avoidance of contradiction, closer to *The Comical Revenge* than to *The Man*

of Mode. The two rake-protagonists, Courtall and Freeman, promise
the gay and witty Gatty and Ariana that they will avoid all female company until their next assignation. Of course, within a matter of minutes
they secure an introduction to a pair of eligible and wealthy young
country girls. Thus Etherege manufactures an essential dramatic tension
between the lovers. But he deprives it of content and significance by
making the potential rivals none other than Gatty and Ariana themselves,
whose names the errant rakes had never learned. The action of *She
Would If She Could* is made up of a series of similar episodes, which
consist of tension without conflict and which tend to establish the
sexual conservatism of the rakes despite the explicit libertinism of the
play's surface. Etherege wants his protagonists to appear to be aristocratic rakes, but without arousing any of the serious sexual and social
contradictions that libertinism implies.

In keeping with this consistent avoidance of conflict, the affair between Courtall and Lady Cockwood—the "she" of the title—does not
involve a lewd, illicit January and May reversal, but rather a formal
diatribe against female libertinism, in which Lady Cockwood serves as
an example of unacceptable female behavior. To our relief, Courtall
narrowly escapes Lady Cockwood's embraces, and is finally made permanently safe from her only by his marriage. His "affair" is actually
a testament to and guarantee of his chastity. Thus, though the play's
title suggests promiscuity, its action represents the flight from illicit
sex, and Courtall, in vivid contrast to Dorimant and to his own name,
is the perfect contradiction in terms: a Virgin Rake.

The empty tensions of the plot are resolved with the prospective
marriages of the two gay couples, to which there has been no impediment but misunderstanding, and with the reformation of the insatiable Lady Cockwood.[18] Thus the conclusion, perfectly consonant with
the sexual conservatism implicit in the whole development of the
action, affirms an orderly and totally efficacious social solution to all
the problems that the world of the plot can envisage. The form of
She Would If She Could, from the inception of the action to its resolution, commends society as it is, its traditional institutions, the status
quo.

In general, Etherege's early comedies, like Dryden's, can best be
understood as kinds of social satires in which the invocation of a recognizable social context and the operation of a recognizable set of social
standards is largely free from any implicit criticism of the "rightness" of
those standards. The intriguelike elements of these plays tend to direct
expectations away from the specific deserts and fates of individual characters, and thus away from any potential discrimination between social
justice and moral judgment. The evasion of actual conflict, especially
sexual, contingent on this neglect of differentiated characterization,

produces a workable dramatic action which can be resolved easily and automatically and which thus assumes that social tension is "all in fun" and, concurrently, that an adequate solution is always available in the status quo. The care that Dryden and Etherege must take to remove any sources of actual conflict, and the tricks and coincidences of which they must avail themselves to make their rakes virginal, all suggest that contradiction and moral discrepancy are inherent implications of the form against which the "all in fun" dramatist must consciously struggle. Very few of these "all in fun" plays are fully devoid of potentially subversive satiric implications, despite the predominant conservatism of their actions. In *She Would If She Could*, for instance, when the unfaithful rakes are confronted by Gatty and Ariana, they defend themselves in turn:

> *Courtall.* Why should you be so unreasonable, ladies, to expect that from us, we should scarce have hoped for from you? Fie, fie, the keeping of one's word is a thing below the honor of a gentleman.
> *Freeman.* A poor shift! Fit only to uphold the reputation of a paltry Citizen.
> [II.ii.199–204]

This momentary irony is not developed or repeated sufficiently to imply a full alternative standard of value to the traditional aristocratic assumptions by which the rest of the action operates. But its presence, like Frances's brief critique of aristocratic prerogative in *The Wild Gallant*, suggests the pervasiveness of this kind of social criticism in the comedy of the period, however weakly developed its satire.

The formal category of social satire, then, enables us to perceive the coherence of the drama over these years, while at the same time distinguishing from that larger group the particular characteristics of the early manners comedy. As we have seen, the evolution from intrigue to intriguelike and "all in fun" social satire entails an increasing formal discrimination of individual characters and fates. It also entails a concurrent progression from entertainment for its own sake to entertainment with an explicitly social context that provides terms for the judgment of the characters and the resolution of the action. The major dramatic satire exploits the implicit contradictions of this social context. It fills the form with actual and unresolvable conflict, and it develops fully all the potential disjunction between social and moral that social satire implies. In *The Man of Mode* Etherege seeks out the collisions of character and value that he avoids in *She Would If She Could*. The polarizations in the play reproduce the ideological contradictions of the aristocratic society that it depicts. That society is examined and finally affirmed, but simultaneously exposed and judged in the unique manner of Restoration dramatic satire.

Libertinism, or some reference to it, is the distinguishing ingredient

of the major social satire of this period. It effectively discriminates the
Restoration social satirists as a group from such predecessors as Jonson,
Shirley, and Molière. The formal centrality of libertine philosophy for
the Restoration dramatists results from its direct implication of the
essential social contradictions of their time and class: writers of social
satire naturally turn for their material to the issues they perceive as
problematic in their particular society. In these plays, the ambivalence
toward the social status quo—or the disjunction between represented
social reality and the implicit moral judgment upon the "rightness" of
that reality—represents an aesthetic expression of the ambiguous aristocratic attitude toward the subversive content of libertine ideology, as
revealed to us in its links with the rhetoric of the radical Puritans.

Though libertinism has a long and distinguished intellectual history,[19]
Restoration libertinism is more than an ideological or philosophical
fossil in postrevolutionary England. During and immediately after the
revolution and Restoration, the aristocracy lost much of its economic
and social distinctiveness and even preeminence. Politically, it remained
dominant into the eighteenth century and beyond. Economically, however, it derived the preponderance of its income from capitalist enter-
prises, primarily in agriculture, but also in trade and industry. In the
nation as a whole, moneyed interests were more powerful than landed
interests by the 1690s at the latest. Thus, as the aristocracy increasingly depended on the same sources of wealth as the bourgeoisie, it became less distinguishable from that class, in its economic position and
in some aspects of social relations and ideology.[20]

A segment of the youngest and most embittered members of the
aristocracy sought refuge in the advocacy of a loose social and philosophical system diametrically opposed to that of the increasingly
prominent, often Puritan, bourgeoisie. Not surprisingly, this system
includes a whole spectrum of social values that parallel those expressed
by the Ranters, the Diggers or True Levellers, and the Muggletonians
during the early revolutionary years. In general, the radicals and the libertines share a common studied opposition to the beliefs and programs
of the Presbyterians. Both the Ranters and the court wits encourage
profanity and exercise their considerable talent for cursing and swearing, in obvious opposition to the moderate Puritans' obsessive verbal
purity. Both radicals and libertines advocate free love and the abolition
of traditional marriage, in opposition to bourgeois sexual constraints.
Both declare an aversion to labor, expressed specifically by the Diggers
as a principled rejection of labor beyond the amount necessary for
subsistence, in opposition to the capitalist, middle-class work ethic.
Both practice nudity and thus challenge the notion of original sin.
Both voice an explicit theoretical rejection of all authority and hierarchy, which on the part of the Diggers is expressed as the advocacy

of a classless society. And both espouse antimonarchism, radical republicanism, and atheism—in Gerrard Winstanley the gradual substitution
of a rational principle for the divine being.[21]

As these similarities suggest, though the aristocratic Restoration libertine retains and protects what remains of a privileged class position,
he is also provided with the ideological material for a radical assessment
not only of the bourgeois, moderate Presbyterians, but also of the monarchy and the aristocracy itself, especially in their accommodation to
capitalist society. The libertine advocacy of freedom, with its deliberate
subversion of social order and hierarchy, constitutes an implicitly radical attack upon the status quo, launched from an ideological vantage
point outside an increasingly capitalist society and reflecting the discontent of a class whose partial exclusion from traditional routes to wealth,
power, and prerogative provides it with a critical perspective upon that
society. For this reason, libertinism is inevitably viewed as a threat and
ultimately repudiated, even by the Restoration libertine himself.

Rochester's inconsistent and occasional republicanism, his atheism,
his rejection of monogamy as a restraint on human freedom, and his
satires upon monarchy and traditional values provide the most obvious
example.[22] But many of the comic dramatists of the seventies express
specific social criticisms of a similar nature. Jeremy Collier himself, in
his attack upon what he clearly perceived to be a subversive literary
form, links manners comedy with Leveller revolutionary rhetoric and
suggests that the two share a parallel, radical purpose.[23] Like many
conservative spokesmen, he knew his enemy, and his assessment of the
radical implications of libertine ideology is accurate, though his readings of the plays are not.[24] The best of the courtier playwrights, in their
adoption of a satiric form, dealt, each in his or her own particular
manner, with the most fundamental social contradictions that they
could perceive. The turn to satire in this period of a reinstated but
economically and socially transfigured aristocracy is the aesthetic consequence of those contradictions.

Dramatic social satire, then, is the formal expression of a peculiarly
vexed and conflicted ideology, fundamentally conservative in its allegiance to traditional values and to the status quo, but daringly radical in
its exposure of the hypocrisy, the immorality, and the materialism of
the society it must finally accept. The complexity of this ideological
contradiction is typically not apparent to critics who see the phenomenon of libertinism ahistorically. Such a perspective has produced, on
the one hand, a view of the libertine as an honest, self-conscious, or un-
sentimental hero, the embodiment of a momentary assertion of sexual
or psychological liberation. For critics of this school, the plays are not
satires, but either uncritical descriptions of contemporary aristocratic
mores or actual celebrations of libertine freedom.[25] This prolibertine

position is balanced by an equally incomplete antilibertine argument, which emphasizes the traditional morality of the drama and documents its rejection of libertine behavior. [26] The polarities of this critical dispute reproduce the structure of the formal and ideological contradiction that I have taken as the basis of my definition of mature dramatic satire: the contradictory interpretations elicited by the form can be seen as evidence of its contradictory nature.

The Man of Mode (1676) begins with a seemingly irrelevant confrontation between Dorimant and a succession of outspoken lower-class characters: the Orange-Woman, the Shoemaker, and, by proxy, the whore. Each of these characters in turn disparages the aristocratic rakes —their behavior, their morality, and their class. The Orange-Woman, who expresses open disgust at her client's sexual corruption, [27] spits at the sight of Dorimant and Medley's morning embrace and, cursing Medley, likens him to her peer, "the shoemaker without" (I.82). The Shoemaker himself compares the morality of the gentlemen to his own: "There's never a man i' the town lives more like a gentleman with his wife than I do. I never mind her motions; she never inquires into mine. We speak to one another civilly, hate one another heartily, and because 'tis vulgar to lie and soak together, we have each of us our several settle-bed" (I.282–86). He challenges the prerogatives of the aristocracy, asserting a kind of egalitarianism in sexual behavior: "'Zbud, I think you men of quality will grow as unreasonable as the women: you would engross the sins o' the nation. Poor folks can no sooner be wicked but th'are railed at by their betters" (I.253–56). The rakes themselves condone and even contribute to this disruption of traditional class distinctions. When, at the end of the act, Dorimant receives a request from his whore for "a guynie to see the operies," he decides to send her the money specifically so that she can "perk up i' the face of quality" (I.471–75).

The presence of these characters, their outspoken observations, and their unique relationship to their "betters" distinguish the social world of *The Man of Mode* from that of *The Comical Revenge* or from Jonsonian social satire. This lower class is not amenable to the simple formal authority that Frederick exercises over Wheadle and Palmer in *The Comical Revenge*. Significantly, the Orange-Woman and the Shoemaker, not one of the gentlemen, are the first to verbalize Dorimant's libertine philosophy, thereby distinguishing it as much as possible from traditional aristocratic morality.

The opening scene thus introduces libertinism almost as the corollary of the rejection of class hierarchy advocated by the most radical revolutionary sects. The conjunction is also made explicit, in this scene and throughout the play, in the character of Lady Woodvill, who nostalgically recollects "the forms and civility of the last age" and fears and detests Dorimant and "the freedoms of the present" (I.117–20). In addition, Medley's debate with the Shoemaker and the Shoemaker's apologia for his own morality, which he claims is "like a gentleman['s]," initiate the critique of libertinism that constitutes the play's satire. Echoing Courtall's ironic comment in *She Would If She Could* (see above), Medley remarks to the Shoemaker: "You have brought the envy of the world upon you by living above yourself. Whoring and swearing are vices too genteel for a shoemaker" (I.249–52). In short, this first scene serves at once to define the social and historical context of libertinism, to applaud its witty representation in the gay and liberal rakes, and to suggest an implicit criticism of its moral and social assumptions. It establishes the formal prerequisites of the drama.

From this introduction until his final triumph in Act V, Dorimant dominates the action of the play. His libertinism, moreover, has greater substance than Courtall's in *She Would If She Could.* We see him involved in two affairs, one of which comes so close to represented consummation that we witness Handy's tying up of the linen (IV.ii.opening *s.d.*). And as a libertine, Dorimant is the epitome of social accomplishment and "genius" (I.232). He is the subject of every conversation, the preoccupation of every woman, and the model for every man. Even the old-fashioned Lady Woodvill is enamored of his wit and charm when he entertains her in disguise. His sexual pursuits generate the action of the play and his social success sets the standards of his dramatic world.

But the implicit moral judgment upon the libertine hero diverges from this assessment of his preeminence in the social world of the action. Though literally triumphant in the context of the plot, Dorimant is the object of a consistent moral criticism, supplied through the details of characterization, incident, and dialogue. The disjunction between this moral criticism and the social approval asserted in the action is the essential formal feature of Etherege's dramatic satire. For instance, we know from Bellair's commendations in the first scene of the play (I.337–38) that Dorimant takes particular care of his appearance. Fopling, who is introduced as the epitome of social affectation, immediately recognizes Dorimant as a compatriot in the French style of dress and manner (III.ii.140ff.). The parallel between these two "men of mode" is pursued consistently throughout the play,[28] and Fopling's obvious and exaggerated affectation is made to infect his more graceful and self-conscious counterpart. Thus the local ridicule directed against the person of Fopling, though also an end in itself, becomes an important device for the implicit assessment of the libertine hero; a device, however, that does not interfere with our admiration for the hero's preeminence or with our sense of the appropriateness of his success in the social context of the action.

The central tension between Dorimant and Harriet further contributes to this implicit judgment of the libertine. Harriet's consciousness of social role-playing serves to reveal Dorimant's hypocrisy: "He's agreeable and pleasant, I must own, but he does so much affect being so, he displeases me" (III.iii.23-24). This contrast in their characters is reiterated in each of their disputes and keeps them at odds until the resolution of the action, despite the fact that they are obviously designed for each other.

The implicit criticism of Dorimant extends beyond this juxtaposition of his social accomplishment with Harriet's naturalness; his relationships with Loveit and Bellinda give rise to the same satiric judgment. For instance, when his scheme to rid himself of Loveit backfires and she flouts him with Sir Fopling, we do not feel her temporary victory over her tormentor to be undeserved. Significantly, Etherege chooses to portray at length Dorimant's coldly calculated plot against Loveit (I.222-31) and his quickly forgotten protestations of eternal love for Bellinda (IV.ii.36-43). By this means Dorimant's whole represented relationship to his cast mistresses is weighted toward a sympathy for them, at his expense. The accumulating judgment upon libertine morality acquires further substance from Loveit's singularly convincing attacks on Dorimant, which contain all the criticisms expressed only implicitly in the juxtapositions and confrontations of the characters. When she accuses him of artificiality (V.i.112), we know from his own comments in previous acts that she is justified. When she confronts him with his lies (V.i.155-60), we know that he has no answer. When he claims she never loved him (V.i.167-68), we are able to reverse the charge. And when he reproaches her with her attentions to Fopling, we feel the perfect justice of her response:

> You, who have more pleasure in the ruin of a woman's reputation than in the endearments of her love, reproach me not with yourself and I defy you to name the man can lay a blemish on my fame. [V.i.183-86]

In short, the force of her eloquence, joined with the force of moral judgment communicated more indirectly in the rest of the action, permits her to carry the day. Thus, when the libertine hero is confronted and bested by his two cast mistresses and forced to flee the field (V.i.256-82), we are prepared to enjoy his confusion.

In general, then, the form of *The Man of Mode* presents us with two contrasting judgments of the libertine hero, one social and one moral. First, in response to the most overt workings of the action, we admire Dorimant as the epitome of triumphant wit and success according to the social values of his world, and on those grounds we feel, throughout the play, that he deserves the ultimate reward of Harriet's love. Second, through the many details of characterization, representation, and dialogue, as well as through the underlying implications

of the central conflict between Harriet and Dorimant, we find that our
hero is cruel, unscrupulous, affected, hypocritical, false: in short, a
damned libertine. The coexistence of these two judgments makes *The
Man of Mode* a dramatic satire.

The conclusion of the play is the resultant of both these formal forces.
True to the social standards of the action, the libertine hero secures
a happy fate: he exits, triumphant, with the most desirable woman of
his world. He undergoes no reformation, he has no lines of repentance
or regret; in fact, his hapless victims Loveit and Bellinda, for whom
the satiric implications of the form had engendered considerable sympathy, must suffer defeat and, in the case of Loveit, open disgrace
(V.ii.351-52). But the social stability produced at the play's conclusion
is strangely incongruous with Dorimant's libertine conduct throughout. His prospects for a permanent happy marriage with Harriet attest
to Etherege's affirmation of a hierarchy of values, including wedded
love, quite different from that expounded by the libertines at the beginning of the play. In fact, the traditionalist Lady Woodvill validates the
relationship herself after Harriet has sworn to remain a dutiful and obe-
diant daughter. Dorimant's evident love for Harriet gives further force
to Etherege's final affirmation of the social status quo. Significantly,
Dorimant's feelings are communicated by means of repeated asides, in
which his love is shown to grow from an initial attraction (III.iii.121-
23) to a disturbing "disease" (IV.i.149-50). Since Dorimant never de-
ceives himself in sexual matters, we can assume that his "I love her and
dare not let her know it" (IV.i.139) is meant to be understood as utterly
unlike his hypocritical protestations to other women.

By representing Dorimant's love for Harriet as fundamentally different from his relationships with Loveit and Bellinda, and by showing
that Harriet possesses all the prudence that her predecessors lacked
(IV.ii.179-80 and V.ii.301-07), Etherege clearly encourages the belief
that Dorimant and Harriet will marry, but he carefully omits the representation of that marriage on the stage. By this means he avoids the
imputations of insincerity that might have attached to Dorimant if
the final union had been arranged with indecorous haste. But he also
avoids any suggestion of a reformation on the part of the celebrated
rake. The libertine hero ends his action unmatched, in the full possession
of his libertinism, and even equipped with the typically cynical rakish
references to Harriet's fortune and his own material necessities (IV.ii.181-
83 and V.ii.265-66). In keeping with the contradiction of values in
the body of the play, Etherege simply continues that contradiction into
the conclusion: Dorimant is both libertine and loyal husband.

Unlike Etherege's early plays, *The Man of Mode* is filled with actual
and serious conflict—so serious that it does not submit to resolution.
Here for the first time, Etherege exploits the form's full potential for

disjunction, and in this respect his masterpiece resembles the other major social satires of its period. But the close proximity between the source of moral judgment and the overt motivation of the action distinguishes the play's form from that of the other major Restoration dramatic satires. The simple mechanics of the plot, which define the social standards of judgment and establish Dorimant's preeminence, also produce the central conflict of the action: that between Dorimant and Harriet. Since this conflict itself engenders much of the satiric criticism directed against Dorimant, the moral judgment offered by the satire cannot be severed from the social judgment asserted in the action. The play's conclusion thus presents Etherege with a difficult formal problem: how to resolve an action based on both social and moral assessment. And Etherege can solve this problem only by unabashed evasion. Dorimant achieves his expected social success, but the moral criticism directed against him is so close to the action that it too finds its way into the resolution of the plot in the form of Harriet's "victory" over the libertine hero. Thus, though the disjunction in *The Man of Mode* between social and moral judgment is typical of social satire, the simultaneous entertainment of libertine and traditional values in the conclusion of the play is peculiar to this social satire.

The unusual critical controversy over *The Man of Mode* itself illustrates the polarities of its satiric form. Interpretations of this play fall into two opposing categories, one emphasizing the social genius of the libertine protagonist and the other the implicit rejection of libertine amorality. Those critics who register Dorimant's social merit alone describe him as an unqualified hero, an invulnerable representative of the freedom to follow one's own inclinations, or a model for the dramatist, the audience, and the age. Consequently, they view the play as inherently amoral.[29] Those critics who note only Etherege's condemnation of Dorimant supply a simple moralistic reading of the drama, emphasizing either the rake's immorality or his reformation.[30] A few readers feel both social and moral forces, and conclude that the comedy is contradictory, ironic, ambiguous, or complex.[31] Clearly, the play presents two faces to the critical world, one social and one moral. Together they constitute its unique satiric form.

Finally, though the means are different, the formal ends of *The Man of Mode* are identical to those of *The Conquest of Granada*. Dryden's juxtaposition of subversive Herculean radicalism and political stability, his incorporation of an antisocial hero into a royalist form, produces the same neatly unresolved contradiction as Etherege's simultaneous affirmation of libertine ideology and traditional social values. Etherege, like Dryden, has it both ways, and his resolution of the formal problems presented by his satire expresses perfectly the ideological contradiction that the dramatist, and his age, were unable to resolve.

Though Etherege finds it almost irresistibly attractive, libertine morality, like Ranter ideology in the mouths of a precariously reinstalled aristocracy, is judged to be destructively antisocial and immoral. Libertine philosophy supplies Etherege with a terminology, like that of the Ranters' republican rhetoric, for a critique of traditional social institutions and class distinctions and even of the aristocracy. This terminology creates for Etherege a fundamental ambivalence about libertinism itself in its implicit challenge to a status quo that neither he nor any other members of the court circle would want to relinquish. Etherege finds the form of his greatest play in this contradiction. Wycherley's less evasive dramatic satire derives its moral bitterness from the same formal source.

III

William Wycherley, like Etherege, wrote two less serious, more intrigue-like comedies before he reached satiric majority in *The Country Wife* and *The Plain Dealer*. Both of his early works have sources in Spanish intrigue drama, both depend upon disguise or mistaken identity as a motivation for their actions, and both accept without question a royalist status quo against which the machinations of their characters are seen to be "all in fun." *Love in a Wood* (1671) consists of a loose and weak action that pits a large cast of potential lovers or mates against one another by means of innumerable incidents of mistaken identity and disguise. Typically, the plot depends upon mere error rather than serious conflict. In one portion of the diffuse action, for instance, Valentine, who loves Christina, is brought to doubt her when his friend Ranger, as a result of a separate misunderstanding, tells him that he has seen her flirting in the park. Mistakes like this multiply and intermingle for all the characters, until they are resolved by the ultimate mistaken identities that permit Christina to confess her innocence to Valentine because she believes him to be Ranger, while Ranger, in an identical scene with his estranged lover, confesses his love because he believes her to be Christina. Needless to say, this reconciles both couples and produces two happy marriages and a conclusion to the action. Except for a kind of conventional anti-Puritanism like that of *The Comical Revenge*, the play is completely uncritical of the characters and antics it depicts.

In *The Gentleman Dancing Master* (1672) Wycherley turns from this diversity of character and incident to a single action dominated by a single marriageable couple. The witty and lively Hippolita, who takes it upon herself to find her own husband when her father's choice turns out to be a vain, Frenchified dandy, dominates the plot in a manner quite unlike that of any of the numerous undifferentiated characters of

Love in a Wood. This ingenious heroine invents the play's central trick, passing off her new suitor and eventual husband as her dancing master to avoid the wrath of her father, who has adopted the ridiculous sexual jealousy of the Spanish. The play, with its lengthy local satire of Spanish manners and Spanish honor, is almost a parody of *capa y espada* drama, except that its protagonists are excluded from the ridicule.[32] The nationalistic intention of this parody serves to distance it from the contemporary London society that constitutes its setting and to make the play, for all its local satire, an "all in fun" social form. Wycherley does not provide an implicit judgment of the social standards that shape the action of the witty protagonists, who are unconditionally admirable, but only a local and specific satire upon individual, non-English idiosyncrasy. Nationalism operates in this play, like anti-Puritanism in *Love in a Wood* or *The Comical Revenge*, to reinforce a blind allegiance to the status quo. This allegiance forestalls the serious conflict of full formal satire and emphasizes instead local satiric objects outside of the dramatist's own class or nation that in turn validate the social status quo by negative example.

Thus, like Etherege, Wycherley moves from an intriguelike form with a myriad of characters to be paired off to a form that depends upon more clearly differentiated characters and upon the discrimination of individual deserts and fates. This attention to specific character assessment, as we have seen in the earlier social satire, is generally linked to a simplification of the plot, to the inclusion of or focus upon a witty gay couple, and, stylistically, to a notable increase in repartee and similitude. These formal steps away from intrigue precede, in Wycherley's career as well as Etherege's, the exploitation of the full disjunction of dramatic satire. While reflecting these essential differences from intrigue, *The Country Wife* (1675), the first of the major manners comedies, retains an old intriguelike trick—Horner's impotence disguise —as the central device of its action. This distant echo of the neutral intrigue form is the material out of which Wycherley creates a full dramatic satire, where the ways of the world are in complete contradiction with what is "right" and where moral judgment is kept scrupulously separate from the social standards of the action.

Like *The Man of Mode, The Country Wife* takes as its satiric subject not the London lower classes, as Jonson does in his social satires or Etherege in *The Comical Revenge*, not City Puritans or foreign caricatures as Wycherley does in *Love in a Wood* or *The Gentleman Dancing Master*, but its author's own class. As Sparkish observes:

> Their predecessors were contented to make serving-men only their stage-fools, but these rogues [the contemporary dramatists] must have gentlemen, with a pox to 'em, nay, knights. And, indeed, you shall hardly see a fool upon the stage but he's a knight; and to tell you the truth, they have kept me these

six years from being a knight in earnest, for fear of being knighted in a play,
and dubbed a fool. [33]

Wycherley's satire is based upon the same social material as Etherege's,
but each dramatist's version of the form is unique. In *The Country
Wife*, our admiration and sympathy for the protagonist are uncontested.
There are no episodes, like Dorimant's defeat at the tongues of Loveit
and Bellinda in *The Man of Mode*, that induce us to side against the libertine intriguer. And there is no direct incorporation of moral judgment into the motivation of the plot, as in the central conflict between
Dorimant and Harriet.

Horner's sexual scheme generates the action of *The Country Wife*,
and his social success supplies the play with its primary standard of
evaluation. In this respect, Horner, like Dorimant, is the formal arbiter
of the comedy. He fools every man and sleeps with every eligible woman, except Alithea, and his sexual triumph is both appropriate and inevitable, in terms of the materialistic standards of his world. Since
Horner is an isolated manipulator—not even his best friends are admitted
into his confidence—Wycherley supplies the Quack, who is present at
all of Horner's sexual victories in order to give the hero the applause
necessary to substantiate our sense of his ingenuity and social supremacy. The Quack's initial failures of confidence stimulate our expectation of Horner's success, which we know to be imminent, and which of
course is always even more complete than we dared hope. The general
environment of male libertinism in Act I wins further sympathy for
Horner's sexual ambitions. And this atmosphere is reproduced in the
honor debates of the Fidgets and Squeamishes of the play. These
characters' incessant references to sexual intercourse and social expediency provide an additional context for the assessment of Horner's
exploits. In short, the social world of the drama, in all its detail, establishes a standard of judgment based upon sexual success and prowess,
against which Horner must be judged as the most successful and profi-
cient member of his society.

And Horner is rewarded for this success. According to the social
standards of the action, his fate is consistent with what we feel to be
his deserts. In this comic world, as the Quack's testimony suggests,
anyone as clever as Horner deserves to succeed. In fact, in comparison
with the officious fool Fidget and the violently jealous idiot Pinchwife,
Horner would easily win our approbation, even by default. In the last
act, when Horner's trick comes close to disastrous exposure, our tensions and expectations arise from our urgent desire to see him saved.
Our sense of the play's implicit rules tells us that Horner does not deserve to be exposed by Pinchwife; in fact, such an exposure would
be a disappointing violation of the terms of the action. But, like Dori-

mant, Horner is judged by another set of standards as well—standards implicit in the dehumanizing nature of the hero's own activities, in the grotesque characters with whom he is surrounded and compared, and finally in the contrasting subplot, which provides an unstated alternative to Lady Fidget's "honor" and Horner's "honesty." None of these sources of moral assessment, however, is allowed to infect our hopes for Horner's success in the action or our anxiety, in the last scene, about his exposure. The course of hopes and expectations for the protagonist in this satire flows smoothly and consistently from our opening assessment of his ingenuity to his appropriate concluding victory. Wycherley maintains a complete disjunction between social and moral judgment.

First of all, Horner's trick—and, because his trick defines his character, his whole being—is the epitome of compulsive and mechanical sexual desire, from which Wycherley has taken pains to exclude any sense of enjoyment or fulfillment, or even satiation. The play's deservedly famous "china scene" provides the central example of this dehumanizing and pleasureless appetite. The metaphor of china serves to reduce an unmeasurable aspect of human intercourse to a matter merely of volume and number:

> *Lady Fidget.* What, d'ye think if he had had any left, I would not have had it too? For we women of quality never think we have china enough.
> *Horner.* Do not take it ill, I cannot make china for you all, but I will have a roll-wagon for you too, another time. [IV.iii.192-96]

In addition, the locked door, behind which this mechanical act is being perpetrated, the bustle on stage, and the presence of the oblivious Sir Jasper all make Horner's dispensing of china an act of cuckoldry, of insatiable appetite, of depraved sensuality; anything, in short, but an act of pleasure or of love. The women's incessantly repeated epithets for Horner: "the confounded toad," "the unmannerly toad," "this woman-hater, this toad, this ugly, greasy, dirty sloven," "the odious beast," "clownish beast" (IV.iii.79-144), all reinforce the animality and depravity that underlie Horner's greatest moment of triumph. And this high grostesquerie is manifest in all of Horner's actions throughout the play.

Horner occupies a world of mechanical sensuality, the depiction of which serves both to emphasize by association the satire that we have seen directed specifically at the libertine hero, and ultimately to generalize that satire to include society as a whole. The Quack's appreciation of Horner's exploits provides, in the context of the action, a conduit for our enthusiastic social assessment of Horner's ingenuity. But implicit in each of the Quack's comments is a judgment upon the characters whom his patron either fools or possesses. He is repeatedly astounded at the behavior of the cuckolds and their wives (e.g., IV.iii.132-33).

In fact, his initial lack of confidence in Horner stems from his ignorance of the baseness of Horner's society (IV.iii.19–20), and as he becomes convinced of Horner's ingenuity, he grows more sophisticated in his assessment of Horner's compatriots.

The prime example of the depravity of Horner's world, and its implication of Horner as well, is the collection of repulsive women whom Horner labors to possess. We are shown, to the detriment of our moral estimate of the hero, Horner's constant prostitution to these women, and his self-abasement in submitting to their name-calling as well as their physical attacks. More significantly, these ladies, by consensus, redefine the notion of honor as social expedience, the universal tool of self-interest (V.iv.98–103). Their open hypocrisy, connected as it is with their simulated fastidiousness before each other and Sir Jasper (II.i.374–75 and 395), and their self-centered sexual snobbery, all elicit a disgust from which Horner cannot be excluded. In fact, Horner's own behavior, his attitudes, and even his cynical language echo theirs (V.iv.167–69). He is condemned not only by association, but also by implicit analogy.

In a similar way, Wycherley allows part of the moral judgment against Horner to emerge from the characterization of Sir Jasper Fidget, Pinchwife, and even Sparkish. Sir Jasper's pursuit of business and contempt for pleasure, his unwillingness to attend to his own women, plays into the hands of the libertine intriguer and establishes, in the male world of the play, the sense of a materialistic, money-dominated society exactly analogous to the mechanical sexual world of the women. Sir Jasper's use of the central terms "business" and "pleasure" defines the reductive society that the play portrays:

> Well, well—that your ladyship is as virtuous as any she, I know, and him all
> the town knows—he, he, he! Therefore, now you like him, get you gone
> to your business together; go, go to your business, I say, pleasure, whilst I
> go to my pleasure, business. [II.i.566–70]

The designation of Horner's "pleasure" as a kind of "business" validates the implicit judgment passed on Horner's pleasureless business from the opening description of his trick, and ties it to the materialistic City sensibility that Wycherley explicitly condemns.

Pinchwife, likewise, consistently assigns a monetary value to women, and specifically to his marital relationship (I.i.383–88). His jealousy springs not from any love for Margery, but from his sense that she is his property, a personal possession with material value which, for that reason, he is bound to protect (II.i.298–301, III.ii.345–46, V.ii.78–81). He inhabits the same reductive world as Sir Jasper, and suffers the same ignominious fate, but, more significantly, his attitudes and even his language are echoed by his tormentor. Horner insistently applies the same metaphor of money and property to all relationships with women.[34] Finally, Sparkish provides a parallel of another sort that nevertheless enforces the effect of the more substantial comparisons of Horner with Sir Jasper and Pinchwife. Though about to marry, Sparkish repeatedly and loquaciously defines himself as a wit and a libertine. His openly professed lack of affection for Alithea derives from a crass sexual materialism that duplicates, in a more blatant and visible form, the philosophy of the libertine hero:

> I never had any passion for you till now, for now I hate you. 'Tis true I might have married your portion, as other men of parts of the town do sometimes.
> [V.iii.66-69]

Like Fopling in *The Man of Mode*, though to a lesser extent, Sparkish is a partial means to Wycherley's satire, and he too comes to be incorporated into the grotesque world of the play as an end in himself. While Sir Jasper and Pinchwife represent the materialistic world of business, Sparkish stands for the apparently contrasting world of pleasure. Horner's doings as a libertine "man of pleasure" are carefully distinguished from Sir Jasper's City affairs, and the effect of this distinction is to enforce our admiration for Horner and our desire to see him triumph over the foolish cuckolds. But in the end, the distinction becomes an analogy, and the libertine is shown to be no more human and no less materialistic than the City businessman.

The satiric exaggeration and reductiveness inherent in Wycherley's presentation of Horner's exploits and environment are complemented, in the moral estimate of the hero, by the values presented in the subplot. While the ladies and Horner redefine honor as social expediency and while Margery, the "innocent" tabula rasa, learns to follow the same hypocritical rules, albeit clumsily, Alithea's allegiance to her honor suggests a moral alternative: "I was engaged to marry, you see, another man, whom my justice will not suffer me to deceive or injure" (IV.i.16-17). While Horner assumes universal cynicism and self-interest, Harcourt and Alithea are falling honorably in love. And while Horner and Pinchwife reduce female companionship to material language, Harcout pledges: "If you take marriage for a sign of love [rather than interest], take it from me immediately" (II.i.220-21). The subplot opposes the possibility of real love to Horner's obsession with appetite, and a sense of human affection to Horner's materialistic cynicism: it provides a glimpse of a different moral universe.[35] At the end of the play, only Harcourt and Alithea marry. Horner, unlike Dorimant, remains an unmatchable libertine, and hence, again unlike Dorimant, a consistent and unqualified object of satire. In the context of the action, his fate is appropriate and inevitable. In the context of the moral assessment of his depravity, the contrast between his fate and Harcourt's further reinforces the satire.

In general, then, *The Country Wife* presents two distinct judgments of its hero. The moral condemnation of Horner does not interrupt our hopes for his triumph at the conclusion of his action. But that moral judgment, though it must share the stage with Horner's success in the social world, is never weakened by the indirect terms of its expression. Because the form of *The Country Wife* maintains this complete distinction between social and moral judgment, the play has a history of contradictory explications. Those critics who see only Horner's social preeminence invariably describe him as an ideal of freedom, dominance, or naturalism. They consequently claim that the play is not a satire, that it has no moral assumptions, and that it makes no moral references. [36] And relatedly, they tend to argue that the Harcourt-Alithea subplot is not a source of moral contrast, but rather an example of the near-disastrous failure of natural self-interest: to the extent that Horner is an ideal, Alithea must be a dullard, a hypocrite, or a fool. [37] Those critics who define the play as moral usually see it as a satire and consequently either believe that Horner is judged or condemned, [38] or dismiss our troublesome admiration for him by claiming that Pinchwife and the other cuckolds are the center of the plot and that Horner is only a representative of the satiric voice of the dramatist. [39] The controversy over this play thus closely parallels that over *The Man of Mode* and arises from the same formal source, but in the case of *The Country Wife* the polarity of interpretation is even more marked. Whereas in *The Man of Mode* moral criticism of Dorimant is so entwined with his social career that it can hardly be missed, in *The Country Wife* the moral dimension is never made explicit. Etherege finally evades a full confrontation with the anarchic logical conclusions of libertine philosophy by bringing his advocacy of traditional morality to the surface at the end of his play. Wycherley, on the other hand, does not permit his drama to elude the contradiction that constitutes the basis of its satiric form. While Etherege makes full use of the formal resources of social satire, filling his action with actual and irreconcilable conflict, Wycherley, by segregating the terms of assessment, takes the form to its logical conclusion: he finds no moral resolution.

The formal differences between these two dramatic satires are embodied in the differing social visions expressed most eloquently in their conclusions. In *The Man of Mode*, Dorimant finishes his career with a testimony to the bonds of monogamous love, and his libertine amorality is subsumed in the happy affirmation of the status quo. Wycherley's satire, however, seeks no such affirmation. It portrays a grotesque and claustrophobic world that offers few alternatives to cuckoldry or depravity. Horner ends his play in isolated and cynical triumph, while Harcourt and Alithea are given only two lines to negotiate their match. The play's final scene presents, in the dance of cuckolds, the ultimate closing off of alternatives, confirming Horner and his several sexual partners in their pleasureless trick. The traditional aristocratic values of honor and personal loyalty that Alithea embodies have little force, except as an implicit source of moral criticism. Wycherley does not imply that the cynical libertine can be happily reincorporated into a stable and traditional society.

The Country Wife, then, is more consistently satiric and more moralistic than *The Man of Mode*. In fact, Wycherley's moralism dictates the radical disjunction of his satiric form, and his direct confrontation with the contradictions of his society inevitably produces a satiric pessimism that suggests little possibility for the kind of social reconciliation that Etherege is eager to affirm. Wycherley voices the discontent of the economically challenged aristocracy in his depiction of the materialistic "man of business," who deserves all that Horner can contrive. But in his portrayal of the "man of pleasure," he condemns the contemporary aristocratic libertine reaction to a changed social environment. For Wycherley, both alternatives finally manifest the same cynical and materialistic values; both are the products of the major social transformation of his century. Both must be rejected. Thus, disdaining formal and ideological evasion, he is left with the complete disjunction of full dramatic satire.

Wycherley's last work, *The Plain Dealer* (1676), provides another example of the elasticity of the formal notion of social satire. The play seems at first even more vicious and brutal than *The Country Wife*, but the vehemence of this particular social satire is mainly on its surface. It is populated with individual satiric butts who, by the diversity of their characters, professions, and sexes, and by their very numerousness, expand and generalize Wycherley's local criticism of society so that it seems to implicate all the world. Formally, however, *The Plain Dealer* is a more compromising and less fully disjunctive satire than *The Country Wife*. By mingling social and moral judgments in the assessments of his protagonist, Wycherley effectively eliminates the rigorously separate moral criticism that characterizes his earlier play. The mixing of judgments enables him, while portraying an immoral and hypocritical world, to temper his satire with social expediency. This special relationship of social and moral in *The Plain Dealer* is prefigured in its dedication and most fully realized in the fates of Manly, the moralist, and Freeman, the play's "complier with the age."[40]

Wycherley's satiric dedication to the notorious London procuress Mother Bennet, prefixed to the published version of the play, celebrates the virtues of his patroness. The lengthy commendations of Mother Bennet's modesty, her public-spiritedness, her generosity, and her hospitality are obviously meant as a satiric criticism of prostitution. But when Wycherley takes the additional step of comparing Mother Bennet

to the ladies of fashion his satire acquires a second object, without
losing its first. He chooses to extol the honesty of whores compared to
that of other women, because whores, at least, are not hypocrites
(ll. 197-201). Here, as in the play, Wycherley demands sexual morality
or honesty, but not necessarily both. As a result, his satire in *The Plain
Dealer* and in its dedication seems always to be retreating from a standard of behavior to one merely of honest admission of one's behavior.
Men and women should behave morally in sexual affairs, but if it is
impossible and foolish to legislate such morality, they should at least
give the true name to their actions. The form of *The Plain Dealer* is
based upon this tendency to retreat.

Manly, the titular character and center of the play's action, is introduced immediately as the epitome of honesty, courage, and plain deal-
ing (I.44-58). He is a radical moral hero, fully dissociated from the
amoral world in which he appears. He criticizes the hypocritical ways of
the town, he cares nothing for money, business, or social status, and
he sacrifices his own comfort for that of his honest sailors (III.746-48).[41]
The process of the action validates all of Manly's allegations against
society, and we come to participate fully in his judgment of the corrupt
world to which he has unwillingly returned. In this respect he serves
as the agent of Wycherley's criticism.

But the social context of his action provides us with another means
of judging Manly: in terms of simple social survival. In Act I, Freeman
criticizes Manly for his impossible idealism (I.247-52), and Manly's
subsequent behavior fully substantiates Freeman's complaints. As a
result, our admiration for the plain-dealing moralist is always tempered
by our recognition of the social world of which he is a part; our moral
judgment is constantly compromised by our urgent sense of social expedience. While we continue, with Manly, to condemn the moral transgressions of men and women in society, we are made to doubt the
efficacy of his behavior and the reliability of his particular judgments.
Indeed, his misplaced trust in Olivia and Vernish shows that he does
not know the world, that his affections are too violent and too hastily
bestowed, that, in fact, his defiant ignorance of society causes him
more pain and loss than even the current immorality necessitates. And
Manly's failure to discern his true friends, Fidelia and Freeman, derives
from the same uncompromising inability to see beyond his own particular standards of conduct.

Those very moral virtues for which we admire Manly and with which
we judge, as he does, the world at large bring about the central conflict
of his action, a conflict that operates by the rules of society. Manly returns to the world to find his absolute moral standards are consistently
problematic when applied to real individuals. In the confrontation with
society that ensues, he discovers not only that his trust has been mis-

placed, but that his distrust has failed him as well. He is forced to adjust his rigid morality to the terms of social existence: he is forced to live and scheme in the world. Formally, our moral assessment of Manly is joined by a simultaneous social assessment that is enacted in the process of the plot and expressed through the character of Freeman, through the sailors' and Freeman's specific criticisms of Manly's behavior, and through Manly's own blindness. Manly's action appropriately ends with his acquisition of the social skills that Freeman commended to him in Act I, and simultaneously with his decision to accept life in society. His fate is defined in social terms and achieved by social means. Though our moral estimate is never negated, it is finally simply superseded by the inescapable workings of the social world.[42] Manly's characteristic moral virtues are shown to be social defects, and his action reflects the lesson of that satiric disjunction, not the denial of one or the other of its formal components.

The subplot provides further illustration of the mechanics of this formal balancing act. Freeman, the Restoration "man of pleasure," immediately sets out to provide for his financial needs by means of a highly practical marital scheme that enacts the essential contrast between his character and Manly's. He is repeatedly willing to compromise himself in order to survive in society, and he explicitly calls upon his special social talent when he realizes that Manly is incapable of providing for them (V.ii.90–92). As a typical rake in a world where such behavior is necessary to survival, Freeman pursues and eventually captures the rich Widow Blackacre, whom he in effect robs to provide himself with a lifelong settlement. But significantly, the action of this plot does not openly contradict any of the reigning moral standards of the main plot. Wycherley is careful, for instance, to supply a scene that demonstrates the Widow's own dishonesty, so that Freeman's consequent triumph over her is felt to be justified. Likewise, Wycherley avoids the final loveless marriage, which would be morally compromising, by granting Freeman an annuity instead, though he is quite prepared for matrimony. Most important, Freeman is never judged for his amoral behavior, either explicitly or implicitly, despite Manly's (and Wycherley's) outspoken morality. In fact, our frustration at Manly's inability to function in the world guarantees our unconditional admiration for Freeman, who, to our relief and in open contrast with his uncompromising friend, is adeptly able to provide for himself. In addition, of course, Freeman receives Manly's full approbation and friendship at the conclusion.

Thus, in the primary plot the moral hero, with no qualification of his morality, is supplied with a social fate: he learns to live in society as a social being. In the subplot the amoral social hero also receives a social reward for his acts of ingenuity and manipulation. Manly's moral

worth is never compromised by Freeman's social success. The relationship between Freeman's and Manly's fates reproduces the balance of
social and moral judgment that characterizes Manly's action itself and,
more generally, the peculiar satiric form of *The Plain Dealer.* This
mingling of moral and social evaluation produces first a vehement critique of the moral corruption of society, and finally a retreat to a
position of sensible and wary acceptance of social necessity. *The Plain
Dealer* represents Wycherley's acknowledgment that, despite our most
fervently held moral standards, the necessary operations of society
must remain essentially amoral, or only partly or occasionally subject
to moral norms. The moral critique of the play, for all its urgency,
leads back to the status quo. Freeman's compliance with the age is un-
compromisingly affirmed, and Manly, the misanthrope, abandons his
ill-conceived plan to sail away forever from the civilized world.

The coexistence of social and moral assessment in this play has
created a critical dissension much like that over *The Man of Mode* and
The Country Wife. Critics who feel that Manly is an unqualified moral
ideal or an embodiment of Wycherley's hatred of the world find the
play overwhelmingly bitter and pessimistic, since they omit the social
qualification of Manly's rigid and ineffectual moral stance.[43] Critics
who do observe that qualification believe that Manly himself is condemned and that the play is largely an exposure of his blindness, folly,
and hypocrisy.[44] Again, the nature of this disagreement is a sign of
the satiric disjunction characteristic of mature dramatic satire, in which
the social world and the moral judgment upon it are, like the critics
of this comedy, continuously at odds. In *The Plain Dealer,* as in its dedication, Wycherley's form retreats from a moral prescription for behavior to an acknowledgment of the ways of the world. Though Manly's
attacks are never too harsh, his fears are exaggerated: society does
provide one loyal lover and one true friend.

Wycherley is thus able to criticize the status quo, but unable or un-
willing to stand by that criticism. In this respect *The Plain Dealer,* like
the other major social satires of the period, is fundamentally conservative. Through Manly's rejection of the corrupt materialism of contemporary society, Wycherley provides a radical evaluation of the new
bourgeois social order. As in *The Country Wife,* Wycherley's moral
criticisms derive directly from his contempt for business, represented
both by the urban moneyed interests and by the commercialized aristocracy. At almost every point in the play the prevailing hypocrisy
against which Manly rails is rooted in a profane love for money, a materialism from which the "rough and angry" sailor is completely and explicitly excluded (V.ii.82–89). Significantly, Manly is compared to a
"tarpaulin" (I.125–27), the term historically applied to the naval cap-
tains who had served during the Commonwealth and who remained

indispensable to the royalists after the Restoration, despite their deplorable love of liberty.[45] In some sense, then, the "unmannerly" hero's rejection of the world is conceived as a revolutionary rejection.

But Manly's perspective ultimately represents too radical a challenge for Wycherley to accept, and the form of his last dramatic satire, like that of *The Man of Mode* and even *The Conquest of Granada*, entails a final return to and affirmation of the status quo. For Etherege, as we have seen, that status quo is fundamentally moral and secure. For Wycherley, who eschews evasion here as in *The Country Wife*, it is corrupt and precarious. The traditional values of love and honor barely survive their incongruously romantic representation in Fidelia, who must serve as the sole counterweight to the whole hypocritical population of the play. Significantly, she is less real to us than the vicious characters by whom she is surrounded, because, as we have seen in our definition of the form of *The Plain Dealer*, Manly's return to society is a function of the play's acceptance of social reality, not a result of the moral promise of a reformed social world. Wycherley does not intend Fidelia to overturn Manly's harsh assessment of society at large or to make the play's conclusion a simple affirmation of traditional morality. He keeps her consistently at the outskirts of the action, a barely realized romantic character in an antiromantic comedy. In this case, the special contradictory form of Wycherley's dramatic satire explains the problematic weakness of one aspect of its characterization. Fidelia is not an oversight or a failure, as several critics have argued,[46] but a very effective local means to a clear formal end.

While *The Plain Dealer* is perhaps no less pessimistic than *The Country Wife*, then, it is certainly more compromising in its formal acceptance of the pragmatic ways of the world. From the strangely congruent perspectives of the alienated aristocracy and the revolutionary "tarpaulins," Wycherley is able to display and assess the major changes in Restoration society. But formally as well as ideologically, he can only criticize and condemn; by its very nature his social satire presents no alternatives to the status quo that constitutes its subject. Thus, while *The Country Wife* ends in the contradiction of full dramatic satire, *The Plain Dealer* concludes with the contradictory compromise of satiric retreat.

IV

The satiric disjunction that we have defined by means of our examination of the plays of Dryden, Etherege, and Wycherley is not confined to the major drama of this period, though it is perhaps most fully realized and most seriously enacted in those works which, for that reason, continue to have an audience long after their particular time and society have

passed away. *The Rover* (1677), by Aphra Behn, was produced only
three months after *The Plain Dealer*, a year after *The Man of Mode*, and
twenty-six months after *The Country Wife*, at the height, that is, of
the period of major dramatic satire. Because of Behn's particular interest
in the problems of women, her concern with marital relationships, her
unusual sensitivity to poverty and individual suffering, and her sympathetic evocation of romantic love, *The Rover* is significantly different
from Etherege's and Wycherley's social satires. But those differences are
only the local details of a form essentially similar—in its disjunction of
social and moral values as well as in its problematic reconciliation of libertinism and royalism—to the dramatic satire of *The Man of Mode*, *The
Country Wife*, or *The Plain Dealer*. *The Rover* derives its peculiar power
from the seriousness with which Behn presents the contradictions most
visible to her in Restoration society.[47]

Behn's early plays roughly resemble the formal preliminaries to social
satire that we have seen in the work of Dryden, Etherege, and Wycherley. Even *The Rover*, her best drama, is full of the Spanish effects of disguise, mistaken identity, honor duels, and nighttime escapades, as well
as of the pure entertainment of farce and stage business.[48] Like the early
comedies of Etherege and Wycherley, the play is crowded with characters and episodes that give its subsidiary plots the kind of variety associated with intriguelike social form and that typify Behn's less important
drama. The main plot of the comedy, however, contains the essential
formal contradiction, powerfully enacted in the conflict between the
Rover, Willmore, and Angellica, the prostitute, that is the prototype of
Behn's serious social satire in this play as well as in *The Second Part
of the Rover* (1681) and *The City Heiress* (1682), though the latter substitutes a gay widow for the prostitute. This central conflict juxtaposes romantic love, which Behn associates with libertine free love, with
the inevitable and reductive economic relationships that reign in society.
And it does so by emphasizing the particular fate of women in a materialistic world.

First, we are made by various means to understand and sympathize
with Behn's loose women in their attempts to survive in the social world.
We are shown the social causes that explain and in part justify the
prostitute's trade, and Angellica is provided with a pragmatic companion who advises her repeatedly, and we feel correctly, not to succumb
to love for Willmore. Our knowledge of Willmore's character fully substantiates her fears. We assume, as does Angellica herself, that if she
gives in to love she will be ruined, and we come to hope that her genuine love for Willmore can be conquered so that she will be able to
survive in society. In this respect, our evaluations of and expectations
for Behn's independent women are directed by our recognition of
the pressures of a corrupt, materialistic world upon the relatively help-

less individual; society operates in such a way that if this noble woman fails to conform and attempts to substitute romantic for economic values, she will be broken.

On the other hand, the argument for true love is presented so eloquently and is allowed to become such a force in these plays that we are compelled to make another kind of assessment, which directly contradicts our hopes for the pragmatic female protagonists' social survival. In his wooing, Willmore voices the argument for freely granted love, described explicitly as the defiant opposite of the commercial love arrangements of contemporary society, whether illicit or marital.[49] Angellica shares the same contempt for mercenary marriage (II.ii.90–96). Together, these two characters define another sort of love, a love that cannot be treated as a commodity, and that raises the lovers, in their blank-verse passages of antimaterialist transcendence, to a strangely incongruous near-heroic stature (II.ii.99–155). Angellica, like La Nuche in *The Rover II* and Lady Galliard in *The City Heiress*, is torn between free surrender and economic survival, between romantic love and pragmatic social necessity. The free love that she finally grants to Willmore is, by definition, potentially transient and thus, for the female victims of society, destructive. At this point romantic love and libertine morality come together for Behn, who assumes that because both contradict the contemporary commercial operations of society—one in its link with the human relations of a past aristocratic tradition and the other in its assertion of a radical alternative to bourgeois sexual propriety— both designate the same emotional relationship. She gives the lovers the language of romance, but the inevitable promiscuity of contemporary libertinism.

In the context of their lofty arguments we admire and applaud their union, though it belies the cautious worldliness with which we assess the process of the action. Thus, Behn's use of romantic convention forces us to make a moral judgment of our social allegiance to economic survival. And, with the characteristic disjunction of the most sophisticated social satire, the form implies a condemnation of that very society whose standards constitute the terms of its action. Angellica chooses love and loses all, as the inconstant Willmore, despite his admiration for her, marries the witty Hellena. The prostitute's fate is socially just, and we have approvingly anticipated Willmore's legitimate match with Hellena, but, by that separate set of romantic standards which operates outside the social context of the action, we judge Angellica's end as nearly tragic.

For Behn, then, the introduction of free or romantic love as a momentary possibility in an action governed by the rules of commercial necessity produces a central formal disjunction that generates all the contingent terms of moral judgment. Typically, she bases her moral criticism of society, as does Wycherley, on its reduction of human

relationships to economic exchange. Prostitution, of course, is the
epitome of that reduction, where love, the essentially spiritual, is ex-
changed for money, the essentially material. But her assessment of
the inevitable ways of the world enables her to criticize society at large
rather than its particular victims. Her sympathy for the fates of individual women permits her to provide a social context in which their
actions are justified in relation to the general materialism of her whole
depicted world.

Behn's dramatic satire voices her special concerns, but it also resembles the major comedy of its time. Her criticism of the restraints on
genuine love parallels Etherege's admiration for libertine free love, but,
like Etherege, she is a staunch royalist. She perceives and describes the
major contours of Restoration society from a near-radical perspective,
but that perspective can only lead her to ideological contradiction
and formal satire. Her conservative criticism of society, like Wycherley's,
envisages no alternative to the status quo. In fact her inability to look
forward is precisely what permits her to equate traditional romantic love
and libertinism. It is her very lack of alternatives and her dogged royalism that enable her to pose the contradiction so elegantly and so ines-
capably for her prostitute protagonists. Thus Behn's originality, while it
distinguishes her drama from the major social satire of her age, finally
provides further evidence of the coherence of dramatic form in the early
Restoration.

V

Together, these comedies provide the material for a comprehensive
definition of dramatic social satire. The definition does justice to the
diverse and unique comic works of the early Restoration, but it also
demonstrates their coherence, their relation to the heroic action of the
period, and their place in the process of formal evolution. It reveals
the history of the genre. The judgmental neutrality of the early imported
intrigue form is a popular common denominator, which provides the
basis for the strange bifurcated tragicomedy of the Restoration, and
from which dramatic social satire gradually and fully differentiates itself.
The formal vacuum of the intrigue is filled with social material as soon
as it is naturalized by its English imitators, and this is the first step toward the realization of the full satiric potential of social comedy. Significantly, this first step is marked also by the increasing prominence of
the gay couple and of the witty love debate, as character and conflict
gain precedence over the ingenious intrigue plot reversal. The similitude
and repartee that have come to be recognized as the distinguishing
stylistic hallmark of the mature comedy of manners are a specific consequence of this formal shift and its manifestation in the love-game

formula. The intriguelike social forms of early Dryden, Etherege, and
Wycherley merge at many points with "all in fun" social satire, since
both attach social material to an action motivated either by mechanical
tricks and revelations, or by an illusion of conflict that is simply set
aside at the end of five acts to produce a happy and easy resolution.
Thus these early or minor social forms are invariably conservative in
their blatant royalism, their anti-Puritanism, their nationalism, and their
unquestioning allegiance to the social status quo. In this respect they
resemble the simplistic early versions of the heroic action.

The imitators of Jonson, notably Thomas Shadwell, produce a variation upon "all in fun" satire, since their formal reliance on humors
characters as local satiric butts permits them to construct their actions
without serious conflict. In Shadwell's early plays, *The Sullen Lovers*
(1668), *The Miser* (1672), and *The Virtuoso* (1676), the idiosyncratic
characters simply dominate the stage, with the result that local replaces
formal satire. A similar effect, though less strictly dependent upon the
humors convention, is produced by plays like *The Soldier's Fortune*
(1680) and *The Atheist* (1683), by Thomas Otway, and *The False Count*
(1681) and *The Younger Brother* (1696—posthumously), by Behn.
But in the careers of the major dramatists, the intriguelike avoidance of
individuated character and the "all in fun" evasion of actual conflict
are gradually replaced by specific judgments passed on particular characters and by serious and ultimately unresolvable contradiction. Though
the early or minor forms, merely because of their social material, are
potentially or occasionally satiric, only the major comedy of manners,
in all its particular versions, fully realizes the formal disjunction of
dramatic satire, and that full realization is the source of its distinctive
seriousness. In this sense, the merits of Restoration comic form transcend the rather dubious tribute paid it by many of its adherents in the
recent critical debate. The excellence of the major social satires of
this period resides not in their amorality, their artificiality, their freedom, their wit, their game-playing, their self-consciousness, or their
ambiguity, but in their daring formal and ideological representation of
the fundamental moral and social contradictions of their time and
place.[50]

The disjunction of moral and social assessment that we have used
to define dramatic satire can also be the basis for our understanding of
the resemblance between the major social satire and the best heroic
actions of the Restoration. As noted in the comparison of *The Man of
Mode* and *The Conquest of Granada*, both forms represent a juxtaposition of royalist and radical that seriously confronts but finally
leaves unresolved the essential conflicts of the age. In view of the major
changes that take place in both comedy and serious drama over the
next two decades and that lead ultimately to the decline of the drama

in the eighteenth century, the heroic action and social satire of the early Restoration represent a crucial segment in a continuous formal evolution. These two forms establish limits on the options available to future playwrights and thus affect, for better or worse, the later fate of the genre. As we have seen, Restoration drama is by formal definition centered on a single social subject: the upper class. In fact, this reduction of its range is the very quality that enables it to present so eloquently the contradictions of Restoration society. In the comedy, the form is only fully serious and successful when it abandons Jonsonian social breadth, which it invariably interprets with blind royalism and anti-Puritanism, and takes up the philosophy of a small segment of a single social class: courtier libertinism. In the serious drama, the fulfillment of the form coincides with the most arbitrary assertion of its antiquated aristocratic standards. Inevitably, then, both of the major dramatic forms of the Restoration omit any fully realized expression of an alternative to the status quo. Thus, the social scope of the drama is initially limited by the development of the mature heroic action and the fully satiric comedy of manners.

Furthermore, both of these forms are predicated on dramatic assumptions that preclude any complexity of character depiction. In the serious drama, static characterization is an integral part of the episodic, hierarchical, aristocratic world of the heroic action. In the comedy, simple, recognizable social relationships and standards are the primary and indispensable substance of dramatic satire. For this reason the final social reconciliations that we have observed in plays like *The Conquest of Granada*, *The Man of Mode*, and even *The Plain Dealer* are always achieved by fiat, by evasion, or by mere assertion, and never by character transformation or development. The absence of complex characterization in the major Restoration comic and serious drama is an immediate consequence of the irreconcilable contradictions that define its form and ideology. Thus, again, the potential range of characterization in future drama is conditioned by the necessary absence of character development in the mature heroic action and social satire.

Finally, the immediately succeeding transitional periods for both tragedy and comedy represent an essential preliminary to the full moralization of the drama in the eighteenth century. Just as the heyday of the heroic action precedes by about half a decade the primary period of mature social satire, the major affective tragedy precedes the major transitional comedy. (We will later have occasion to consider the reasons for this disparity.) But in both early Restoration forms the moment of greatest contradiction and greatest seriousness is followed by significant change. The conventions of the earlier drama, however, are not simply and completely superseded. Though the form of the heroic action and social satire of the Restoration does not predict the future of the drama,

it does dictate the specific limitations of social range and characterization that come to differentiate the dramatic moral action from the
novel. Thus, ironically, the fate of eighteenth-century drama is in part
the product of the seriousness and excellence of its much more notable
predecessors.

PART II
TRANSITIONAL FORMS, 1677–1707

THREE
Affective Tragedy

Restoration affective tragedy substitutes the unfortunate and undeserved situation of its central character for the aristocratic status of the heroic protagonist. The unique and defining characteristic of this form is its dependence upon the audience's pitying response. The characters and episodes of an affective tragedy are comprehensible not in terms of an internal standard of judgment that directs our assessments and expectations, but rather in terms of the expressed pathos of the situation. In the fictional world posited by such a form, merit is either ignored or assumed, and action and meaning depend upon the affective power of the protagonist's plight. This emphasis on situation at the expense of assessment corresponds to a diminished interest in characterization and a diminished ability to create and sustain consistent characters. Furthermore, it requires a simplification of depiction and an inattention to motive that inevitably exclude character development or complexity and that frequently imply, to augment the pathos, that the protagonist is perfectly innocent. It leads to the replacement of aristocratic heroes by private citizens, to the frequent use of women in supporting roles and—more significantly—as protagonists, as well as to the turn to domestic material and, ultimately, national as opposed to exotic history.[1]

Though affective tragedy differs fundamentally from the heroic action that precedes it, it is directly and closely derived from that earlier form. In effect, it drains the heroic play of evaluative efficacy and meaning, and substitutes the affective response of pity for the judgmental one of admiration. Thus, its ties to prior conventions perpetuate the limitations in scope and characterization of the heroic form, despite its specific elimination of aristocratic values. Ultimately, affective tragedy is a consequence of the changes in the evolution of the heroic action from Davenant and Orrery to Dryden and Lee. The fragmentation of the neat love-and-honor standard, leaving love alone as the preeminent and potentially most pathetic choice; the general disintegration of assessment, especially in Lee's incoherent characterization; and the growing interest in "natural" pity and sympathy at the expense of the heightened and exaggerated mode of the artificial heroic action all presage the evolution of a new drama able to rationalize and incorporate these impulses into a form that ignores or eliminates judgment, replaces it with pathetic situation, and designates empathetic response as its determining formal principle. The changes that occur in serious drama from 1660 to 1677, then, are significant in themselves and in their relevance to the definition and evolution of the heroic action, but in retrospect they represent the initial quantitative signals of a qualitative shift that results in the new formal and ideological coherence of affective tragedy.

The major tragic dramatists of the late Restoration—Lee, Dryden, and Otway—along with many playwrights of the second rank, like Banks and Southerne, share a set of assumptions and priorities that we will be able to recognize and define as formally affective. And within these general similarities, affective tragedy, like the heroic action, undergoes a subsidiary evolution of its own that, interrupted by the period of dramatic inactivity occasioned by the union of the theaters and the political instability of the 1680s, results in the fulfillment of the implications of its formal assumptions and anticipates the moral action of the eighteenth century. The early affective and near-affective tragedy of Lee and Dryden maintains the legendary and exotic aristocratic characters typical of the heroic action, though it either gives those heroes an effectually antiaristocratic ideology, or depicts them at the tragic and passive close of their careers and consequently defines them not so much by their status as by their unfortunate situation. But because early affective form continues to depend, at least nominally, upon heroic material, it sustains an interest in aristocratic character that becomes unusual in later pathetic tragedy.

With the advent of Otway, Banks, and Southerne, affective assumptions are brought to their logical conclusion by the depiction of a domestic situation and the designation of a passive, innocent female protagonist or, in the absence of an appropriate woman, a Stupid Hero [2] who is at the physical and psychological mercy of her or his environment. A private citizen, a Stupid Hero, or, even better, a woman, effectively eliminates the issue of character assessment by removing the traditional source of such assessment in social status. This frees the form for the single-minded pursuit of the pathetic situation and for the unadulterated advocacy of classless pathos. For Banks, domestic history operates as a corollary to the domestic situation, and justifies his experiments in the new form. In fact, historical drama acts as a catalyst in this period, freeing playwrights for formal innovation that might otherwise seem to violate the ideals of standard tragedy. These writers are close predecessors of eighteenth-century moral dramatists like Rowe, who combines domestic history with a female paragon protagonist to produce his moral she-tragedies.

The stages in the evolution of affective drama serve to define the form with increasing precision, since each subsequent variation of the general model reveals some particular aspect of its essential assumptions. Thus, as we develop a comprehensive definition of affective form in itself and a specific means of distinguishing each affective play from the others, we also discover the particular history of affective tragedy that eventuates in the moral action of the eighteenth century, as well as the necessary mediation of affective form in the larger generic evolution from a drama of social status to a drama of moral worth.

I

The past grandeur of Lee's and Dryden's declining emperors in *The Rival Queens* (March 1677) and *All for Love* (December 1677) defines the initial stage in the evolution of Restoration affective tragedy. These plays, performed within nine months of each other, both depict the last, passive days of their heroes' careers and both carefully recollect the terms of a previous heroic assessment. Dryden's play is formally affective, consisting of an action and apotheosis determined and achieved not by Herculean merit, but by the pathos of despair and death. Lee, however, remains primarily a transitional dramatist, experimenting often incoherently with character assessment, and betraying a symptomatic rejection of the aristocratic hierarchy of values affirmed in the heroic action. But the particular incoherence of *The Rival Queens* begins, indirectly, to suggest the ideological basis of Lee's formal experimentation in the direction of affective tragedy. *Lucius Junius Brutus* (1680) brings that experimentation to its logical conclusion, by attaching a specific ideological content to a coherent affective form. Thus the latter half of Lee's career provides an idiosyncratic but significant model for the initial, transitional stages in the evolution of affective drama. *All for Love*, then, can be seen along with *Lucius Junius Brutus* as a formal response to *The Rival Queens*, perfecting and refining that initial experiment.

The incoherence in Nathaniel Lee's presentation of his protagonist in *The Rival Queens* duplicates the problems of characterization in his earlier plays, except that Alexander's particular inconsistency reveals the implicit source of Lee's attack upon the heroic action. The hero is depicted in the hours before his death, surrounded by portents and prognostications of doom that are to be realized through the combined effects of a violent love rivalry and a hellish political conspiracy against his life. Alexander is both a suffering lover who repeatedly and explicitly chooses love over empire and a vicious tyrant who is ambiguously reprehensible in the arbitrary assertion of his imperial power. These two definitions of his character alternate unpredictably in the process of the action, and the inconsistency that ensues is a sign of the fragmentation of the heroic standard as well as a corollary to the antiabsolutist ideology expressed in the play.

Alexander is described as a demigod, "the master of the world." [3]
Though we observe him after his battles have been fought and his doom
is already foretold, he makes his delayed entrance in Act II as a conquering hero amidst the fanfare of a noisy triumph. But Lee qualifies
the conventional definition of the Herculean protagonist in two distinct and unrelated ways. First, despite those numerous claims to active
heroism, Alexander repeatedly chooses love over honor for the sake
of Statira (e.g., III.294–97), even forcing his army, the physical embodiment of his honor in an action that represents no battles, to submit
to the commands of love:

> But first kneel with me [to Statira], all my soldiers, kneel. *All kneel.*
> Yet lower, prostrate to the earth. [III.392–93]

Clytus's reiterated accusations clarify the issue: "While each hand does
beauty hold, / Where is there room for glory?" (I.i.66–67). Love and
honor are evaluative opposites, eternally at odds, and either choice is
inevitably defective. Unlike the neat and comprehensive hierarchy
of the heroic action, where the proper act eventually ensures both love
and honor, Lee's drama offers only one or the other. The disintegration and depoliticization of that heroic hierarchy and the consequent
absence of an efficacious ethical standard imply that the choice of
love must bring disaster, suicide, and death. Consequently, the play is
pervaded with gloom. Every scene repeats the foreboding that is expressed directly through the vows of the conspirators (I.i.130–47), Statira's ill-fated oath (I.ii.87–92), and the ghosts (I.i.282 *s.d.*), portents
(II.1–36), and spirits (V.i.1–19).

Thus, out of Alexander's choice of love over honor, Lee constructs
a pathetic situation in which the conquering hero becomes, at least for
the moment, an object of pity rather than admiration. His appearance
on the stage in conjunction with the weak and innocent Statira is calculated to augment this pathos. He pleads (III.272–75); he faints (III.
339); he falls upon the floor (III.277–78); he seems to die (III.406–09).
In short, we are forced to see him as a victim, a suffering lover, or a
"child" (I.ii.30) [4] and to respond to his plight with the kind of pity that
the magnanimous Alexander is said to have bestowed upon others
(II.281–87). This pity, as we will see, is a common quality of the period's pathetic protagonists, and it illustrates the degree of identification that the form requires of its audience. [5]

The "rival queens" serve, in Alexander's absence, to maintain the
continuity of this pathetic effect through the course of the action. They
epitomize the suicidal choice that Alexander has made, and their dispute, with Roxana's consequent violent schemes, represents the direct
realization of Clytus's ominous predictions. Roxana plots revenge upon
Alexander, while Statira, in the role of the wronged wife, weeps and

declares her innocence to an appreciative audience. Her reiterated weakness in the opening scene, in the confrontation with Roxana, and finally in her pathetic death, as well as in the central pleading scene with
Alexander, all serve to increase the affective force of the action and
to connect that pathos with Alexander's antiheroic choice of love over
empire. If the "rival queens" appear to usurp preeminence in the play, [6]
it is because they must perform the task of locating and enacting the
specific formal implications of Alexander's choice. With the destruction
of the heroic action's controlling hierarchy, Lee is left without an internal means of judgment; comprehensibility now depends upon pathos.

But the subversive turn to pathos is not the only modification that
Lee is tempted to make in Alexander's heroism. At other moments,
Alexander remains a Herculean figure, but his aggressive dominance is
interpreted as tyranny. In these scenes he is not a simple Herculean
villain—like Maximin in *Tyrannic Love*, who uses his heroic virtues to
evil ends—but an example of the potential tyranny of any absolute
power. The Lysimachus-Parisatis subplot serves primarily to unmask
this tyranny implicit in the Herculean ideal. Lysimachus is the emblematic victim of Alexander's excesses. His true love for Parisatis, whom
Alexander has promised to Hephestion, the court favorite, makes him
the innocent object of Alexander's violent and autocratic decrees, which
even include an order for his death (II.400–03).

Lee's depiction of the scheme against Alexander's life casts further
doubt on the heroic values by which the protagonist is initially defined.
The conspirators explicitly attach their condemnation of Alexander
to his heroic stature. He "would be a god" but is "cruel as a devil"
(I.i.217–19). The lurid descriptions of Alexander's hideous retribution
against his suspected enemies (I.i.201–43) lend credence to the conspirators' accusations of tyranny. The conspirators themselves, however,
are not admirable agents of justice, but rather, as conspirators invariably are in Restoration drama, evil schemers associated with horror and
hell (I.i.272–80 and IV.i.269–82). Thus, even when Alexander remains
a heroic figure, Lee vacillates in his depiction of the nature of that heroism: Alexander is sometimes an admirable Herculean demigod threatened by the illegitimate schemes of a pack of unprincipled conspirators,
sometimes an arbitrary and vicious tyrant, deserving death.

The inconsistent views of Alexander are most neatly epitomized in
the central scene of "honest Clytus's" criticism of Alexander and subsequent death. Early in the play, Lee established Clytus as the legitimate spokesman of Alexander's downfall. Consequently, Clytus must
speak two "truths." First, refusing to wear the luxurious Persian cos-
tume that Alexander offers (IV.ii.71 *s.d.*), Clytus accuses the king of
choosing women over empire (IV.ii.140–42). This accusation echoes
the criticisms that Clytus has expressed throughout the play, but it is

joined, a few lines later, by a separate charge: that Alexander is a tyrant.
Clytus recollects for us, this time with the voice of honesty, the crimes
that have accompanied Alexander's power, and, defying his incensed
emperor to murder him as well, he lists the same victims named earlier
by the conspirators (IV.ii.188-97). But Clytus is both a loyalist (IV.i.29-
30) and a critic of monarchy (IV.ii.115), and thus when Alexander
strikes him down in a further enactment of the tyrant's power, he can
repent and rescind all his accusations:

> O Alexander, I have been too blame.
> Hate me not after death, for I repent
> That so I urged your noblest, sweetest nature.   [IV.ii.217-19]

We are left, by this scene, in an evaluative chaos that precisely reflects
the particular incoherence of *The Rival Queens.* In Lee's simultaneous
stories, as in Clytus's simultaneous accusations, Alexander is both a
pathetic protagonist, sacrificing all for love, and a reprehensible heroic
tyrant, judged by his misuse of power. It is to the "noblest, sweetest"
Alexander, the admirable heroic lover, that Clytus tenders his repentance, proclaiming the justice of his death (IV.ii.221-22) and affirming
the legitimacy of Alexander's sentence: "Let bold subjects learn by
thy sad fate, / To tempt the patience of a man above 'em" (IV.ii.214-
15). But a few lines later, the violent and autocratic Alexander admits
to the tyrannical injustice of which Clytus had accused him:

> Death, hell, and furies! You have sunk my glory.
> O, I am all a blot, which seas of tears
> And my heart's blood can never wash away.   [IV.ii.251-53]

Ultimately *The Rival Queens* presents two parallel and absolutely
irreconcilable accounts of Alexander's story. Alexander is the pathetic
victim of an inevitable and disastrous choice of love over honor, whose
fate we anticipate and understand in terms of the pity evoked by his
distressing situation—or he is the rash, hasty, violent tyrant who sends
the innocent and loyal to their deaths and thus brings about his own
destruction. The dichotomy between pathetic lover and tyrant is reproduced again in Alexander's death. Technically, the hero dies of the
poison given to him by the conspirators, but Alexander feels the first
pangs of death as an immediate result of Roxana's curse: "I already
feel the sad effects / Of those most fatal imprecations" (V.i.235-36). In
fact, the poison administered by Cassander has conveniently taken
five hours to work (IV.i.251-52), but we are not unprepared to believe
that Alexander might be dying of the effects of love. After all, his love
confrontations in the previous scenes frequently left him sick, fainting,
and avowedly near death (e.g., II.409-11, III.406-09, and IV.i.97-99).
Lee simply uses the same death scene to conclude both versions of his

Alexander story; the Herculean hero perishes as a direct consequence both of his tyranny and of his love.

The two separate accounts of "the death of Alexander the Great" are mechanically combined in the opening scene, where the Lysimachus subplot is joined with Clytus's exposition of Alexander's unmanly romantic inclinations. This superficial conjunction is repeated when the injured lover Roxana is brought temporarily into the antityranny conspiracy. The overlapping themes of love and tyranny serve to make the plot appear whole: when Alexander exercises his tyranny against Lysimachus, he is implicitly flouting the power of true love, though in another guise he is himself a lover. But the substance of these apparent connections quickly melts away upon closer examination. In his tyrannical moments, Alexander's hypocrisy as a lover is never mentioned, and when he appears as the victim of passionate love, he abandons the identity of the tyrant. His two careers remain unreconciled.

Lee's tragedy thus displays a major incoherence so pervasive that the resultant ambiguity dominates the play. This ambiguity is not the deliberate and artful ambiguity of complex characterization—which some critics have claimed to find in *The Rival Queens*[7]—but rather the inchoate and involuntary ambiguity of formal transition. Such a distinction is absolutely essential to an understanding of generic history. The interpretation that automatically transforms a formal or ideological contradiction into a positive aesthetic value systematically precludes any discussion of change or evolution in literary form. There is no history from such a critical perspective, because there is no conceptual criterion that defines the formal status of the particular effects of character, motif, or theme. In *The Rival Queens*, the significance of Alexander's ambiguity is only apparent from the structure of the whole play, and furthermore, the historical significance of the play itself is only apparent from such an initial assessment of its form.

Implicit in Lee's incoherence is a juxtaposition that reveals the ideological basis of this early affective form: the juxtaposition of pathos and antiabsolutist sentiment. These effects are interchangeable in the process of the action: Lee finds it unnecessary to distinguish between Alexander the pathetic victim and Alexander the absolutist tyrant. The coexistence of pathetic effect and antimonarchism suggests that the play assumes a natural and necessary analogy between the two. Lee's tendency to weaken the heroic action, to undermine its inclusive aristocratic hierarchy of values, to divide love from honor, and to depict the inevitable and disastrous choice of love over empire and even life results in an increasing recourse to pathetic situation at the expense of definable merit. It reflects as well a loss of confidence in the efficacy of assessment and a lack of attention to consistent characterization in general, and a concurrent prevailing sense of gloom and pessimism. These

are the initial, defining qualities of early affective form, and they are,
for Lee, perfectly synonymous with an inchoate and incomplete but
parallel loss of confidence in the aristocratic ideals that govern the world
of the heroic action, and ultimately with an uncertainty about monarchy itself.

Thus, in its persistent analogy of pathos and republicanism, the form
of *The Rival Queens* reveals the ideological basis of Lee's transition
to affective tragedy. In a period when the qualification of absolute monarchy had begun to appear not only inevitable but also desirable,[8] the
"new" dramatists could no longer supply an admirable heroic protagonist, complete with his neat list of Platonic or epic virtues, and hence,
they could no longer produce the straightforward character assessment
that had marked the prime of the heroic action. Most of them, of
course, never stated, and felt no need to state, an alternative to the aristocratic values that their affective forms subverted or ignored. In this
respect Lee's forthright republicanism in *Lucius Junius Brutus* represents
a unique achievement of ideological and formal self-consciousness, well
before its time. The unrealized analogy in the form of *The Rival Queens*
is its necessary predecessor.

Lucius Junius Brutus solves the problems attendant upon the formal
dichotomy of *The Rival Queens.* In the earlier play Lee qualifies the
conventional definition of heroic merit through his incongruous depiction of an alternately pathetic and tyrannical protagonist. But in the
explicitly republican *Lucius Junius Brutus* he effectively combines consistent pathos and consistent antimonarchism in a single coherent
action. The subversion of heroic values which in Lee's earlier plays had
been merely disruptive finds explicit and simultaneous formal and ideological expression in *Lucius Junius Brutus.*

Brutus is apparently a hero in the old manner, with all the conventional epithets of Herculean merit. Most important, though, our admiration for him is sustained without confusion or qualification throughout
the play, and his consistent heroism differentiates him sharply from
Lee's earlier protagonists. In effect, Lee transforms his constitutional
disaffection with the judgmental hierarchy of the heroic action into
an overt advocacy of an alternative ideal in his depiction of a republican
hero. Brutus can be consistently heroic because his merit is everywhere
and always tied to his republican virtue. He declares himself the savior
of Rome, the upholder of liberty, and the opponent of the tyrant Tar-
quin from the beginning of the action, and he is seen and applauded
as such by the population of the play.

Thus, the admiration evoked for Brutus, though couched in the familiar hyperbolic language of the heroic action, is associated not with
aristocratic values, but with republican and bourgeois ideology. Lee's
play in this respect is almost a manifesto of the Whig constitutional

position during the exclusion controversy,[9] and, except for its radical antimonarchism, a full expression of the dominant ideology of Britain after the Glorious Revolution. Brutus explicitly associates for our admiring consumption: freedom, liberty, commonwealth, justice, law, magna carta, constitutionalism, profit, trade, mercantilism, manufacture, imperialism, plenty, and peace.[10] To complete the ideological picture, Lee provides the opposing values of tyranny, loyalism, absolutism, factionalism, restoration, royal prerogative, courtier libertinism, Catholicism, murder, and cannibalism (e.g., III.i.107-12, III.ii.50-58, and IV.103-29). Brutus can be a consistent hero for Lee, but only in explicit opposition to the aristocratic ideology of the old heroic action. In this play, then, Lee turns his characteristic subversion of heroic values to a positive formal purpose.

In addition, the pathetic effect that, as we have seen in *The Rival Queens*, represents the other front of Lee's fragmented war upon heroic form is in *Lucius Junius Brutus* made to serve the coherent ends of an ideologically republican action. Whereas Alexander must provide Lee with an inevitably incoherent source of both pathos and heroic tyranny, in the later play the soft and suffering Titus, Brutus's wayward son, shares with Brutus the role of protagonist, and those two characters divide the pathos and heroism between them. We recognize Titus as a character who is to be defined and understood in terms of his pathetic situation: "My constant suff'rings are my only glory" (V.i.41). He is "fond, young, soft, and gentle, / Trained by the charms of one that is most lovely" (II.378-79), and hence prone to emotional outbursts, to tears, to physical prostration, and to suicide (III.iii.22-30). Like the pathetic Alexander in *The Rival Queens*, Titus encounters a dilemma that arises from his allegiance to women and to love, and that is repeatedly contrasted with Brutus's virtuous choice of heroic duty. As his suffering increases, Titus becomes progressively more pathetic and more affectingly attractive to us, as well as to his lover, Teraminta (III.iii.53-56).

The choice of love over "kingdoms" is made not only by the suffering lovers in their affecting and defining dilemma, but also by the audience in its assessment of these characters and its comprehension of the form. Titus's death in this sense provides the pleasurable and anticipated fulfillment of our response to his pathetic situation, and we share the admiring pity of his executioner:

> Come then, I'll lead thee, O thou glorious victim,
> Thus to the altar of untimely death,
> Thus in thy trim, with all thy bloom of youth,
> These virtues on thee, whose eternal spring
> Shall blossom on thy monumental marble
> With never fading glory. [V.i.169-74]

The women in the play, especially Teraminta but also Lucrece and
Sempronia, support and increase the pathetic effect centered in Titus's
fate. They enter mainly to plead—Lucrece for revenge, Teraminta and
Sempronia for Titus's life—and thus to fortify the action with those
begging scenes endemic to affective form. In short, by dividing pathos
from heroism, Lee maintains his characteristic fragmentation of the
love-and-honor hierarchy with its attendant implications of disaster and
doom, but without destroying the coherence of his drama.

Titus and Brutus are, then, joint protagonists, representing separate
formal forces, who share the action of the play. But despite their significant differences, the two characters are deliberately knit together,
and they function formally, especially in the climactic last acts, to
embody Lee's coordination of republican heroism and pathetic effect.
Even when, early in the action, the contrast between Brutus and his
son is first and most explicitly defined, we are warned that in some special sense they are to be identified (II.293–95). Later that identification
is reiterated in both physical and spiritual terms. Titus is Brutus's self
(IV.330), the "flatt'ring mirror of [his] father's image" (IV.488).

The similarity is reaffirmed in the climactic episodes of the play,
when Brutus decrees Titus's execution. With perfect formal symmetry,
Lee uses each half of the composite protagonist as a foil for the other.
Thus, Titus's rather innocent crime provides us with the fullest and
most majestic definition of Brutus's heroic merit. His determination to
treat "his darling Titus" (V.i.3) according to the strictest rigor of the
law, despite the universal pleas for leniency, specifically earns him those
heroic epithets which define his republican virtue: the upholder of
liberty, the "father of his country," "half a god" (V.ii.69). But Brutus's
heroism likewise supplies Titus with the climactic fulfillment of his
pathetic situation. Though technically guilty, he is actually an innocent
victim of a combination of coercion and coincidence, since he signed
the list of conspirators only to save Teraminta's life, and then returned
to revoke his agreement only seconds too late. His farewell scenes
with his father and Teraminta, his scourging, his confrontation with
the "mangled" Teraminta, also scourged, and his death all serve to
prolong and intensify our pitying response to his plight. It is through
this lengthy suffering and leave-taking that Titus becomes, for us and
for the population of the play, all pleading together to save his life, a
"glorious victim."

The two protagonists are formally wedded in their reciprocal definition of each other's essential function in the play. But in addition,
those separate functions themselves are explicitly merged in the scene
of their fullest expression. Brutus, when he declares his heroic resolution to perform strict justice upon his son "without a groan, without
one pitying tear" (IV.531), reaches a height not only of stoical repub-

lican heroism but also, strangely enough, of pathos. The scene in which "the father of his country" establishes forever through his transcendent example the justice, liberty, prosperity, and imperial power of Rome is also the scene in which he becomes an object of pity. His tearful farewell to Titus epitomizes this uncharacteristic emotionalism (IV.583-84), but throughout the whole scene he groans, weeps, sighs, and throws himself upon the ground, declaring his love for his "best beloved" son (IV.451). In fact, Titus's death is described as if it were Brutus's suicide, "the sacrificing of [his] bowels" (V.ii.38), drawing out "blood, the heart blood of Brutus, on his child" (IV.494). In this sense, Titus is used to provide the pessimistic and emblematic final suicide that invariably concludes the affective action, though in Lee's unique version the protagonist both dies and lives on in the person of the republican hero.

Titus analogously exchanges his characteristic pathos for the resolution and majesty of republican heroism. When Brutus falls to the ground, his son is the one who emblematically stoops and raises him (IV.561-62). Before his father can reveal to him the rigor of his exemplary justice, Titus has declared, in the language of Herculean grandeur and republican virtue, his unflinching willingness to die for Rome:

> Titus dares die if so you have decreed;
> Nay, he shall die with joy to honor Brutus,
> To make your justice famous through the world
> And fix the liberty of Rome forever. [IV.479-82][11]

Thus, when Brutus declares Titus to be the "mirror of thy father's image," he only verbalizes the merging of their characters that has already been enacted on the stage. Titus demands republican justice as energetically as Brutus seeks to implement it (IV.564-72) and earns, like Brutus, "a throne . . . in heav'n" (IV.575), the tribute of the gods (V.ii.180-81).

In *Lucius Junius Brutus* Lee has discovered a form that can contain both pathos and republican heroism without tension or incongruity. The two ultimately merge because they represent simultaneous consequences of the same career-long formal and ideological process. Both republican heroism and pathetic effect are, for Lee, the products of the fundamental instability of aristocratic evaluative standards. Brutus is possible as a hero because he aggressively defies royalist hierarchies. Titus is viable because his action ignores determinable merit entirely in favor of simple pathetic response. The two can be paired and merged because both assume that tragic fragmentation of the love-and-honor standard which is the formal core of Lee's rejection of heroic values. The fate of the composite protagonist of *Lucius Junius Brutus* demonstrates the disastrous and affecting result of that fragmented choice: love and its implicit escape from public concerns is inevitably doomed, and honor, even republican honor, is tragic in its triumph. The form of *Lucius Junius Brutus* is this elegantly conceived consistency of pathos and republicanism.

Lee's career is a model, though a unique one, for the major transition in serious drama from the heroic to the affective action. As we observed in his early plays, Lee's casual neglect of character consistency, his systematic fragmentation of the love-and-honor ideal, and his constitutional allegiance to disaster and gloom all approximate the initial formal steps of the major shift to affective drama. But for Lee, at least in the first half of his career, these steps produce only confusion and formal incoherence. In these respects, *The Rival Queens*, though one of his later plays, is essentially like *Sophonisba* and *Gloriana*: it undermines heroic assessment, but puts nothing in its place. On the other hand, in the second half of his career Lee's formal rejection of aristocratic standards begins to take on the specific ideological content that we have seen in the analogical form of *The Rival Queens* and that rationalizes the undirected incoherence of his earlier dramatic experimentation. Thus, while *The Rival Queens* remains a problematic work, it unites a formal fragmentation of the heroic hierarchy with an ideological criticism of tyranny in such a way as to suggest the precise direction of Lee's desultory progress toward formal coherence.

From this perspective Lee's least imperfect and in many ways most successful play, *Lucius Junius Brutus*, is the natural conclusion to the growing ideological self-consciousness of his dramatic experimentation. Lee begins by taking the heroic action apart with every formal tool at his command. With *The Rival Queens* he discovers meaning in the disassembled pieces, specifically in the rejection of judgment embodied in the fragmented, suicidal choice of love over honor. In welding that formal rejection to an ideological rejection of political tyranny, Lee begins the reassembly completed in *Lucius Junius Brutus*. That play attains formal coherence through its alignment of pathetic effect and republican ideology. Significantly, this alignment, achieved with such difficulty by Lee, later becomes the trademark of the eighteenth-century moral action.

Lee's career reveals, with unique formal and ideological explicitness, the particular place of affective tragedy in the evolution of serious drama in this period. To the extent that affective form simply eliminates assessment, it is an evaluative placeholder between the explicitly aristocratic form of the heroic action and the bourgeois form of eighteenth-century moralized tragedy. The rejection of heroic evaluation, then, is the necessary prerequisite of formal pathos, and it links the early depoliticized affective tragedy with the later middle-class drama. Lee's precocious advocacy of the Whig ideals that become formally dominant

only in the moral action anticipates the subsequent gradual moralization
of affective form, and reveals the ideological dimension of the movement away from character assessment that marks the major serious
drama of the late 1670s and early 1680s. That ideological dimension,
as Lee's later anti-Whig *Constantine the Great* (1683) suggests, does
not necessarily include the advocacy of a political or social alternative.
Alternatives can and inevitably do emerge, but the defining essence
of affective tragedy is ideological failure or rejection. The aristocratic
and absolutist hierarchies are no longer formally viable for Lee and
for the other major dramatists most sensitive to the social and political
realities of their time. Even a conservative and a royalist like Dryden
chooses in his best play to depict Herculean values with nostalgic recollection. *All for Love* is in this sense, like *The Rival Queens*, an elegy
for absolutism.

II

All for Love (1677) is full of material that marks it as a clear and consistent affective tragedy, and thus, unlike *The Rival Queens* and *Lucius
Junius Brutus*, it can serve as a relatively pure example of the form.
Every represented exchange between the two protagonists, and almost
every subsidiary episode as well, is calculated to increase our pitying
response to their plight. Cleopatra's successive pleading scenes, for example, like innumerable similar scenes in other pathetic plays of this
period, exercise her audience's affective faculties. This standard pathetic
device is directed not so much at the unresponsive auditor on the stage,
whose stubborn deafness provides the dramatist with an excuse to prolong the pleading, as at the emotions of the audience. Cleopatra pleads
nominally to Antony, but formally to us. Her begging defines her as a
victim, and our emotional response elevates and justifies her victimization. Because we feel for Cleopatra, we feel her suffering to have meaning. This assumption defines the form of the play.
  But aside from evoking the simple pathos of their situation, Dryden
presents Antony and Cleopatra as a pair of prodigies from a past heroic
age. The play's references to gods and heroes establish a sense, sustained
throughout the action, that these weak, despairing lovers are, concurrently, awesome giants who have outlived their proper time.[12] The opening image of huge "forsaken" river creatures cast up "flound'ring" on
an unfamiliar shore contributes to this general sense of stranded and expiring grandeur (I.11–15).[13] These analogies are combined with constantly reiterated evocations of loss and nostalgia at the passing of an
age: " 'Tis past recovery" (I.50), "But now 'tis past" (II.28), "Now
'tis past forever" (II.217), " 'Tis past" (III.373), "Egypt has been; our

latest hour is come . . . / Time has unrolled her glories to the last, / And now closed up the volume" (V.71-75), "What ages have we lived!" (V.393).[14]

Thus Dryden augments the affective formal assumptions of his play with a sense of heroic glory quite incompatible with the actual demeanor of his characters. In fact he must construct separate identities for both Antony and Cleopatra, outside the realm of the presented action, in order to create the illusion of heroic conflict and to motivate the plot. *All for Love* describes an apparent heroic dilemma—a choice between love and honor—where there is actually no conflict at all, but rather the simple affective mechanism of pathos. By making that pathos appear to belong to a world of heroic actors, Dryden supplies his play with a plot and its conclusion with a recollection of grandeur beyond the capacities of pure pity.

By historical and literary precedent, as well as by his reputation within the play, Antony is a hero in the old style, a Herculean demigod. The "real Antony" in the world of this play, however, neither does nor even decides anything for himself. He is the Antony who, we learn from the very first, is "a prey to black despair" (I.61). He is the lost and ruined Antony, "unbent, unsinewed," "the blank of what he was" (I.173-79). Like Alexander and Brutus, he enacts his own "ruin" by throwing himself upon the ground (I.215 *s.d.*). As helpless as an infant (II.235), he is swayed first one way and then another by the real agents of the plot, Ventidius and Alexas. In fact, Ventidius's exalted descriptions of Antony, and even Antony's momentary heroic response, are a reminder of past heroism, not an expression of present capacity. In contrast to his heroic claims for Antony, Ventidius serves formally to absolve his hero from any implication of independence or initiative.

The "real Antony" is defined and understood, as he defines himself in his death speech, not by his heroic merit or moral worth, but by his pathetic situation, his "last disastrous times" (V.388). The heroic epithets that are attached to Antony represent a deliberately fabricated illusion, unsubstantiated in the action and actually belied by the conduct of the characters. Significantly, among the many illusory definitions of Antony's heroic merit, the only quality that is shared by the "real Antony" in his pathetic action is the propensity for pity. He is said to be "more pitiful" after battle than "praying virgins" (I.186-87), and even godlike in his "soft pity to th'oppressed" (II.151). And indeed, Antony weeps and sighs repeatedly throughout the play. Pity is obviously the cause of his change of heart in favor of Cleopatra. But, more important, it is also the source of Ventidius's initial and subsequent temporary ascendancies over him (I.266-73). The sole attribute of the legendary heroic Antony that is enacted in the plot is that very response of pity which the form itself demands from its audience.

Pathos is the defining quality of Cleopatra's character as well. She is wholly innocent, completely virtuous, and, in fact, from the first moment we see her on the stage, "no queen" but "a captive," a lover, and "a slave" (II.7-15). She refutes all the charges brought against her by Ventidius—charges that are justly made of Shakespeare's queenly courtesan—so effectively as to be extolled as "wronged innocence" by Antony, who accuses Ventidius of nothing short of blasphemy for impugning her (II.436-37). She proves her undying loyalty to Antony by revealing Octavius's offer of immunity (II.390-400), justifies her flight at Actium by her weak and womanly fear of battle (II.374-77), and even explains away, to Antony's satisfaction and our own, her early years of dalliance with Caesar. This Cleopatra is effectually and explicitly "a wife, a silly, harmless, household dove, / Fond without art, and kind without deceit" (IV.92-93). She is, in fact, more true than Antony's true wife, Octavia, who finally uses up her love and leaves him (IV.414-17). Cleopatra's love admits no impediment, even of Antony's hatred (IV.582-85) and, ultimately, of death. Her perfect innocence and virtue, substantiated by the closing benediction, "Sleep, blest pair" (V.514), inspires, in the observers within the play as well as in the audience, protestations at the injustice of heaven, an injustice that further augments the pathos of the action:

> *Charmion.* Be juster, heav'n: such virtue punished thus
> Will make us think that chance rules all above,
> And shuffles with a random hand the lots
> Which man is forced to draw. [V.1-4]

The rival-queens scene constitutes a brief formal epiphany of the pathetic assumptions of the play. Though in the absence of Octavia Dryden is capable of describing Cleopatra as Antony's wife, that affective device is not legitimately open to him in the tour de force of the two ladies' collision. In fact, Octavia's recent appearance with her pathetic children has greatly increased her power with the audience.[15] But Cleopatra carries the day, not by bullying Octavia, but by fainting (III.470-74). The conclusion of the scene shows us that Cleopatra is weaker and more pathetic than Octavia, that she has "suffered more," (III.459), that she, like Antony, is a "harmless infant" (III.484) at the mercy of the vicissitudes of her situation. In this central scene, then, as in the whole play, response determines the shape and significance of the action. Cleopatra's victory over Octavia in our sympathies is produced not by the superior merit of the Egyptian "wife," but by the greater affective power of Cleopatra's plight. As Antony accurately observes: "Pity pleads for Octavia, / But does it not plead more for Cleopatra?" (III.339-40).

To maintain the passivity and pathos of Cleopatra's situation, Dryden

must keep her not only innocent, but also, like Antony, inactive. Cleopatra too does nothing for herself. Alexas initiates and implements
the gift of jewels that restores Antony to Cleopatra in Act II. He con-
cocts the scheme to arouse Antony's jealousy of Dolabella in Act IV.
And he, this time unknown to Cleopatra, announces her suicide to Antony in Act V.[16] Each of these maneuvers not only excludes Cleopatra
from blame, but actively augments her innocence and virtue. Her momentary mock flirtation with Dolabella, for instance, conceived and
coached by Alexas, is ended by that primary affective resource, a fainting fit, which serves as physical proof of innocence and weakness at
once (IV.166 *s.d.*). Cleopatra, just like Antony (IV.432–34), is unable
to disguise her feelings.

    Thus, while Cleopatra's virtue is maintained, the action is motivated
by a collection of other characters, led by Alexas. Their combined
effect creates the illusion of another set of characteristics for Cleopatra,
and this "other Cleopatra" absorbs the morally questionable qualities
of the literary and legendary queen, leaving the "real Cleopatra" an un-
sullied wife. Alexas's machinations, the Egyptians' cowardice, and
Ventidius's unjustified accusations and exhortations all conjure up for
the purposes of the plot a seductress, a courtesan, a liar, a conniver,
and a traitor. This "other Cleopatra" conspires to arrange the defeat of
Antony's navy at Actium, contemplates a separate peace with Octavius, and conducts an affair with Dolabella. These apocryphal activities
lend a superficial plausibility to the "real Cleopatra's" occasional incongruous claims to a defiant heroism parallel to that of the legendary
Antony. More important, the "other Cleopatra" supplies Antony with
a dilemma where the "real Cleopatra" can provide only pathos. As long
as Antony is undeceived about her virtue and her love, he remains
true to her and his choice is simple and automatic (II.430–42). In short,
Dryden's particular form requires that Cleopatra be a wife but seem to
be an evil seductress who brings about Antony's ruin. The first is necessary for the play's pathetic effect, and the second for the action upon
which that effect must be based.

    The central pathetic situation of *All for Love*, then, arises not from a
real dilemma but from a formal trompe l'oeil perpetrated by the "other
Cleopatra" and the hearsay heroic merit of the passive Antony. The
affecting emotional torture that Antony and Cleopatra endure is the
product of a series of carefully contrived misunderstandings that produce an equivalent series of eloquent and unsubstantiated assertions
of heroic grandeur. Indeed, the illusory characteristics of both protagonists serve the same formal purpose.

    Antony's and Cleopatra's deaths constitute the last and most fully
pathetic step in the definition of their affective power, and thus satisfy
our expectations and resolve the plot not through the meaningful

fulfillment of a logical process of evaluation, but through the pitying response that marks our comprehension of the form: because our feeling for the characters reaches a climax at their deaths, we feel their deaths to have meaning. Emotion is an end in itself. Affective form thus automatically assumes the world to be "well lost." But, as we have seen, *All for Love* also attaches a distinctive air of heroic grandeur to this loss. The heroic recollections associated with Antony and Cleopatra serve not only to manufacture a dilemma that can motivate the plot, but also to elevate the pathos of that dilemma, so that the "loss" appears grandly rather than merely pathetic. Thus, though within the world of the play both characters are portrayed as passive victims of their private situation, explicitly denying even the significance of their public roles (III.396–98 and V.401–02), [17] their deaths, the ultimate expression of powerlessness and passivity, can appear simultaneously as a kind of heroic conquest, a moment of glory and grandeur in which they outdo the nominal conquerer, "the boy" (III.63) Octavius.

The pathos of Antony's and Cleopatra's deaths, then, is determined by the actions, or inactions, of the "real" Antony and Cleopatra, caught in the insoluble dilemma of the plot. Their heroism is asserted through the illusory evocations of the heroic Antony and the "other Cleopatra," who make it appear that empires and eternal glory are at stake. The final simile of the tragedy expresses exactly this relationship between affective form and heroic assertion: "See, see how th'lovers sit in state together, / As they were giving laws to half mankind!" (V.507–08). As a lost and ruined lover and a poor, weak woman, the "real" Antony and Cleopatra give no laws, direct no fates, and attain no glory. They are only like the monarchs whose names they bear. But that likeness is the special achievement of Dryden's particular affective form. In general, then, *All for Love* includes a residual heroic dimension, superimposed upon the "real" pathetic definition of the protagonists' character and plight, that elaborates their action and accounts for its preeminent position in the serious drama of the period.

Other affective tragedy confronts the same problem as that solved by Dryden's dramatic simile in *All for Love;* it must motivate a plot and produce a pathetic situation with characters who are essentially passive and innocent. But the younger dramatists, not so concerned as Dryden with consistency, are most likely to solve the problem with a simple contradiction in characterization. Dryden, unlike Lee and Otway, sustains a firm allegiance to the determinacy of character. [18] The "other Cleopatra" is an elaborate formal means of upholding that determinacy which in *Sophonisba, The Rival Queens, The Orphan,* or *Venice Preserved* is necessarily sacrificed to the immediate requirements of the action. As we observed in the context of his heroic drama, Dryden, at least in this respect, does not make as fundamental a break with early Restoration dramatic practice as do his younger, "newer" contemporaries.

Dryden's play, like Lee's *Lucius Junius Brutus* and *The Rival Queens*, documents the formal proximity of early affective tragedy to the heroic action. Both these dramatists choose heroic subjects, and both seek to maintain, almost against the internal propensities of their forms, the demigodlike stature of the old heroic protagonist. But both writers, in separate ways, discover formal alternatives to the heroic action. Lee's essentially ambiguous experiment in *The Rival Queens* is followed immediately by Dryden's masterful formal simile in *All for Love*, which even builds upon many of the specific details of the earlier play: the emblematic rival queens' confrontation, the all-too-honest advisor to the emperor, and the crucial choice of love over empire. Significantly, Otway's serious drama depends less on the recollection of heroic form and more on the simple affective force of domestic, statusless characters. This domesticity, as we will see, is the inevitable conclusion of the formal and ideological assumptions of affective tragedy, as well as the necessary prelude to the "classless" moral tragedy of the eighteenth century.

III

Thomas Otway's mature affective drama, represented by *The Orphan* (1680) and *Venice Preserved* (1682), but clearly prefigured in the early near-heroic *Don Carlos* (1676) and *Titus and Berenice* (1676), reveals the depoliticization characteristic of the purest versions of the form. The simple domesticity of Otway's tragic plots entails not merely the choice of love over empire, which we have seen to be common to Dryden and Lee, but the elimination of empire altogether. Along with honor and empire, Otway necessarily eliminates status, even as a nominal label attached to a primarily pitiable character or as a nostalgic reflection of past heroism. Otway's protagonists are neither princes nor kings, but private men or, more important for the subsequent evolution of serious drama, women. The beset heroine is the natural recourse of affective form, since she is by definition a weak, domestic being excluded from issues of honor and empire and thus both pitiable and statusless. To guarantee the pathos of his protagonists, who can evoke none of the nostalgia of an Alexander or an Antony, Otway gives them innocence and, when necessary, virtue. In fact, in keeping with their particular version of affective tragedy, Otway's plays provide a notably clear example of the reciprocal relationship between pathos, innocence, and the consequent inconsistencies in plot and character motivation congenital to the mature affective tragedy and later to the tragic moral action.

Significantly, the first lines of *The Orphan* do not introduce the unhappy protagonists, but rather the subsidiary character Acasto, their father, whose virtues and idiosyncracies are expounded at seemingly unnecessary length, and whose sudden illness interrupts the action. Acasto has puzzled critics of this drama, whose explanations of his role range from the suggestion that his illness is meant to symbolize his sons' deviation from a standard of manly virtue[19] to the less plausible argument that his presence is essential to the plot because he sleeps next door to Monimia: when his seizure forces him to retire to bed Monimia and Polydore must be silent to avoid disturbing him, and this instigates the whole tragedy.[20] But there is a much less ingenious explanation of Acasto's significance, one which also illuminates the place of *The Orphan* in generic history: Otway uses Acasto as a means of establishing and justifying the formal premises of the drama.

Acasto is a true soldier, a conqueror, a loyalist, and a man of glory and honor.[21] But, strangely enough, he has rejected the world of heroism (I.1-4). He is given considerable space, quite outside the apparent requirements of the plot, to enumerate his criticisms of the "corruption, envy, discontent, and faction" of "courts and camps" (II.18-60). Notably, he includes even the king in his pronouncement upon the inevitable corruption of public life: "He is . . . so just, that were he but a private man, / He could not do a wrong" (II.122-25). More important, Acasto effectively denies the world of heroism to his sons, Castalio and Polydore, whom he forbids "to launch for fortune in th'uncertain world; / But warns to avoid both courts and camps" (I.65-66). In the early scenes of the play, their constant objections to his strict antiheroism serve to establish, on the one hand, their admirably heroic tempers, and on the other, and more important, the essential domestic assumptions of their action. Acasto, emblematically as well as explicitly, would substitute a domestic world for the disillusionment of honor and empire. His otherwise rather unaccountable appearances in the play all enforce this effect. His incongruous and pointless "death scene" in Act III, for instance, from which he immediately recovers, permits him to summon his dependents and pronounce a lengthy pathetic and antiheroic death speech (III.67-96). That antiheroism constitutes the formal backdrop of the play. As Acasto denies the world of "courts and camps" to his sons, Otway denies the choice of honor and empire to his audience and to the form of his most daring domestic tragedy. Acasto's crucial formal role, then, is to create and maintain the elimination of honor and status essential to the particular affective action of *The Orphan*. Significantly, these explicit or enforced rejections of the values of heroism are repeated only in the first half of the tragedy, before the plot is completely under way and the pathos of the action is established.

In conjunction with Acasto's embittered criticisms of the court,

Otway also uses pastoral lament as a corollary to this denial of a public context. In a passage that, like Acasto's antiheroic comments, contributes to the domestication of the drama, Castalio envies the "happy shepherds" and longs for the bucolic countryside (IV.80–96). In fact, pastoral allusion is a congenial companion to pathetic effect not only in *The Orphan*, but in affective tragedy in general.[22] Here and elsewhere, the pastoral theme adds concrete imagistic detail to the evocation of pity. In this sense, it serves as an essentially empty conventional adjunct to the form: Castalio seeks pastoral escape even though, as Acasto and the opening exposition of the servants make clear, he is already in the country. This bold neglect of meaning is characteristic of Otway's tragic drama.

The action of *The Orphan* is centered upon a simple, insoluble domestic imbroglio in which the innocent and virtuous female protagonist, Monimia, is, through a combination of coincidence and malice, violated by her husband's twin brother and thus forced, Lucrece-like, to suicide. Monimia is, by repeated definition, "a poor and helpless orphan" (I.328), "a little tender flower" (IV.296), "the trembling, tender, kind, deceived Monimia" (V.453). She is said to possess herself the very sympathy which the audience is asked to extend to her. Her "little breasts," which Otway uses throughout the play as a concrete emblem of her character,[23] are the visual equivalent both of feminine vulnerability and weakness and of feminine compassion. Thus, like Alexander and Antony, Monimia serves as the object and also as the model for our response to her action. The heroine's pathetic plight is effectively coupled with the accidental and pitiable violation of the brothers' oaths of eternal love, and these interconnected transgressions lead to a group suicide and a multiplication of pathetic parting scenes. Thus the dilemma of Monimia's violation produces not one but three innocent victims who fill the last two acts of the play with intertwined and overlapping pleadings and misunderstandings. These scenes are the meat of Otway's affective form, preceded as we have seen by the essential first course of Acasto's antiheroism. They are characterized by despair, hysteria, violent language, self-accusation, and physical prostration, and gauged, in effect, to exploit every opportunity for pathos.

In keeping with this purpose, Otway builds a telltale inconsistency into his characterization of Polydore. This honorable youth, who so eagerly runs upon Castalio's sword and confesses his guilt in Act V, admits openly to jealousy and malice in his prosecution of the tragic trick in Act III (e.g., III.370–429). Attempts to discover consistency in this play have produced an inconclusive variety of critical readings, all seeking to explain away the problems presented by Polydore and by the implausibility of the plot.[24] The very diversity of these explications suggests that the problems are real, but that they cannot be resolved through any simple reassessment of the internal motivation of the tragedy. They cannot be explained away, but they can be explained. They are a sign of the reigning hierarchy of formal choices that determines the shape of the play. At the end of the action, Polydore's innocence and honor are essential to the triple-headed pathos of the confessions, as well as to the coordinate tragedy of love and friendship. In the middle of the play, his malice is required to create the dilemma without implicating the essential innocence of the virtuous Monimia. Otway permits such an inconsistency because his primary concern in this play is not character but effect, and because the preeminence of effect so overshadows such issues of character and motivation as to make them irrelevant to the mechanics of the drama and thus largely invisible to its audience. The mistake in the characterization of Polydore is a deliberate one.

The Orphan, then, represents the full exfoliation of the mature affective form. The passive female protagonist, the assertion of innocence and virtue, the incessant gloom and foreboding, the emphasis on response at the expense of meaning, the neglect of characterization and the proliferation of character inconsistency, and the pervasive simplification, domestication, and depoliticization of the drama all reflect implicitly the formal rejection of the heroic hierarchies that Dryden elegizes and Lee attacks. The royalist Otway simply puts pathos in their place, and in so doing leaves that place open for the bourgeois values of the later moral action.

Despite many noteworthy differences, *Venice Perserved* is formally parallel to *The Orphan*, and the central similarity between the two plays demonstrates the consistency and predictability of Otway's affective tragedy. The play depends upon a dilemma of precisely the same nature as its predecessor's, though with a shifted emphasis in victimization. The statusless male protagonist, Jaffeir, takes the place of Monimia, though the coordinate pathetic situation—a tragic love relationship and a tragic friendship—remains the same. More important, the particular relationship between character inconsistency and depoliticization in *Venice Preserved* provides a basis for the further delineation of the special nature of affective form.

The action of the play consists of Jaffeir's related betrayals, first of his wife, then of his friend. In effect, the protagonist's plight is defined in terms of the tragic fates of his victims, and this derivation of pathos from pathos—Jaffeir's from that of Pierre and Belvidera—characterizes the particular affective form of *Venice Preserved*. Because of her sex, the "kind, good, and tender" (I.324) Belvidera is the most affecting and most obvious victim in the play. Her scenes of farewell—"Part! Must we part?" (II.iii.187)—are prominent from the beginning of the action, and her madness and death sustain their pathos to the last possible moment. Belvidera's violently pathetic career is rivaled in effect and centrality by the unfortunate fate of the noble and generous Pierre. Pierre is not only "the honest partner of [Jaffeir's] heart" (I.121) but also "a soldier, who has lived with honor, / Fought nations' quarrels, and been crowned with conquest" (V.iii.75–76). His role is more restrained than Belvidera's, but no less instrumental in generating and then generalizing the pathetic situation.

Jaffeir's betrayal of Pierre, then, serves not only to generate pity for the victim but also to raise sympathy for the self-castigating traitor, who suffers the contempt and shares the death of his friend. Similarly, though Belvidera is the actual victim, Jaffeir's fumbling attempt to murder her while she *"leaps upon his neck and kisses him"* (IV.ii.409 *s.d.*) results in a heightening of Jaffeir's pathos as well, when he curses himself for his cowardice and love (IV.ii.413–16). In fact, every appearance of the emblematic dagger arouses pity not only for the victim, but equally for the aggressor, and Jaffeir characteristically responds to his own threats of violence toward Belvidera with an emotion at least as affecting as hers (e.g., II.iii.228–38). This formal transubstantiation of aggressor to victim becomes explicit at Jaffeir and Belvidera's final parting scene, where Jaffeir turns the dagger against himself (V.ii.195–200), and it is ultimately realized when Jaffeir stabs first Pierre and then himself upon the scaffold.

These scenes of violence serve as brief epiphanies of the pathetic effect that dominates the plot and controls the characterization of the tragedy.[25] In fact, the dagger becomes the physical symbol of the play's particular affective mechanics.[26] Violence is tied to pathos, in the action as well as in the language of the play, in such a way that the wielder of the dagger is both agent and object of affect. As the drama reaches a climax, Otway need only display the dagger to arouse our pity (e.g., V.ii.206–07, V.iii.106–09). Jaffeir is thus himself the victim of Pierre's and Belvidera's plights, and in the general mingling of pathetic expostulation he answers them in kind, emphasizing, for even greater emotional effect, his guilt and repentance (IV.ii.175–79), his wretchedness and regret (IV.ii.296–302). The result is a chorus of pleadings and partings that accumulate, as in *The Orphan*, in the last acts of the play and that produce in the audience the pleasurable pity that is both the consequence and the sole significance of the action.

In general, Jaffeir's claims of guilt serve to make him the supreme victim, and the dilemma he faces is posed not as a legitimate choice but as a formal locus for pathos. His own description of his situation appropriately subordinates the significance of the choice to the pain of choosing (IV.i.72–78). Pain is not only the essence of his character, but also, in terms of the inverted logic of affective form, the source of both personal and aesthetic pleasure:

Come, lead me forward now like a tame lamb
To sacrifice. Thus in his fatal garlands,
Decked fine and pleased, the wanton skips and plays,
    Trots by the enticing flattering priestess' side,
    And much transported with his little pride,
    Forgets his dear companions of the plain,
    Till by her, bound, he's on the altar lain;
    Yet then too hardly bleats, such pleasure's in the pain.   [IV.i.87-94]

The characterization in *Venice Preserved*, like that in *The Orphan*, is
the servant of that pleasurable pain which dictates the progress of the
action. Amidst his self-accusations, Jaffeir's innocence is sustained by
Otway's manipulation of our attitudes toward the conspirators, especially Pierre. The nobility that Pierre exhibits in the last acts of the play
is strangely unlike the explicit villainy that Otway attaches to his first
meeting with Jaffeir. There Pierre speaks of "revenge" and "mischief"
(I.287 and 305), calls Jaffeir his "proselyte" (II.ii.13), offers him an
apparent bribe (II.ii.33), and is, throughout these midnight scenes, explicitly associated with hell, the devil, and damnation (II.ii.34-38).
Otway uses the other conspirators, particularly the lecherous Renault,
to substantiate our suspicions of Pierre. After Renault's attempted
rape of Belvidera and the conspirators' bloody resolutions to murder
the innocent bystanders of Venice, we are prepared to agree, at least
temporarily, with Belvidera's assessment:

Can thy great heart descend so vilely low,
Mix with hired slaves, bravoes, and common stabbers,
Nose-slitters, alley-lurking villains! join
With such a crew, and take a ruffian's wages,
To cut the throats of wretches as they sleep?   [III.ii.161-65]

In short, Pierre and the conspirators appear at times the saviors of
Venice (I.151-64) and at other times a pack of devilish fiends. This
inconsistency is essential to the maintenance of Jaffeir's innocent victimization. It transforms his apparent choice into a simple series of
pathetic situations in which suffering, and not choosing, is the formal
principle. Thus, Jaffeir is innocent in joining the conspiracy both because it is a noble and honorable enterprise and because he was tempted
to do so by no less than the devil himself. He is innocent in offering to
sacrifice Belvidera because his loyalty to his noble friend demands it.
And he is innocent in betraying Pierre because the conspiracy is a treasonous attack upon the "reverend" Senate (IV.ii.60) and because that
same Senate, now corrupt and "faithless" (IV.ii.356), had promised to
pardon the conspirators.

More important, the inconsistency in Pierre's characterization permits
Otway to maintain Jaffeir's affecting innocence despite the magnitude

of his crimes. We feel all the emotional effects of Jaffeir's betrayal of
his friend and his attack upon his wife without attaching any of the
responsibility for those acts to the protagonist, who remains the innocent victim of his own pathetic situation. When Pierre and the other
conspirators are bound for death, Otway permits no recollection of
their previous iniquity (V.iii.51–54). And Pierre himself appears at that
moment irreproachably noble (V.iii.6–9). In this manner, Jaffeir's
plight acquires the added poignancy of Pierre's perfect innocence, while
Pierre's initial villainy motivates the action without endangering our
sympathy for Jaffeir. The deliberate and functional inconsistencies of
the characterization in this play are formally identical to those in *The
Orphan* and have provoked a similar critical debate. The attempt to
justify them in terms of the internal motivation of the action has recently
led several critics to the conclusion that Otway's purpose is the delineation of verisimilar psychological complexities.[27] But as we have seen,
Jaffeir's or Pierre's "complexities" appear only in the immediate service
of the play's affective form.

The inconsistency in *Venice Preserved*, like the "mistake" in the
characterization of Polydore in *The Orphan*, is a weakness that is pro-
tected by those very formal premises which it fulfills: the more we
feel the pathos of the tragedy, the less important matters of characterization and motivation become. The inconsistency in this play
supplies not only the essential innocence of Jaffeir's character, and thus
the means to his victimization, but also the corollary depoliticization
that we have seen to be a central tenet of affective tragedy. Otway uses
the same means to arouse our pity as to detach that pity from the
public world of kings and empires or of specific political factions. To
the extent that Jaffeir's "choice" is transformed, by Pierre's inconsistency, into simple victimization, assessment is necessarily replaced
by situation and public concerns become irrelevant to the affective
preoccupations of the form.

Broadly speaking, the analogies between republican Venice and
monarchical England are singularly inappropriate. More specifically, the
association of the conspiracy with the ambiguous character of Pierre
renders it politically meaningless. Furthermore, Shaftesbury enters the
play both as the lecherous, antityrannical conspirator Renault and as
the repulsive, perverted Senator Antonio. Yet the Catholic priest appears
as an agent of these supposedly Whiggish Senators and is symbolically
and nobly rejected by Pierre (V.iii.15–23). Such hopelessly tangled local
references express in themselves Otway's consistent royalism, and their
confusion may reveal the influence of the new, democratic Toryism that
was beginning to form in opposition to the consolidation of the aristocratic Whig oligarchy.[28] But they serve in the context of the action to

short-circuit evaluation entirely and to sustain the private, domestic reference essential to pathetic form.[29] In *Venice Preserved* Otway eliminates the choice of heroism not by retreating to the pastoral countryside, as in *The Orphan*, but by providing a host of specific, indiscriminate, and contradictory allusions in an explicitly political context.

This elimination has a moral and ethical dimension as well, since Otway's affective form requires the neutralization of all possible evaluative standards. In *The Orphan* Castalio's crucial reticence about his marriage is not meant to cast ethical aspersions on his character, but simply to motivate a plot in which blame is entirely irrelevant to effect. His inexplicable secrecy, which is never justified, is merely used to augment the pathos surrounding the final act. Similarly, Jaffeir's decision to betray the conspiracy is robbed of all moral or ethical import by the ambiguity of Pierre, the conspirators, and the Senate. Jaffeir himself is never sure for long where his "honor" truly lies. When Belvidera finally convinces him of the necessity of betraying the conspiracy to the Senate, he concludes:

> Th'art my soul itself; wealth, friendship, honor,
> All present joys, and earnest of all future,
> Are summed in thee. [IV.i.80-82]

Soon after, however, when confronted by Pierre, his first words are:

> To thee I am the falsest, veriest slave
> That e'er betrayed a generous trusting friend,
> And gave up honor to be sure of ruin. [IV.ii.147-49]

Not only does an act of honor quickly become an act of dishonor, but Jaffeir cannot in retrospect offer any motivation at all for his betrayal of his friend. He can only beg for pity. In excluding the choice of heroism and the world of public commitment, Otway simultaneously denies his drama all other standards of positive judgment.

The evasions, the confusions, and the "mistakes" in these two masterful and powerful pathetic plays expose for us some of the working machinery of a self-conscious and exclusively affective form. Otway's initial choice of situation over status as the organizing principle of his drama leads him to the selection of an innocent, private, passive protagonist, and that selection in turn demands the evasive depoliticization and the inconsistent treatment of character that we have seen to be reciprocal effects of the same, initial affective intention. Monimia and Jaffeir are comprehensible not as social or moral beings with social or moral merits or defects, but as simple sufferers and victims whose fates display the pleasurable extremities of pathos as the inevitable consequence of their accumulating sorrows. Polydore and Pierre are significant not as autonomous individuals with the verisimilar complexities of actual psychologies, but as specific formal generators of the affective action.

Otway's mature tragedy, then, breaks with heroic form not as Lee's does by direct attack or by the active substitution of bourgeois ideals, and not as Dryden's does by the nostalgic location of aristocratic hero-ism in a past age, but by the simple elimination of status and character assessment. In this sense, despite his personal royalism, Otway, even more than Dryden and Lee, produces a full development of the form's implicit assumptions. As a Tory dramatist in a period of political in-stability, he repeatedly reminds his audience of the local issues upon which his political sentiments are built. In *The Orphan* we learn that Monimia's loyal and honest father had lost his estate in the civil war (I.55–56). In *Venice Preserved* we are presented with a vehement and libelous attack on Shaftesbury as well as a criticism of Whig consti-tutionalism in the Venetian Senate and in the bloodthirsty conspirators. But as we have seen, Otway's royalism never finds its way into the form of his plays, simply because a pure affective form assumes no ap-paratus of judgment, either political, moral, social, or metaphysical. In *Venice Preserved* even the ostensible villain, Pierre, cannot be con-sistently named and assessed, since such a discrimination would imply a hierarchy of values that would contradict the essential affective assumptions of the action. Otway, like Lee and Dryden, abandons the evaluative standards of the heroic drama, rejects the public choice of honor, and turns to a form that is essentially empty of assessment, of issues, and even of meaning.

Otway's sense of the inefficacy of aristocratic and absolutist ideals constitutes a manifestation, in literary form, of the ideological turmoil attendant upon the last days of English absolutism.[30] The gloom, the foreboding, the tragic failure, the corruption, and the disillusionment that haunt Otway's plays reflect the pessimism that results, as in Lee's tragedy, from the disintegration of formal assessment, the fragmenta-tion of the aristocratic hierarchy, and the disturbing, shifting insuffi-ciency of judgment and discrimination. Both *The Orphan* and *Venice Preserved* are permeated by this cynicism and disgust,[31] and each play, appropriately, ends with an emblematic expression of pessimism and despair:

> *Castalio.* Confusion and disorder seize the world,
>   To spoil all trust and converse amongst men;
>   'Twixt families engender endless feuds;
>   In countries, needless fears; in cities, factions;
>   In states, rebellion; and in churches, schism. [*The Orphan*, V.516–20]

Jaffeir. Final destruction seize on all the world!
  Bend down, ye Heavens, and shutting round this earth,
  Crush the vile globe into its first confusion;
  Scorch it with elemental flames to one cursed cinder,
  And all us little creepers in't, called men,
  Burn, burn to nothing. [*Venice Preserved*, V.ii.93-98]

Otway's affective tragedy abandons the formal and ideological security of assessment for the pleasing pain of pathetic situation. His plays, in their relative formal purity, provide the clearest proof of the necessary mediation of affective form between the aristocratic social drama of the Restoration and the bourgeois moral drama of the eighteenth century.

IV

Though Lee, Dryden, and Otway are the deservedly preeminent practitioners of affective form in this transitional period, the pathetic assumptions that we have defined in their tragedies are also discoverable in the less renowned and less successful plays of dramatists like Banks and Southerne. Banks's revival of English history and his consistent use of the pathetic female protagonist or, when she fails, the Stupid Hero provide an enlightening example of the role of historical drama in formal evolution. Southerne's increasingly explicit morality and its attendant formal consequences illustrate the beginnings of the change from affective to moral drama. In general, the fundamental similarity of the two writers, both to each other and to the major dramatists who have supplied us with a definition of the form, suggests the pervasiveness and variety of affective drama in this period, as well as the nature of its gradual evolution toward moral tragedy.

At first examination, John Banks differs significantly from Otway in his choice of the historical English monarchy as subject matter. Otway selects an unknown central European orphan; Banks hits upon Queen Elizabeth or Anne Boleyn (in *The Unhappy Favourite: or the Earl of Essex*, 1681, and *Vertue Betray'd: or, Anna Bullen*, 1682). But as we shall see, this important distinction is a sign of the fundamental affinities between the two dramatists, since Banks uses history as his particular roundabout route to affective form. Like Otway, Banks deliberately drains his historical drama of political reference. First of all, he relies almost exclusively upon female protagonists, who, even as queens and princesses, can be depicted as weak, mourning, and expiring lovers. His heroines, despite their status, have no public role and make no reference to the fortunes of the kingdom, except to reflect enviously upon the happier fates of private citizens.[32] His heroes, when they share the stage with their suffering or wounded counterparts, resemble them in passivity, pathos, and ineptitude, and achieve an almost feminine reduction in effectual status as a result.[33] Royalty is for Banks not a mark of status, but simply a means of establishing a uniquely pitiable situation, and aristocracy becomes synonymous with pathetic misfortune.

In the context of the action, Banks goes to almost ridiculous lengths to eliminate public motive from historical events. Essex's rebellion is carefully reinterpreted as the result of a fit of pique on the part of a proud "favourite" with the taint of stupidity, who, for some unaccountable reason, takes his cause to the populace when Elizabeth, jealously in love with him, boxes him on the ear. Likewise, Anna Bullen is sentenced to death as a result of a series of tricks and machinations perpetrated by Elizabeth Blunt, who is simply jealous of her, and Cardinal Wolsey, who is not supplied within the play with any motivation at all, except that he may be "a devil" (V, p. 68). The result is a form, much like Otway's, in which the characters are seen and assessed as victims in an evaluative vacuum so complete that, as in *Venice Preserved*, it is not even possible to identify and judge the evil agents of their destruction. They plead, they weep, they misunderstand one another, and, most important, they indulge in choruses of lengthy farewells, all of which, aside from the necessary exposition, account for the bulk of the represented stage business. Consequently, in Banks's drama, as in *The Orphan*, the action itself is slight or nonexistent. *The Unhappy Favourite* describes Essex's return and his consequent execution. *Vertue Betray'd* opens after Anna's marriage to Henry VIII and depicts only her subsequent death. In both cases action as well as characterization are designed to produce the proper pathetic response rather than to provide judgment, motivation, or psychological verisimilitude.

Despite their subject matter, then, or perhaps even because of it, Banks's history plays are fully pathetic. In fact, the use of English history seems to supply Banks with a justification for the formal experimentation that characterizes his best tragedy. When he attempts pathos without this historical framework, as in *The Rival Kings* (1677) or *Cyrus the Great* (1695), his drama is weak, ineffectual, or absurdly sensationalist. Within the hallowed convention of the necessary historical reference of tragedy, Banks embarks upon a nationalistic campaign for domestic history which, he argues, is more probable and verifiable than the romantic, exotic material of heroic drama (dedication, *Vertue Betray'd*, sig. A2^r–A3^v). Granted this argument for historical verisimilitude and tragic propriety, Banks is free to select the appropriate historical subjects and to invent an essentially private, apolitical affective form. In the same way that Otway uses profuse

political allusion to depoliticize *Venice Preserved,* his contemporary
uses historical reference to disguise the private assumptions of formal
pathos. In addition, the local and comparatively prosaic material of
English history provides the drama with familiar, life-size characters
with whom the audience can identify and who can more properly
be supplied with simple human emotions than can the superhumans of
the exotic heroic action. In short, the advocacy of domestic history
leads Banks directly to the delineation of domestic passions.[34]

In terms of the evolution of serious drama in this period, Banks is a
uniquely transitional figure. He maintains all the status and historical
significance of the aristocratic hero, even to the depiction of some of
the most politically crucial events in English history; the material of
his plays, except for the local setting, is identical to that of the heroic
action. But he restricts his protagonists, in general, to beset or mar-
tyred women or Stupid Heroes, and his concerns to strictly private passions. In effect, this permits him to take a decisive formal step away
from the heroic action, which defines its characters in terms of social
status, and toward the moral forms of the eighteenth century, which
repudiate aristocratic class judgment by searching out the inherent
moral worth of the individual.

In addition, Banks's conflation of domestic history and domestic
passions suggests the utter irreconcilability of heroic and moral form
without the mediation of affective tragedy. It is only the resolute
omission of public acts and thus the arbitrary denial of the formal
efficacy of social assessment that make Banks's drama a connecting
link between a drama of kings and princes and the bourgeois moral
tragedy of the eighteenth century. Significantly, Banks's recourse to
the female protagonist is the essential catalyst in his skillful and surprising equation of English history and private pathos. In making this
equation, Banks gives precisely the same justification for his depiction
of domestic passions as does the official inventor of the moral she-
tragedy, Nicholas Rowe. The location of private woes in public places
substantiates the formal significance of the use of historical material
in periods of major generic transition, and illustrates the close continuity between affective and bourgeois moral drama.

Thomas Southerne's tragedies provide concrete formal evidence of
the increasing moralization of serious drama at the end of the century.
Whereas Cleopatra's wifely virtue, Titus's pardonable treason, and
Jaffeir's contrived innocence are all functions of the pathos of their
respective actions, the moral perfection of Southerne's Isabella is displayed, in part, simply for its own sake. *The Fatal Marriage: or, the
Innocent Adultery* (1694) describes the rather horrible consequences
of inadvertent bigamy. Isabella, the suffering heroine, takes a second
husband in the belief that her first, most beloved mate, who has left

her with a precociously pathetic infant, has perished in the wars. He
returns too late to prevent the marriage, but in time to produce a kind
of morally scrupulous distraction in his wife, and the play ends with
an excruciatingly morbid scene of pathos and death.

Unlike any of those innocent affective protagonists whose virtue is
achieved by formal default, Isabella is supplied from the beginning of
her action with moralistic sententiae explicitly defining "the Beauties
of [her] Soul."[35] Cleopatra's moral perfections are only registered at
those specific points in the play when she must be excused from the
crimes of the "other Cleopatra," or when her pathos is in specific need
of emphasis. Isabella is always perfect; in fact, in the early scenes of
the play, descriptions of her moral merit actually supersede emotional
evocations of her suffering. Unlike Otway, Southerne maintains the
innocence essential to affective form by providing a specifically moral
excuse for Isabella's "crime." She is approached by her second husband
at the moment when her creditors, having stripped her of all her pos-
sessions, are about to carry her away to an unspecified fate, leaving her
infant child to starve along with her loyal nurse. Isabella is morally
obligated to save the lives for which she is responsible by marrying her
generous and honorable suitor.

Thus, while *The Fatal Marriage* remains primarily a pathetic play,
reveling in the emotionally charged misunderstandings, self-accusations,
and farewells attendant on the ill-fated Isabella's reunion with her beloved Biron, Southerne is inclined, at least in the initial acts, to emphasize virtue over suffering and to describe a consistent and fully realized
moral paragon. Subsequently, of course, Isabella's virtue serves the
ends of accumulating formal pathos, and the madness and death scenes
gain added fervor from the assumption of Isabella's perfect innocence.
In general, though the morality of Southerne's paragon protagonist is
not necessarily separable from the pathos that is the formal consequence
of her perfection, it is evidently able to assert a kind of independence
signaled by its brief and occasional interference with the exploitation
of suffering, which anticipates the later turn to morality as an end in
itself. The serious plots of *The Disappointment* (1684) and *Oroonoko*
(1695) provide similar examples of the moralization of Southerne's
affective drama, focusing on chastity, the sine qua non of the eighteenth-century female paragon. As we will see, the appeal for sympathy
made by the moral action is frequently similar to the emotionalism
of formal pathos, but while the affective dramatist seeks to maximize
effect regardless of morality or character consistency, the moral dramatist begins with the formal given of the paragon protagonist and
seeks to construct a viable action around that central figure. Southerne's
mature drama is poised just on the affective side of that water-
shed.

V

The common distinguishing formal characteristics of all these plays, then, provide a general definition of affective tragedy that can include drama as apparently diverse and unique as *All for Love*, *The Orphan*, and *The Unhappy Favourite*, without reducing the idiosyncracies of individual artists to irrelevant anomalies. The designation of situation instead of merit as the principle of order and comprehension corresponds to a loss of confidence in the aristocratic and absolutist ideology embodied in the heroic form as well as to a functional failure of evaluative discriminations in general. It leads to the gloomy and restricted domestic focus of this drama, to its conscious neutralization of political, social, and moral issues, to its preference for innocent, suffering female victims, to its tendency toward functional inconsistencies in characterization, to its pervasive stylistic sensationalism, and, of course, to its singleminded and overwhelming pathos.

These elements are linked initially, in the pioneering plays of Lee and Dryden, to the recollection or critical reassessment of heroic ideals. In this sense, though formally pathetic, *The Rival Queens* and *All for Love* are closer to the heroic action than are Otway's mature plays. In effect, Lee's precocious *Lucius Junius Brutus* uses the style and conventions of the heroic action to construct an alternative republican ideal that materializes out of the ideological void of affective form. At its evolutionary midpoint, affective tragedy explicitly detaches itself from any hierarchy of values, either recollected or radical, and presents simple suffering, unqualified by cause or blame. But by the end of the century the evaluative vacuum of the form begins gradually to be filled by the moral assertions that had, in the heyday of pathos, merely signaled an increase of effect. The claim for virtue in the name of pathos is transformed into the creation of the paragon protagonist, who is formally significant and meaningful in herself. In addition, the recourse to domestic characters, and specifically women, provides the necessary ideological buffer between social and moral form. Since women are, for obviously related reasons, both especially pathetic and specifically statusless, they are particularly suited not only to the affective action, but also to a moralized drama that deliberately seeks to repudiate status and to put inner moral worth in its place. In this respect, the history of serious drama is closely wedded to the changing position of women in English society. The evolving attitudes toward property marriage, toward women's economic functions, toward the nature and importance of the family, and toward female chastity, which result, in part, in the eighteenth-century bourgeois cult of womanhood,[36] produce a new female prototype that is reflected in the crucial role of the passive, virtuous woman in these plays. In the evolution of dramatic form, as we shall see, women serve to mediate between Almanzor and George Barn-well, between the aristocratic hero of the Restoration and the middle-class hero of the eighteenth century, just as the absence of judgment in affective form mediates between the aristocratic social standards of the heroic action and the bourgeois moral standards of eighteenth-century tragedy.[37]

Thus, the preliminary material essential to the moral action of the eighteenth century is already implicit, in however adulterated a state, in the pathetic plays of the 1670s and 1680s. The formal change that takes place between that time and the performance of *The London Merchant* (1731) is fundamental, but so continuous that even those first near-heroic works can be seen as the formal and ideological predecessors of eighteenth-century sentimentalism.[38] In effect, the bourgeois ideals that achieved their long-delayed official ascendancy in 1688 embark on their voyage to ideological and formal preeminence in the drama with Lee's incoherent subversion and fragmentation of the heroic action and Dryden's elegiac admission that the formal coherence of the age of aristocratic values had passed away.

Hence, although the serious moral action of the eighteenth century is a decisive formal innovation, it is also the heir of a continuous dramatic tradition in which all of its significant single elements are fully and repeatedly anticipated. Affective tragedy likewise bequeaths the partic-ular constraints of its form to its less fortunate successor. Pure formal pathos seems to require the simplicity that permits an expansive develop-ment of the central emotional scenes, and, for related reasons, it eschews an elaborate protrayal of motivation or contingency. In this sense affec-tive tragedy erects its own formal edifice around the conventions that it inherits from the heroic action. The narrow scope and flat characteriza-tion of the heroic drama are perpetuated in the formal assumptions of its closely allied successor. The substitution of pathetic situation for evaluation, and the subsequent denial of public reference and social or moral meaning, inevitably maintain the narrow focus of serious drama, though its aristocratic basis disappears. And the related general affec-tion for simple and "single" plots and "regular" structures arises from and reinforces these inherent restrictions upon its range. Furthermore, in eliminating assessment and repudiating or subverting evaluative judg-ments, the form perpetuates the additional, but related, constraint upon characterization. In an evaluative vacuum, motivation is not only irrelevant but impossible. Thus, when pity replaces admiration, it brings with it no potential recourse to the inner life of its beset protagonists. Perhaps the most graphic example of this concurrent stifling of motiva-tion and character complexity is in the Restoration adaptations of Shakespeare's tragedies, which systematically substitute innocence for blame and simple misunderstanding for responsibility.[39]

Affective tragedy is therefore by definition restricted to simple, flat characters who answer only to the pathos of their situation. Without the resource of psychological verisimilitude, which arouses our sympathy by convincing us that a character is a full and complex human being, the affective dramatist can produce the sympathy essential to his form only by making his simple characters perfectly innocent and implicitly virtuous. Claims to moral perfection, when they occur, are thus an automatic reflex in the affective action, and it is the concentration upon pathetic effect, in the absence of complex characterization, that produces the inconsistencies common to the form. A dramatist like Otway willingly sacrifices the consistency of his characters in order to make them innocent and virtuous, and he must do this because he cannot make them psychologically complex. For this reason, the plots of affective plays invariably hinge upon mechanical rather than psychological complications, and Dryden, for instance, must rely upon the catalysts Alexas and Ventidius to produce any action at all.

Affective form, to the extent that it serves as the necessary intermediary between social and moral and provides a partial anticipation of the statusless middle-class protagonist and the irreproachable paragon, represents a genuinely transitional stage in the evolution of serious drama. But equally important, it is the carrier of specific constraints in scope and characterization to which the moral action is particularly vulnerable. In fact, the moralized drama of the eighteenth century evolves out of precisely those functional assertions of innocence and virtue to which, as we have seen, the stereotyped characterization and restricted scope of the affective tragedy is formally tied. Because of the nature of their formal proximity and the special sort of continuity in the evolution of serious drama in this period, the tragic moral action inherits the limitations of affective tragedy. But the restrictions of scope and characterization that combined to produce the enduring dramatic achievements of affective form, including the greatest serious play of the period's major playwright, prove to be a liability to the moral action, producing generic problems beyond the capacities of the age's most talented dramatists to resolve.

FOUR———————————————————
Transitional Comedy

The transitional comedy of the late Restoration, like the affective tragedy, abandons the simple and single judgmental mechanism of its formal
predecessor. Well before the turn of the century, the social assessment
typical of dramatic satire begins to give way to an entirely different evaluative criterion: that of inner moral worth. The change consists not
only of a separate set of values enacted by the characters, but also of a
separate set of assumptions about the comprehensibility of the drama.
A social satire is based upon the potential implicit disjunction between
social and moral judgment, and does not assume that its audience will
adopt and internalize what it sees presented on the stage, but rather that
it will scrutinize and perhaps reject that world. A moral action, on the
other hand, claims to express directly the morality of its audience, and
it assumes an immediate congruence between that morality and the
represented action. In this respect, there is no formal middle ground between social satire and moral comedy. The transitional comedy of this
period does not constitute a coherent form of its own, but rather a coherent collection of individual responses or capitulations to the forces of
generic change. Taken together, these responses reflect a general rejection
of aristocratic judgments parallel to that evident in the affective tragedy.

The resultant moralization of this drama, however incomplete, is in
itself a sign of the development of a new evaluative standard that, in
its fullest expression, deliberately dismisses the social success of its characters, and concurrently the aristocratic context where that success is
achieved and applauded, in favor of a moral criterion that claims to transcend class and social distinctions. The incipient morality of these plays,
then, constitutes the initial stage of a fundamental formal change and
anticipates the subsequent breakdown of social stereotypes, the neglect
and demise of classical decorum in characterization, and the corollary
rejection of classical generic distinctions and levels of style, which come
to define the form of the full moral action. The moral protagonist who
emerges in this transitional comedy, sometimes only in the last scene, is
potentially a serious middle-class hero whose character and treatment
challenge all the assumptions of aristocratic social satire.

The transitional comedy of this period is defined by the collision of

two incompatible modes. Those dramatists who surrender, albeit ingeniously, to the formal contradiction generally produce comedies in which
social and moral are simply juxtaposed. The plots of these mixed
transitional plays graphically enact the confrontation of the rival formal
forces of the period. *The Richmond Heiress* (Durfey, 1693) begins as
a social satire and ends, inexplicably, as a moral action. *The Wives Excuse* (Southerne, 1691) creates a context of explicit and even "lewd"
sexual pragmatism that is incongruously concluded with a scrupulously
moral assertion of individual virtue. *Love's Last Shift* (Cibber, 1696)
mixes social and moral in unreconciled separate actions that alternate
on the stage. And *Love and a Bottle* (Farquhar, 1698) transforms a
social action into a moral one by means of an ingenious trick that allows the dramatist to have it both ways: sexual profligacy turns out
to be identical with virtue and true love. Minor works like *The Lost
Lover* (Mary de La Rivière Manley, 1696) and *Tunbridge-Walks* (Thomas Baker, 1703) variously illustrate a similar characteristic transitional
incoherence. These plays can handily utilize the energetic plots of social
comedy and still assert the ultimate moral standard of a different dramatic world. Their incoherence solves the problem, later to become an
impasse, of inventing a dynamic action for a moral paragon. In short,
they reflect and appeal to the divided dramatic allegiances of the period, and their repeated inconsistencies testify to the particular incompatibility of social satire and moral action.

But the diminishing predominance of social satire has a more fundamental significance for the best playwrights of the period. The growing
interest in morality for its own sake, reflecting the concurrent pervasive formal and ideological changes of the age, briefly frees some dramatists to experiment with complex characterization. This is because the
intervention of moral values necessarily undermines the working assumptions of satiric form, which depends for comprehensibility on social
stereotypes. And the weakening of satiric form, with its consistent depiction of the external operations and "manners" of society, in turn
permits the examination of internal realities, of motivation, and even of
psychology. *The Way of the World* (Congreve, 1700) is uniquely representative of this transitional drama in its subtle definition of internal
motivations and moral values in an aggressively social context. And
The Relapse (Vanbrugh, 1696) attempts, though in a different manner,
a similar exploration of character complexity.

But Vanbrugh's and Congreve's experiments lead nowhere. They
reflect the special conditions of an incomplete formal shift that, once
completed, specifically excludes the very innovations that these dramatists sought to make. Vanbrugh's and Congreve's plays are written at
a time when the formal changes that eventually produce the full moral

action have not yet replaced the social stereotypes of dramatic satire
with the moral stereotypes of bourgeois drama. Congreve's movement
away from simple characterization succeeds the general transitional
influx of moral standards into the comedy, but precedes the rejection
of classical decorum and the inversion of class stereotypes that eventually accompany the full moralization of the drama. In this context,
the comparative failure of Congreve's best plays forecasts the future
of the new form.

Though it can be said to reach its height in *The Way of the World*,
transitional comedy begins, like affective tragedy, in the period immediately following the triumph of the two major early Restoration
forms. Before the mid-1690s, however, moralized or partially moralized drama is a relatively alien species, and Durfey's plays *The Virtuous
Wife* (1679) and *Love for Money* (1691) both appear to assert their
moral conclusions as anomalous and unexpected innovations. Shadwell's
whole career supplies a lesson in precocious moralization. His early
plays represent a humors variation upon the dominant social satire, but
his drama always suggests a strong, and potentially moral, deviation
from aristocratic standards. After his period of silence and presumable
exclusion from the theater during the troubled 1680s, he returns to
the drama with the moral, and explicitly Whiggish plays, *The Squire of
Alsatia* (1688) and *The Volunteers* (1692). Thus, both Durfey and
Shadwell predate the prime of transitional comedy, and both write
plays in which their moral assumptions appear not as a consensus but
as an embattled anomaly.

The mainstream of the transitional comedy flows primarily in the
1690s, at the time of the gradual moralization of affective tragedy and,
significantly, before the publication of Collier's *Short View* (1698).
After the turn of the century, it becomes difficult to distinguish the
typical incoherence of transitional plays from the similar incoherence
of failed moral drama, except by the form of the dramatist's mature
work. Farquhar's plays, though they resemble Steele's, can be seen as
a very late and ingenious version of transitional comedy, and, in that
guise, they will serve as a convenient argumentative transition to the
definition of the comic moral action. The plays of this period, then, and
even the originality and hard fate of its most accomplished comic dramatist, are comprehensible as the products of a major formal transition
in which the general outlines and limitations of the full moral action
are already visible. In defining the nature of the transition through its
representation in the early embattled plays of Durfey and Shadwell,
the incoherence of Southerne, Cibber, and Farquhar, the tentative experimentation of Vanbrugh, and the brief and brilliant originality of
Congreve, we can discover the immediate sources of the generic problems that plague the major dramatists of the eighteenth century.

I

Thomas Shadwell's lengthy and divided career spans the period of major dramatic social satire and early transitional comedy. His plays, arranged chronologically, provide an example, in an individual corpus, of the formal shift from dramatic satire to moral drama. But even his early works, and his related youthful advocacy of "humors" as opposed to "wit" comedy, set him apart from the dominant vein of Restoration social satire.[1] The special form of Shadwell's humors drama reveals his antagonism to the major manners comedy of his contemporaries and enables him to make a smooth transition to the primarily moral forms of the later segment of his career. Significantly, the black sheep of dramatic satire turns to explicit, and explicitly ideological, morality in the year of the Glorious Revolution, though his censored Whig comedy of the early 1680s contains strong anticipations of the change.

Shadwell deliberately dissociates his early drama from dramatic satire both in his "humors" debate with Dryden and in his dramatic commentary on comic conventions in *The Libertine* (1675). His attack on "the *Playes* which have been wrote of late" in the preface to *The Sullen Lovers* (1668) is gauged not only to endorse humors comedy in preference to the comedy of wit or repartee advocated by Dryden and to refute the detractors of Jonson, but, more important, to extend that local quarrel to the fundamental question of the proper instructive content of comedy. Shadwell's advocacy of humors comedy is synonymous with his denunciation of the immorality of wit comedy, which, he claims, has as its "chief Subject . . . bawdy, and profaneness, which they call *brisk writing.*"[2] From the beginning of his career, then, Shadwell contends in theory and in practice that the purpose of comedy is not merely to please—for "it pleases most to see Vice incouraged"[3]— but "to correct, and to inform."[4] In this respect, his early debate with Dryden represents the first stage of a continuing objection to the formal assumptions of social satire, which ends only with his adoption of the moral action.

In addition, Shadwell provides a dramatic version of his vehement rejection of the contemporary libertine hero in a play produced at the height of that hero's dominance of the major social comedy. *The Libertine*, an adaptation of earlier Spanish and French Don Juan drama, augments the explicit moralism of its sources by depicting a protagonist even more depraved and bloodthirsty than his predecessors, and even more clearly representative of a whole class of aristocratic marauders and rapists.[5] Shadwell's play is an exaggeration of the Don Juan story so outrageous as to be almost ridiculous, but so vehement as to constitute a clear moralistic condemnation of the reigning comic protagonists. Shadwell's deviations from his source are designed to demonstrate at every point the logical extension of libertine behavior. *The Libertine* presents sexual license as a violent attack by the upper class upon the lower, morally equivalent to and accompanied by the most heinous and bloody of crimes, and properly subject to the worst of metaphysical punishments. More important, Shadwell grounds his moral critique of libertinism in the standard conventions of contemporary comedy. Don John and his gang visit a typical hospitable country estate possessed of eligible and beautiful but betrothed young virgins, only to incite a brawl, murder their amiable host, wound the prospective bridegrooms, and escape, leaving the horrified virgins to end their lives in a convent. Like many a venturesome maiden in men's clothes, Maria follows Don John through storm and shipwreck, but to murder, not to marry him, in revenge for the murder of her brother.

In keeping with these manifestoes of his opposition to contemporary drama, Shadwell's plays as a group are superficially more chaste, though ultimately no more moral, than the mature dramatic social satire. The humors characters of his early works dominate the action at the expense of the libertine sexual intrigue mandatory in the major social comedy. In *The Sullen Lovers*, for example, the comic barrage of ridiculous behavior on the part of the "impertinent" humors characters usurps the focus of the form. Even the nominal action of the play, the matching of the two "sullen lovers" who share a violent disapproval of the antics of their companions, itself hinges on the comical behavior of the "impertinents," since the more they plague the couple, the more likely it will be that the lovers will discover their perfect compatibility.

Likewise in *The Virtuoso* (1676) the title character steals the show. The play contains a standard love chase, but that action, like the plot of *The Sullen Lovers*, is both chaste and weak. Instead of centering a satiric action upon the conventional rake hero, Shadwell typically substitutes a figure of local ridicule, in this case Sir Nicholas Gimcrack, the impractical philosopher, whose character dominates the plot and significance of the play. In effect, Shadwell deliberately and repeatedly weakens his plots in favor of local ridicule. And significantly, when he abandons his moral principles and concedes to "bawdy and profane" social satire in *Epsom-Wells* (1672), he also abandons the preeminent humors of his best early drama.[6]

Shadwell's advocacy of humors over wit comedy, then, is the theoretical expression of his moral objection to contemporary social satire. In practice, it produces a form which, unlike that of the standard manners comedy, readily gives way to the welcome incursions of morality. As a special kind of social satire, his early plays are not formally moral in themselves. Rather, Shadwell's humors theory, in its advocacy of comic instruction and its aversion to the licentiousness of full social satire, prevents him from writing strong and straightforward actions, muddies the definition of functional desert in favor of local effect, and obscures the evaluative dimension of the form. In so doing, it leaves a space for the consistently moral merit of his later, virtuous heroes.

Shadwell's transition to moral drama begins surreptitiously with his partisan play *The Lancashire Witches* (1681). Once again, the protagonists are chaste and loyal, and the action is dominated by a ridiculous local device: in this case not a single humors character, but a coven of preposterous flying witches. These witches represent the imposition of Whig ideology upon Shadwell's humors satire. They and the characters who believe in them are explicitly associated with Toryism, Popery, and the Popish Plot in particular. Disbelief in the witches is the reasonable and rational product of good humor, good sense, honesty, and Whiggism. The antics of the witches take the place of the plot complications of a standard satiric action. Hence they are essential to the workings of the comedy, though the lesson of their farcical tricks and parodic "spells" is that witches are imaginary. This contradiction is the consequence of Shadwell's attempt to fuse his characteristic humors form with a positive moral and ideological message. The special political morality of Shadwell's admirable characters in *The Lancashire Witches* is a direct function of his local device. In his next play that morality leaves its device behind and becomes a formal end in and by itself. *The Squire of Alsatia* (1688) is the ideological companion of the Glorious Revolution, but the formal successor of Shadwell's earlier partisan drama.

The Squire of Alsatia is Shadwell's first moral action, and, significantly, it combines the ideology of the Glorious Revolution with overt didacticism and a comparatively strong plot. The generous and admirable protagonist, Belfond junior, attains exemplary status by the end of the play and explicitly represents, in his virtues, the consequences of a liberal education, which presumes the natural benevolence of the individual. He is contrasted with his country brother, Belfond senior, whose education has been oppressive, narrow, traditional, and severe. After a few venial sexual transgressions, for which he generously atones, Belford junior proceeds to aid his disagreeable and disapproving parent, save his swinish brother from compound disaster, and vow eternal constancy to his beloved. The errors of his youth serve not to qualify his ultimate virtue but to establish, with the age-old aid of the double standard, his all-important generosity, conventionally exhibited in sexual terms. Shadwell's use of the double standard here is so extreme as to invite an ironic interpretation of the protagonist's virtue,[7] but there is no evidence of such irony in the structure of the play. Belfond junior's cast mistress, Mrs. Termagant, is depicted as violent, vicious, murderous, and apparently insane. She ends the play by producing a pistol and shooting at the all-suffering Belfond junior, who is only saved by the comic good fortune of a misfire. Her apparently unprovoked attacks are gauged to arouse our pity for her victim, and notably not for herself.[8] The substantial difference between Shadwell's Mrs. Termagant and Etherege's Mrs. Loveit is indicative of the essential distinction between Etherege's social form and Shadwell's moral one. While Mrs. Loveit plays a subtle formal role in the implicit exposure of the libertine hero's moral degradation, Mrs. Termagant has no more significance than her name and her surface position in the action suggest. Shadwell's play is evaluatively direct; it offers no disjunctive judgments, no dramatic discrepancies. Nothing is implied.

The definition of Belfond junior's numerous virtues and the concurrent comparison of his character to that of his ill-educated brother give rise to the frequent and formally central debates upon the merits of their separate upbringings. The values that emerge are programmatically Lockean and Whiggish,[9] and they are expressed in a series of moralistic sententiae that label and enforce Shadwell's didactic intention. That intention is directly exerted in the action of the play, which carries out the ideological and moral definition of the two brothers' contrasting deserts. Belfond junior behaves virtuously and receives the reward originally intended for his elder brother: the beauteous Isabella. Belfond senior behaves rebelliously and stupidly—his error is embodied in Shadwell's vivid depiction of the Alsatian underworld—and he ends the play, along with the unscrupulous Alsatians, in disgrace. The ideology of *The Squire of Alsatia* is identical to that of *The Lancashire Witches*, except that in the later play it is expressed in a strong straightforward action that assesses, depicts, and rewards its characters according to that controlling internal moral standard. Shadwell's first moral action is thus a formal derivative of his explicitly stated ideological position, and his later plays repeat the pattern, though with less effect.

The Volunteers (1692, posthumously), Shadwell's last work, places even greater emphasis on the exemplary virtue of its protagonists. In this comedy, no fewer than four characters are repeatedly applauded according to their moral merits. The innocent heroine Clara is so virtuous that she refuses even to answer the unjust aspersions cast on her by her evil and heartless stepmother, and is subsequently expelled from her father's house. She is equipped with such sententious lines as: "The Innocent ne're fear suspition. . . . Ill words shall not make me forget my duty to my Fathers Wife. . . . The Innocent fear no Spies. . . . How Innocence can smile at accusation. . . . I have been used to bear, and for your sake I can do it. . . . Let Guilt look dejected, Innocence will smile."[10] Her male counterpart rivals her in moral excellence. Specifically, he is described as brave, virtuous, and infinitely deserving (II.i, p. 179). And of course the lovers do receive all their expected deserts. The play also includes the necessary ideological accessories to

Shadwell's moral drama. Education is defined and praised; freedom of religion is defended; the military is honored and preferred to fortune; Frenchified court manners are deplored; the old straightforward, honest soldiers, whatever their side, are applauded; dissimulation is rejected; compassion and unabashed sympathy are seen as inherently good; sexual license is disapproved; and virtue is naturally attractive and naturally triumphant.

Shadwell's career, then, from *The Sullen Lovers* to *The Volunteers*, neatly bridges the period of formal transition, and Shadwell comes to write the first important and eloquent dramatic moral action, but only because, to a certain slight but essential extent, he was an anomalous figure in the early Restoration. His first plays, though satiric enough, are not satiric in the libertine manner of the major social comedy of the period, and that significant distinction, founded as it is upon a fundamental theoretical and ideological divergence, causes Shadwell initially to consider himself and eventually to become the spokesman of a rival and finally triumphant comic form.

Thomas Durfey, in some of his early drama, similarly anticipates the subsequent moralization of the comedy,[11] though with considerably less self-consciousness and more incoherence than Shadwell. His moral or partially moral plays, scattered through a large corpus consisting predominantly of farce and intrigue, generally depend upon some version of instant reformation, and they reflect the kind of disunity that characterizes the moral invasion of social form. *The Virtuous Wife* (1679), for instance, is essentially a dramatic satire with an incongruous moral conclusion. It ends with the exemplary reformation of the wayward husband, Beverly, who is effusively and affectionately reconciled with his virtuous wife, Olivia, to the tune of numerous didactic sententiae on marriage. But in the first acts of the play, Olivia and Beverly appear as frank and unsentimentalized marital enemies, since Beverly has married Olivia under rather reprehensibly false pretenses. Thus, though the play makes a random assertion of morality, it does not place that morality in a coherent action.

Durfey's later moral plays, though similarly obscured by farce and intrigue, come somewhat closer to formal coherence. *Love for Money* (1691) presents a genuinely and consistently virtuous pair of lovers, anticipatory of Steele's immortal paragons, whose rigorously unmercenary relationship refutes by example the cynical and false sentiment of the title. Here and elsewhere, Durfey's morality turns on this sense of the corrupting power of money, and on a desire to locate value instead in inner merit. But like many other writers of the period, he does not carry that belief to an extreme. Money is decried as contrary to virtue, yet the virtuous end with three thousand pounds a year.

More interesting and more self-consciously moral is *The Richmond*

Heiress (1693), which reverses the conventional comic formula by introducing the witty-rake-gets-wealthy-heiress plot, only to have the exemplary heiress defiantly reject the mercenary rake in Act V, after he has finally managed to steal her away from her rigorous protector. The heiress's virtue is explicitly proposed as an example to her sex, to be "reverenc'd in succeeding ages."[12] The surprising reversal in this play suggests Durfey's sense of the anomalousness and originality of the moral values he expresses and, more specifically, of the unconventional assumptions of exemplary drama. In playing itself off against the conventions of earlier social comedy, *The Richmond Heiress* succumbs, albeit self-consciously, to the inconsistencies typical of transitional form. Before the moral reversal of the last act, Durfey presents the mercenary Frederick as a standard rake-hero, whom we assess and admire in social terms. Only toward the conclusion of the play do we receive hints that money is perhaps a source of corruption, and Frederick's final ejection from the comic party, foiled and furious, suddenly transforms him from an attractive wit into a criminal. In this sense, *The Richmond Heiress* resembles Durfey's earlier play *The Virtuous Wife* as well as the later comedy of Cibber and Farquhar. It uses the lively intrigue of the social form to motivate its action, and then appends to it an incongruous moral lesson. The morality is not in itself insincere, but it is formally impotent, and this impotence is the common characteristic of much transitional comedy.

Thus, Durfey's moral drama, like Shadwell's early humors satire, includes a sense of its own aberrancy, and even his antimercenary morality seems to be expressed in opposition to its surroundings. These factors date him as the most precocious practitioner of moral comedy. Later transitional dramatists are much more likely to present virtue as the expression of an ethical consensus, though, significantly, they are no more able or willing to adopt fully the form which that consensus comes to demand. The impetus toward moral effect, then, seems to precede its full formal embodiment in the moral action, and dramatists like Durfey, Southerne, and Cibber write moral comedy before the means has evolved to make that comedy coherent. This lapse of formal hegemony is the source of the brief display of dramatic originality that marks the transition from social satire to moral action.

II

Thomas Southerne and Colley Cibber, with different motives and different kinds of success, write the mixed comedy that most accurately embodies the consequence of the collision of formal premises in the 1690s. Both dramatists seek to reproduce the witty banter and sexual parrying of the earlier dramatic social satire, but both add a formally incongruous moral component to that social world. Cibber accedes to moral form like the shrewd politician to his constituency. Southerne gives it a potentially serious place in his best comic work, though he is unable to use it to coherent formal ends. Despite their important differences, however, Southerne and Cibber produce comparable plays, and the basis of their similarity is in their capitulation to the competing formal forces of their age.

Southerne's most interesting comedy, *The Wives Excuse* (1691), resembles his serious plays in its transitional turn to a faint or incomplete moral premise, except, significantly, that it is more strongly tied to the materials and conventions of the Restoration. Thus, while the moralization of Southerne's affective tragedy represents an imperceptible alteration of an intermediary form, the moralization of his comedy entails the introduction of a potentially incongruous element into an explicitly amoral drama. For this reason, *The Wives Excuse* is a more problematic work than *The Fatal Marriage* or *Oroonoko*.

The play is a compendium of the most striking devices and conventions of the major social satire. Southerne reproduces the cynical definition of aristocratic honor that we discovered in *The Wild Gallant* and *She Would If She Could*, causing his rake to advocate lying as "a Necessity that every man of honour must submit to."[13] Furthermore, his wits and fools explicitly echo Wycherley's characteristic equation when they declare that "pleasure is my Business" (II.iii.963, V.ii.2352). Also like *The Country Wife*, the play includes a comic confrontation between a foolish false wit, Friendall, and his rival, Lovemore. Lovemore courts Mrs. Friendall before her husband's eyes while she, Alithea-like, seeks unsuccessfully to advise Friendall of Lovemore's illicit intentions. Meanwhile Friendall, in the manner of Sparkish and Sir Jasper Fidget before him, urges Lovemore to greater intimacy with his wife (I.i.363–430). And finally, like *The Man of Mode*, *The Wives Excuse* presents a "tying up the linen" scene in which the rake, who has just sent off his newly conquered mistress in a chair, contemplates the false oaths that he has sworn to her in the heat of passion and coldly considers how best to be rid of her (II.iii.890–921).

Southerne is clearly marshaling all the material that he can muster from the major social satire to produce the formal context of this comedy, and in fact, *The Wives Excuse* is a late, self-consciously exaggerated version of the earlier drama to which it alludes. Its plot consists entirely of a series of sexual schemes and counterschemes, phrased in explicitly "lewd" language and issuing in deliberately lewd consequences. The sheer volume of this amoral and pragmatic social negotiation dominates the play, to the detriment of a dynamic central action.

But, as Dryden approvingly notes in his commendatory poem, Southerne has another, ultimately incompatible, objective in *The Wives*

Excuse. He seeks to make the "Lewdness" moral ("To Mr. Southern,"
p. 40, l. 17). And to this end he grants his central female character
several moving moments of moral defiance in which she declares her
virtue in the face of sexual temptation (IV.i.1920–36, V.iii.2506–20).
These declarations come after her whole world has unanimously pronounced the inevitability of her fall (I.i.66–81, III.ii.1411–17); her
husband's foolish activities have reached a climax of absurdity; her feelings for her putative lover have grown increasingly favorable; and the
female characters who surround her, with one exception, have fallen in
their turn as fast as the plot permits. But she holds out "to the last Act
of life" (IV.i.1936).

The incongruity of Mrs. Friendall's stance is a consequence of Southerne's attempt to incorporate a moral character into a social context
and to provide a social action with at least an ambiguously moral conclusion. The standards proposed and the expectations aroused by the
play remain unreconciled, but *The Wives Excuse* contains signs of the
interpenetration of social and moral that takes place in the unique
and original transitional forms of Vanbrugh and Congreve. In his depiction of Mrs. Friendall, Southerne lays the groundwork for a potentially
serious treatment of marriage and marital problems—problems that he
is careful to leave unresolved at the conclusion of the play.[14] This kind
of seriousness, which arises from the represented confrontation of a
moral character with a social world, is the basis of the most successful
transitional comedies of the period. Southerne can only flirt with the
reconciliation of social and moral, however, because he fails to find the
means to give it formal coherence. Like Cibber, he is chained to the
conventions of the major Restoration comedy, and even when the matter of his drama calls for the serious representation of inner tensions,
he is unable to alter the manner of his predecessors. Southerne's peculiar impotence is a sign of the strong continuity of this generic history.

Although Colley Cibber's notorious personal and literary opportunism distinguishes him as one of the most idiosyncratic and colorful
figures of the period, his eccentricity can also be seen as a consequence
of the tensions of this transitional time. Cibber's drama, like Durfey's
and Southerne's, typically embraces both possible worlds. It clings to
the liveliness and theatrical vitality of the social form, but inevitably
augments those qualities with the affecting triumph of moral virtue.
Love's Last Shift (1696) and *The Careless Husband* (1704) exemplify
Cibber's characteristic mingling of social and moral. Together they
illustrate the kind of formal incoherence typical of the period, as well
as the course of Cibber's own gradual concession to fully moralized
comedy.

The popular and enduringly successful *Love's Last Shift*, Cibber's
first play, is a mixed comedy, consisting of two plots, tenuously related,

and predominantly divided along social and moral lines. In the primary plot, the virtuous, long-suffering Amanda produces the permanent reformation of her heartless, rakish husband, Loveless, by going to bed with him, unrecognized, as his newly conquered mistress. The second plot describes the attempts of Young Worthy to secure the flirtatious Narcissa, who is intended for his elder brother, while the Elder Worthy simultaneously seeks Narcissa's cousin. A testimonial to Cibber's opportunistic ingenuity, the play is mixed in two ways. First, the Amanda-Loveless plot, with its female paragon, its sententious tributes to selfless virtue and marital constancy, and its affecting depiction of the fainting heroine and penitent rake, is juxtaposed with the primarily social intrigue of Young Worthy's pragmatic love schemes. Appropriately, the second plot contains the ridiculous figure of local satire, Sir Novelty·Fashion, the affected descendant of Etherege's Fopling Flutter. The flirtations of Sir Novelty and the ladies, and the marital efforts of Worthy, who describes himself in Act I as a fortune hunter, provide a striking contrast to the moral assumptions of the main plot. To this extent, the play is divided into concurrent contrasting story lines that, taken together, illustrate the formal indecision of the transitional dramatists.

The more disturbing division in *Love's Last Shift*, however, is the incoherence of each of the separate actions: the primary moral plot begins as a social satire, and the secondary "manners" action ends with a faintly moral taint. As a result, the comedy as a whole opens on radically different premises from those on which it concludes. Throughout most of the first acts the participants of both plots, with the notable and incongruous exception of Amanda, discuss whoring, ridicule virtue, and attempt to procure a quick and easy fortune. The primary plot, of course, ends in reformation, but it is a reformation imposed from without by an arbitrary change of formal terms. Throughout the body of the play, Loveless, in keeping with all the appurtenances of his dramatic world, is simply a conventional rake, railing at his lack of money, unperturbed by the reported death of his wife, leering after ladies in the park, hastening to a rendezvous with a fair unknown, and discoursing eloquently upon libertine sexual generosity. As Cibber admits in his frankly pragmatic epilogue: "He's lew'd for above four Acts, Gentlemen!"[15]

In Act V, however, Loveless not only renounces the whole of his past life and declares genuine and eternal love for Amanda, but also, when he hears that she has conveniently inherited a fortune which she at last gives over to him, disavows any interest in such mercenary concerns (V.ii.218–23). There is nothing in Loveless's characterization that prepares us for this repentance, nor is there meant to be. Technically, the change is based upon a staple convention of social form, the "lew'd" bed-trick, in which Loveless inadvertently sleeps with his own wife. Cibber brings about the reformation not by any kind of character development, but simply by exchanging one set of formal assumptions for another. In the first four acts, Loveless is the libertine hero of social satire, whom we admire for his witty freedom and pragmatic self-interest. In Act V he occupies a different moral world, in which virtue's power is pervasive and absolute and the sources and permanence of his repentance are consequently unquestioned and unquestionable.

Cibber uses the subsidiary plot to keep the first four acts of the play "lew'd." Sir Novelty and his violent whore Flareit belong to the world of Loveless's amorous escapades, and Worthy's pursuit of the elusive Narcissa identifies him, at least in those scenes, as a conventional rake. But Worthy's character suffers from blatant inconsistencies that betray the workings of the form. In the opening scene he is, like Loveless, an admitted fortune hunter scheming to carry off an heiress against her father's wishes. Amanda quite justly suspects him of such motives, and her warnings to Narcissa, as well as Worthy's own reiteration of his intentions, enforce the impression of rakish self-interest.

But in Act V, after Loveless's reformation scene, Worthy too disavows any interest in Narcissa's fortune, which he generously offers to return to her tricked and irate parent. Like Loveless's, Worthy's noble acts earn him both the woman and the wealth, but the juxtaposition of his statements of disinterest with his earlier mercenary pragmatism exposes the formal mixture that characterizes the play. In addition, Worthy's early rakishness explicitly contradicts his simultaneous concern for Amanda, whose virtue he effusively extolls and whom he aids in the reformation of Loveless. And concurrently, his libertine allegiance to Loveless is rather incompatible with his morally motivated plot for the rake's reformation. Worthy does double duty in *Love's Last Shift*, and his inconsistent character is an emblem of Cibber's mixed intention. His pragmatic attitude toward Narcissa serves as a motto for the social segment of the action:

> *Women are changed from what they were of old:*
> *Therefore let Lovers still this Maxim hold,*
> She's only Worth, that Brings her Weight in Gold. [I.i.528-30]

But his contradictory admiration of Amanda's virtue gives the moral plot its title:

> Poor *Amanda*, thou well deserv'st a better Husband: Thou wer't never wanting in thy Endeavours to reclaim him: And, faith, considering how long a Despair has worn thee,
> *'Twere Pity now thy Hopes shou'd not succeed;*
> *This new Attempt is* Love's Last Shift *indeed.* [III.ii.207-12]

Cibber's first comedy is thus an opportunistic tour de force of dual appeal,[16] which combines the simple juxtaposition of a social and a moral plot with the more fundamental incoherence, within each plot, of a mixed action. Cibber himself makes his divided intention explicit in the epilogue, which addresses one after another of the interest groups that he identifies in his audience:

> First, To you
> Kind City-Gentlemen o'th'middle Row;
> He hopes you nothing to his Charge can lay,
> There's not a Cuckold made in all his Play. . . .
>   Now, Sirs, To you whose sole Religion's Drinking,
> Whoring, Roaring, without the Pain of Thinking . . .
> Four Acts for your coarse Palates were design'd,
> But then the Ladies Taste is more refin'd,
> They, for *Amanda*'s Sake, will sure be kind. [p. 84, ll. 1-21]

The play's inconsistencies of characterization and inadequacies of motivation are direct consequences of the transitional dramatist's desire to have it both ways, and this divided intention in turn precludes any exploration of psychology and any complexity or subtlety of presentation. Loveless cannot have an inner life, he cannot rationalize or equivocate, he cannot even seem capable of reformation, or he would cease to be a conventional rake and the first four acts would lose the "lew'd" appeal of social satire. Concurrently, his virtuous female counterpart must also be flatly virtuous, because she shares his dramatic world, because she is a new figure in the established social form, and because any complexity and depth would upset the balance between social and moral that is maintained by her simple, undeveloped assertion of morality. In effect, the mixed form of the play demands flat characterization, in both its social and its moral segments. The simple moral ciphers of which Amanda is an early example arise directly from the juxtaposition of irreconcilable forms, and persist long after the social has given way to the moral in the eighteenth century. Cibber's stereotypes are a sign of the constraints inherent in much of the transitional drama of this period, as well as an anticipation of the ultimate limitations of the full moral action.

Cibber's later plays retain reminiscences of the mingling of effect that characterizes *Love's Last Shift*. To this extent, his whole lengthy career can be placed on a continuum that begins with *Love's Last Shift* and that reflects only quantitative changes of emphasis from its beginning to its end. But the moral action and its didactic intention come to dominate his plots and to relegate the echoes of Restoration social satire to a colorful background. *The Careless Husband*, for example, merely juxtaposes the two forms in two separate plots, neither of which alone exhibits the internal tensions of genuine transitional incoherence. The primary plot maintains a relatively consistent moral tone, and the subsidiary plot is quickly and unobtrusively moralized

as well. Sir Charles Easy, the philandering husband, is reformed by his
virtuous and long-suffering wife's tolerance and patience. When she
finds him in a compromising position with her maid, "*both asleep in
two Easy Chairs*" (V.v.1 *s.d.*), she restrains her anger, blames herself,
and covers his bare head with her steinkirk to prevent his catching
"some languishing Distemper" (V.v.24). This alerts him simultaneously
to her discovery and her generosity, and she is rewarded with his vows
of eternal love. Sir Charles, unlike Loveless, is described from the first
as erring but potentially reformable. He states in Act I that his wife's
generosity toward him has practically cured him of philandering (I.i.268–
72). The terms of his ultimate reformation and reward are thus planted
in his initial characterization, and he and his lady occupy the same
smoothly operating dramatic world.

The subsidiary plot, like that of *Love's Last Shift*, boasts a Lord
Foppington, whose character provides a focus for the satiric elements
of the action. In this plot, Lady Betty Modish, another figure from
social comedy, seems to care nothing for virtue or love, and coquettishly
trifles with the heart of her loyal lover of five years' standing, Lord
Morelove. The witty exchanges and social parlays of their relationship,
combined with the ridiculous behavior of Lord Foppington, give the
play an air of social satire that contrasts with the moral outcome of
both actions. Lady Betty, like Sir Charles, is made conscious of her
genuine love for Morelove, weeps, confesses, and is reformed, and the
play ends with a universal repentance and good feeling that includes
even Lord Foppington and the vengeful Lady Graveairs, one of Sir
Charles's previous mistresses (V.vii.289–90). Unlike Young Worthy, his
counterpart in *Love's Last Shift*, Lord Morelove is a loyal, generous,
and true lover from the beginning of the action. And Lady Betty's cruelty is made to appear only the plausible consequence of an unfortunate but reformable pride, which is overcome by her genuine love for
her constant suitor.

The satiric reference of *The Careless Husband* is so tangential to
either action that it produces none of the inconsistencies that characterize *Love's Last Shift*. In this sense the play's peculiar transitional
mixture of social and moral effect is subsidiary to a predominant moral
intention that reveals the direction of Cibber's dramatic evolution.
From its foothold in the last act, the moral action advances to conquer
the comedy, and subsequently, in *The Lady's Last Stake* (1707), this
gradual turn to a consistently moralized drama is even more fully con-
solidated. But despite the significant change of emphasis between *Love's
Last Shift* and *The Careless Husband*, the later play retains the flat
characterization and undeveloped motivation of its incoherent predecessor. The transition is so imperceptible that Cibber can simply build
upon the moral stereotypes that necessarily populate his most funda-

mentally mixed comedy. Loveless and Amanda are denied an inner life
by the internal logic, or illogic, of Cibber's divided intention in *Love's
Last Shift*. *The Careless Husband* emerges directly from that transitional form, and reproduces its stereotypes even though its inconsistencies have gradually given way to a substantially coherent moral
intention. Thus, the historical significance of mixed transitional comedy
far outweighs its comparatively slight aesthetic merit. Cibber's representative drama helps to explain the continuity of flat characterization
from the social stereotypes of dramatic satire to the moral stereotypes
of the moral action. The dominant transitional form of this period
simply perpetuates the constraints attached to Restoration social comedy.

III

John Vanbrugh and William Congreve discover different answers to the
problems presented by the collision of incompatible forms, and their
solutions depend upon an attitude toward comic characterization fundamentally distinct from that of Southerne and Cibber. Cibber's transformation of Vanbrugh's unfinished play *The Provoked Husband*
(1728) from a complex exploration of marital incompatibility to a
simple assertion of conventional morality demonstrates this distinction.
Where Cibber chooses to force both forms into the same mold, Vanbrugh and Congreve seek to produce a new pattern that will allow for
the exploration of moral values in a social context. But unlike Cibber's
all-purpose product, their experiments involve a revelation of character and motive incompatible with the inherited conventions of the full
dramatic moral action. The result is a unique and isolated moment of
formal innovation that is most notable not for the undeniable aesthetic
merit of its dramatic experimentation, but for its transience.

Vanbrugh's first play, *The Relapse* (1696), is a sequel and answer to
Love's Last Shift. Through his depiction of the continuing dilemmas
of Loveless and Amanda, Vanbrugh discovers an answer to the disturbing incoherence in Cibber's arbitrary conjunction of social and moral
stereotypes. In effect, he invents a coherent form in which the moral
standards now current in the drama are tested and affirmed in a social
context that contains all of the pragmatic self-interest of the "manners"
world. *The Relapse* solves the problem presented by the transitional
collision of social and moral form by internalizing the irreconcilable
values that Cibber merely juxtaposes and by making their disjunction
the basis of an examination of character rather than its simple, external transformation. The unusual coherence of *The Relapse* and its unique
depiction of its characters' inner lives are simultaneously consequences
of Vanbrugh's response to the contradictory dramatic assumptions of

his time, and the new form that results eludes inclusion in the two categories that dominate the period. In this respect, *The Relapse* is an answer to Cibber's formal failure rather than a challenge to the moral values that both dramatists assume. Vanbrugh's morality differs from Cibber's not in its content—that of female chastity and marital fidelity —but in the shape of its achievement.

The nature of Vanbrugh's dramatic world is defined by the social values that share the stage with his representation of moral worth. The "manners" context is supplied obliquely but powerfully by the satiric subplot, which describes the successful fortune hunting of a younger son, Young Fashion, who cheats his elder brother, Lord Foppington, the recent purchaser of a peerage, out of his prospective country wife. This plot, of course, is predicated on the pragmatic assumptions of social satire. The witty hero and his affected, self-centered, ridiculous brother occupy a world of harsh economic realities, where money buys titles, influence, and ladies and the lack of it leads to military service or starvation.[17] In the context of this society, the resourceful hero's scheme earns our support as an ingenious and necessary exercise of enlightened self-interest. Even though he professes no affection or concern for his future wife, we do not judge Young Fashion on moral terms, except to the extent that we feel the corruption of his whole society at that separate level of evaluation available to dramatic satire. Vanbrugh maintains the context of conventional social comedy,[18] much as Cibber does, by including a subsidiary plot that fills out the drama with explicitly social material.

The social environment of the play extends to the main plot, which Vanbrugh grounds in the same world of harsh sexual realities. The transience of the rural ideal expressed in the opening scene is substantiated by the depiction of the pragmatic London society in which Loveless and Amanda subsequently find themselves. In fact the context of their action, once in London, is mainly social, though they themselves, especially Amanda, are finally depicted and assessed by their allegiance to a moral standard. The characters of Berinthia and Worthy are the primary repositories of social judgment in the main plot. Like the characters of social comedy, both are engaging and comprehensible in terms of their practical sexual self-interest.

Berinthia, for example, extolls the freedom of young widowhood (II.581–84), which she utilizes to good purpose in her affair with Loveless. Her advocacy of "hypocrisy, invention, deceit, flattery, mischief, and lying" (III.ii.249–50) shows her to be a self-conscious, amoral, and engaging wit whose attitudes and intrigues reflect the conventions of social comedy. Her sexual pragmatism, especially in her advice to the disconsolate Amanda, is eminently justified by the facts of the social world she occupies, and in this respect even her affair with Loveless engages our temporary advocacy. Worthy shares the social assessment accorded to Berinthia. He too lives in the world of Lord Foppington and the witty Young Fashion, and therefore he cannot even seriously entertain the notion of female virtue (V.ii.25–33). He is, in Berinthia's words, a "devil" (V.ii.63), whose pursuit of Amanda receives all the backing of the pragmatic and energetic social tradition. The expressed beliefs and the behavior of these two characters serve to establish a context of standards and assumptions based directly upon the conventions of social satire. Amanda and Loveless are placed in a dramatic world fundamentally different from that of Cibber's fifth act, or, even more significant for the future of the comedy, from that of the full moral action. It is a world of economic and sexual self-interest, in which the schemes of younger sons, lively widows, and gentlemen libertines are necessary, justifiable, and admirable.

Vanbrugh treads the razor's edge of formal incoherence in introducing his moral ideal into this social world. But the collision of rival forms is transmuted in *The Relapse* into an internal conflict between virtue and the pragmatic facts of social existence. Vanbrugh replaces Cibber's juxtaposition of social and moral stereotypes with an exploration of psychological inner life and motivation that pits individual morality against social temptation. Loveless and Amanda are complex characters whose soliloquies reveal the hesitations and rationalizations that accompany the attempted preservation of virtue in society.

In the first, idyllic scene of the play, Vanbrugh establishes the nature of Loveless's characterization. The reformed rake's vows of eternal constancy are contrasted with Amanda's realistic appraisal of human weakness. Amanda understands Loveless as a complex character of limited self-knowledge, and her understanding is validated in the next act, when the couple returns to London and Loveless reluctantly confesses his admiration for the young lady at the play:

> I happened in the play to find my very character, only with the addition of a relapse; which struck me so, I put a sudden stop to a most harmless entertainment which till then diverted me between the acts. 'Twas to admire the workmanship of nature in the face of a young lady that sate some distance from me, she was so exquisitely handsome. [II.40–46]

Vanbrugh's playful self-reference in this passage emphasizes Loveless's naïve ignorance of his own motivations. We know before he does that he will "relapse," that in fact he has done so already. His succeeding dialogue with Amanda reveals the inner process by which he initially rationalizes and then discovers his own fall from grace. He argues with Amanda, and himself, about the implications of his acts, and the dispute leads him to discover his own hitherto unrecognized motivations:

> *Loveless.* Should you come home and tell me you had seen a handsome man,
>   should I grow jealous because you had eyes?
> *Amanda.* But should I tell you he were exquisitely so, that I had gazed on him
>   with admiration, that I had looked with eager eyes upon him, should you
>   not think 'twere possible I might go one step farther and inquire his name?
> *Loveless (aside).* She has reason on her side. I have talked too much.
>   [II.81–88]

From this realization Loveless proceeds to a tacit lie:

> *Enter* Berinthia
> *Loveless (aside).* Ha! By heavens, the very woman! [II.113]

And he then advances to an explicit and calculated one:

> *Amanda.* How do you like my cousin here?
> *Loveless.* Jealous already, Amanda?
> *Amanda.* Not at all; I ask you for another reason.
> *Loveless (aside).* Whate'er her reason be, I must not tell her true.—
>   (*To* Amanda.) Why, I confess she's handsome. But you must not think I
>   slight your kinswoman if I own to you, of all the women who may claim
>   that character, she is the last would triumph in my heart. [II.420–28]

Thus we are provided with a full inner history of Loveless's "relapse,"
which reveals the state of his consciousness at every point in the process.

Similarly, Loveless's unusual self-revelatory blank-verse soliloquy,
virtually unprecedented in the comedy of this period, displays the strug-
gles and vacillations of his conscience with a striking attempt at psychological detail. The breaks and interjections in this speech, like those
in Amanda's later, equivalent, inner dispute, suggest the incoherence
and sudden insights of a mind in the moment of indecisive contempla-
tion. Loveless begins by surprising himself with his own thoughts, as
in his earlier argument with Amanda: "Undoing, was't I said? Who shall
undo her?" (III.ii.11). He continues by describing, generously and
feelingly, his genuine love for his wife (III.ii.12–28). And he ends, as
in the earlier dialogue, by arguing himself into the realization of his
"relapse":

> Yet hold. If laying down my life
> Be demonstration of my love,
> What is't I feel in favor of Berinthia?
> For should she be in danger, methinks I could incline
> To risk it for her service too; and yet I do not love her.
> How then subsists my proof? [III.ii.29–34]

For the first half of the play, Vanbrugh supplies Loveless with a complex psychology that displays the weakness of individual virtue in

society. After the relapse, Loveless's role in the plot effectually ends, and he becomes merely the means to Amanda's temptation.

The social context of the action impinges upon Amanda's virtue in the form of Loveless's betrayal and Berinthia's repeated advice on such a contingency, and the complexity of Amanda's character, like that of Loveless's, is directly derived from this juxtaposition of Berinthia's social world and Amanda's moral one. Berinthia's wisdom—to repay the philanderer in kind—is in perfect pragmatic keeping with the terms of the society in which Amanda finds herself. But the formal strength of the social convention is brought into the service of psychological complexity. Vanbrugh makes Berinthia's appeal a part of Amanda's inner dialogue, thereby internalizing the potential formal collision and supplying his exemplary heroine with a dramatized inner life. Amanda is shown to feel the attractiveness of the social standards at first presented only externally in the character of Berinthia. This transformation of Berinthia's pragmatic standards into internal psychological material is characteristic of Vanbrugh's transitional form.

Amanda's soliloquy, the exact counterpart of Loveless's, occurs after she has received ocular proof of her husband's infidelity, and just before her final temptation by Worthy. Beginning with "scorn" (V.iv.18), she proceeds to hesitate, vacillate, and reason with herself. Her initial rejection is followed by excuses for Loveless's behavior—"My beauty possibly is in the wane" (V.iv.33)—and by further desires for the very retaliation in kind that Berinthia repeatedly advised (V.iv.35–39). Amanda's final position is far from a stereotypical assurance of her virtue, as her reaction to Worthy implies:

> Virtue's his friend, or, through another's heart
> I yet could find the way to make his smart.
> > *Going off, she meets* Worthy.
> Ha! He here? Protect me, heaven, for this looks ominous. [V.iv.40–42]

This soliloquy is the culmination of Vanbrugh's delineation of Amanda's character from her arrival in London and her first meeting with Berinthia. The initial symptoms of Loveless's "relapse" coincide with Amanda's first signs of interest in Worthy (II.522–39), and further conviction of Loveless's betrayal is matched by her further eager inquiries about her would-be lover (IV.ii.63–66 and 103–04). When Worthy enters to offer the ultimate temptation, in Act V, we are unprepared to predict the result. Amanda's virtue is formally balanced by the standards of the social context, and, in terms of that dramatic convention, we appreciate the strength and reasonableness of Berinthia's internalized appeal. The dilemma thus becomes the genuinely problematic one of the definition and preservation of a moral ideal in a social world. And our sympathy for Amanda is the direct product of the delicately synchronized operation of social and moral values in the play.

Even the ultimate triumph of Amanda's virtue does not upset that balance, for it is explicitly won, not asserted, and the significance of its victory depends upon the tests and impediments provided by the external and internal social context. Amanda's rejection of Worthy proves her morality in a way unavailable to Cibber. Earlier, Worthy and Berinthia have explicitly outlined the rigorous and, they feel, unattainable standards of female virtue:

> I think 'tis a presumptuous thing in a woman to assume the name of virtuous, till she has heartily hated her husband and been soundly in love with somebody else. Whom, if she has withstood—then—much good may it do her.
>
> [III.ii.222–26]

Vanbrugh puts Amanda to precisely the test proposed by the skeptical social characters of the play: she discovers her husband's unforgivable infidelity and is presented, at just that moment, with another man whom she can and in fact seems to love. Her rejection of Worthy and his consequent heightened admiration for her substantiate the value of her virtue, along with the difficulty of its achievement. Significantly, even the central metaphor of the climactic confrontation between Worthy and Amanda enacts Vanbrugh's formal juxtaposition of social and moral values. In Berinthia's scenes, "angel" and adoration represent an ironic tribute to sexual pragmatism (V.ii.61–69). Here, Worthy and Amanda use the same metaphor as a serious emblem of moral virtue (V.iv.168–83).[19] But the social world of Lord Foppington and Young Fashion remains, and the subsidiary plot ends the drama with the blatant cynicism characteristic of social satire. Individual morality is not shown to carry all before it, as indeed, in the special terms of this play, it cannot. Worthy is left in an explicitly temporary state of untested virtue. More important, Loveless's "relapse" goes unpunished, and the future of his relationship with Amanda unmentioned. The peculiar inefficacy of the victorious morality—as Berinthia says, "much good may it do her"—is the last and most obvious signal of the fundamental originality of Vanbrugh's comic form.

In general, *The Relapse* represents a bold and significant innovation in transitional comedy, a successful version of the story Southerne failed to tell in *The Wives Excuse*. Its experiments with psychological complexity provide a direct formal answer to Cibber's warring stereotypes and distinguish it both from social satire and from the subsequent moral action. But the perilousness of its reconciliation of social and moral is faintly evident in the jarring contrasts of conventions and characters. The countryside is represented in the main plot as an idyllic rural retreat and in the subplot as a filthy and backward repository of clownish imbecility. Similarly, our unflagging admiration for Amanda is held in a very tenuous balance with our approbation of the engaging

Berinthia and our amused enjoyment of her contrived seduction by
Loveless. The frequent dialogues between Amanda and Berinthia almost
reproduce, in those scenes, the inconsistency of *Love's Last Shift*. Perhaps more disturbing, but equally symptomatic of Vanbrugh's intention,
is the disappearance of Loveless from the action after he has served his
purpose as a complex character caught between morality and libertine
profligacy. Ultimately, Loveless is only interesting to Vanbrugh in indecision, since that indecision is the source of the drama's unique transitional form. Amanda correspondingly emerges as the unambiguous
protagonist only when her turn comes for psychological trial.

All of these problems are consequences of Vanbrugh's attempt to
find a comic form that accepts the moral assumptions of transitional
drama without abandoning the social context of dramatic satire. Vanbrugh's answer to the rival forces of his age is a new kind of comic
characterization that internalizes the contradiction between those moral
assumptions and social convention, and renders that contradiction as
the psychological struggle of a moral individual in an amoral world. His
defiance of Cibber's moral and social stereotypes, his daring reconciliation of moral paragon and libertine pragmatist, his unusual recourse to
soliloquy to reveal the inner workings of a character's conscience all
distinguish *The Relapse* as a remarkable, original formal effort, but also
as a work that is perfectly representative of its time. It is also representative of its author. *The Provoked Wife* (1697), Vanbrugh's only
other complete standard comedy, provides an additional example of his
exploration of serious marital and moral problems in an unstable comic
context. [20] Vanbrugh, like Congreve, is a preeminent transitional dramatist. Like Congreve's, his innovations depend upon the weakening of
satiric form by the incursions of a new and opposed moral standard of
assessment. And, again like Congreve's, his experiments are unrepeated
once the formal instability of the transitional period is replaced by the
new coherence of the full moral action.

IV

Congreve's transitional comedy represents a more independent growth
than Vanbrugh's, since it is not inspired by any specific, inadequate
antecedent. But although he does not provide a formal answer to any
individual earlier play, Congreve, like Vanbrugh, does consciously
attempt a general revision of comic practice. He is consistently forced
to defend himself against the charge of obscurity in characterization.
In the case of *The Double-Dealer* (1693), he asks his critics to revise
their notion of the necessary attributes of the comic protagonist:
"Another very wrong Objection has been made by some who have not
taken leisure to distinguish the Characters. The Hero of the Play, as

they are pleas'd to call him (meaning *Mellefont*) is a Gull, and made a
Fool and cheated. Is every Man a Gull and a Fool that is deceiv'd?"[21] In
his dedication to *The Way of the World* (1700) he complains that the
deliberate and unique subtleties of his characterization were lost on the
audience, which obtusely mistook fools for wits and wits for fools (p.
390). Apparently Congreve has been tampering with the stereotyped
characterization typical of social satire. Though his brief and abortive
dramatic career begins with a straightforward and conventional comedy
of manners, *The Old Bachelor* (1693), which depends for its lively
intrigue upon a regiment of simple stock characters, he turns immediately in his second play to the formal innovation with which his corpus
ends.

The *Double-Dealer* and *The Way of the World*, like *The Relapse*, are
consequences of the transitional instability of satiric form. Both are
based upon the social conventions of dramatic satire. Both reproduce
the pragmatic values, the conversational wit, and the frequent local
ridicule of that earlier tradition. But both also attempt to incorporate a
new means of assessment, based upon an internal ethical standard. In
his experiments with comic drama, interrupted by the largely traditional
crowd-pleaser, *Love for Love* (1695), Congreve discovers a new formal
coherence in a unique and, in his own period, ultimately unacceptable
portrayal of character. *The Double-Dealer* places moral villainy in a
social context, and thus uses ethical evil to disrupt the conventional
stereotypes of social comedy. *The Way of the World* furthers that disruption by incorporating a means of direct and positive moral assessment into its protagonists' "mannered" relationship. These plays freely
exploit the formal possibilities temporarily available in their transitional
time. And that freedom partly explains their disappointing fate on the
contemporary stage, as well as their much more enduring excellence.

The *Double-Dealer* was criticized not only for the unconventional
gullibility of its hero, but also for the unusual use of soliloquy in the
depiction of its villain. The modification of social judgments that marks
the form of the play accounts for both of these apparent problems, as
well as for the strange preeminence of the evil genius, Maskwell. This
malicious schemer spends the action of the play plotting villainously and
almost indiscriminately against every member of the aristocratic family
of which he is a dependent. Simply in terms of the extent of their activity, the witty lovers, Mellefont and Cynthia, are insignificant compared
to Maskwell. Until the final revelation and destruction of his schemes,
they are the passive victims of their blocking figure. Furthermore, Maskwell's almost unmotivated villainy is formally incongruous with the
primarily social context of the rest of Mellefont and Cynthia's world.
This incongruity is the basis of the form of *The Double-Dealer*.

The context of the main action is supplied by a parade of ridiculous subsidiary characters whose cuckoldry is treated with the finest comic wit of the satiric tradition. These characters are wholly contained within a social standard of assessment. We are not, for example, inclined to invoke a moral judgment of Lady Froth at the moment of her laughing surrender to Brisk; in fact, when Lord Froth suddenly comes upon them, we hope they will escape. We also wish, of course, that Careless and Lady Plyant will manage to convince Sir Paul that the love letter he has intercepted is merely some kind of a test. And, of course, they do. Mellefont and Cynthia mingle with these characters with the aplomb of Restoration Truewits, and comment gently but incisively upon their ridiculous behavior (e.g., II.i.20–44). The satire that they direct against the fools of their world serves to restrict our judgment of those fools to conventional social ridicule.

This material is juxtaposed with the moral depravity of the other cuckolder and schemer of the play, who, significantly, never directly confronts the Froths and Plyants on the stage. As this radical separation of characters suggests, the depiction of Maskwell's villainy assumes an entirely different kind of evaluation from that of the fools' antics. In him, these foibles become sexual transgression, treacherous duplicity, depraved egotism, and monstrous ingratitude. Maskwell's genuine malice transcends simple corrupt self-interest. In fact, the motives for his villainy are applied rather belatedly and incoherently to his burgeoning complex of evil schemes. We discover his affair with Lady Touchwood and his concurrent plot against Mellefont well before we learn of his desire for Cynthia, upon which those former ploys are retrospectively dependent. That desire itself is only a nominal motive, completely unsubstantiated in the action, and confused by hints that he initially felt a sexual interest in Lady Touchwood (III.i.175–79). Furthermore, it is never clear how his schemes with Lady Touchwood will provide him with Cynthia, and the ultimate windfall offer of Lord Touchwood's estate comes as a surprise unanticipated by any prior notice of such an objective in Maskwell's machinations.

While Maskwell's villainy is emphatically clear, his motives are not, and these deliberate obscurities are symptoms of Congreve's attempt to differentiate the representation of genuine immorality from that of self-interested social hypocrisy. Maskwell's character is not comprehensible in terms of social ambition, and therefore he cannot be assimilated into the world of the other comic characters in the play. When we look closely, his pragmatic motives melt away, and we are left with a depiction of unmotivated villainy unaccountable in a world of simple social corruption. In fact, Maskwell is consistently described, by the other characters as well as himself, as a villain and a devil,[22] and that reiterated definition contributes to the sense of his extraterrestrial immorality.

Maskwell's villainy is demonstrated directly by his complete control over all the other characters in his action and indirectly by the formal subservience of those characters to Congreve's depiction of moral evil. Most obviously, the proliferation and interrelation of Maskwell's plots and double-crosses make his extraordinary villainy indisputable. In this respect, Lady Touchwood serves as a means of complicating Maskwell's schemes and of adding sexual trickery to his edifice of lies. Her passionate violence and jealousy provide an explicit and significant contrast to his cold and unmitigated evil (e.g., I.i.323–32). Congreve even puts the witty hero of his comedy at the service of this characterization of unconventional immorality.[23] Mellefont appears to be "a Gull and a Fool" because he is the consistent object of Congreve's irony. He is repeatedly made to remind the audience, at the most inappropriate moments, of his confidence in Maskwell (II.i.405–11) and of his certainty of success (III.i.257–59). But in all other respects Mellefont is the admirable and witty hero of the play. The irony directed at him in these scenes is the consequence of Congreve's attempt to distinguish immoral villainy from the context of social convention. Mellefont must appear to be a fool, in the stereotypical terms of dramatic satire, so that Maskwell can be an extraordinary villain, outside of those terms. In answer to his critics, Congreve himself describes the formal priority of Maskwell over Mellefont: "I would have 'em again look into the Character of *Maskwell*, before they accuse any Body of weakness for being deceiv'd by him. For upon summing up the enquiry into this Objection, [I] find they have only mistaken Cunning in one Character, for Folly in another" (pp. 120–21).

The unprecedented immorality of the title character is the formal center of *The Double-Dealer*, and it assumes an inscrutability and ambiguity incompatible with the stereotyped characterization of social satire. It is in these terms that Congreve defends Maskwell's soliloquies as necessary to the depiction of villainy:

> It oftentimes happens to a Man, to have designs which require him to himself, and in their Nature, cannot admit of a Confident. Such, for certain, is all Villainy . . . when a Man in Soliloquy reasons with himself, and *Pro's* and *Con's*, and weighs all his Designs: We ought not to imagine that this Man either talks to us, or to himself; he is only thinking, and thinking such Matter, as were inexcusable Folly in him to speak. But because we are conceal'd Spectators of the Plot in agitation, and the Poet finds it necessary to let us know the whole Mystery of his Contrivance he is willing to inform us of this Person's Thoughts; and to that end is forced to make use of the expedient of Speech, no other better way being yet invented for the Communication of Thought. [pp. 119–20]

The essential quality of Maskwell's evil, then, is the impenetrability of his character, which is by nature invulnerable to external judgments.

Maskwell himself describes this central assumption of his characterization:

> Why, let me see, I have the same Face, the same Words and Accents, when I speak what I do think; and when I speak what I do not think—the very same—and dear dissimulation is the only Art, not to be known from Nature.
>
> [II.i.460-64]

He characteristically reveals his plots in order to further them, making not only his own face, but truth itself impervious to assessment (e.g., V.i.95-101). In effect, the external ambiguity of Maskwell's moral evil dictates the means of his depiction in the play. In order to understand his actions we must be presented with his thoughts, and his thoughts provide the only means for our comprehension of his immoral nature. Congreve's introduction of extraordinary moral forces into a social form is thus directly tied to his experiment with a new kind of characterization dependent upon the unprecedented revelation of a specific sort of inner life, and embodied in the same technical innovation—comic soliloquy[24]—that distinguishes the form of *The Relapse*.

Maskwell, then, is presented and judged in terms incompatible with those of social comedy. His moral villainy, unrealizable within the conventional social stereotypes of dramatic satire, explicitly defies the direct external judgments applied to those stereotypes. Though his opacity does not result in a complexity like that of Vanbrugh's Loveless and Amanda, it arises from a similar challenge to the conventions of social form. In *The Double-Dealer* Congreve is specifically concerned with the immediate evaluative transparency of social stereotype, and the particular moral villainy of Maskwell is obviously designed to suggest the inadequacy of that transparency. In this respect Congreve's first experimental comedy replaces the social corruption of its namesake, *The Plain Dealer*, with the immorality available to transitional form. Wycherley's satiric depiction of social hypocrisy is comprehensible in the surface conversation and behavior of Olivia, Vernish, or the supple Lord Plausible, whereas the moral evil of *The Double-Dealer* is the product of Maskwell's inner life and is accessible only to the audience and only through the special dispensation of a dramatic device that makes that inner life audible.

The positive moral values thus negatively implied in Maskwell's characterization are faintly echoed by the other characters of the main plot, who acquire occasional moral virtues in order to give legitimacy to their opponent's moral vice. In this context, Lord Touchwood makes explicit reference to the enduring value of moral worth as opposed to the pride of social status: "Honesty to me is true Nobility" (V.i.318). And the morality of his statement is effectively contrasted with the hypocritical falsity of its immediate object, Maskwell. Mellefont

and Cynthia, though both witty satirists of the Froths and Plyants of
the play, are apparently genuine lovers in terms unsuited to the amoral
pragmatism of dramatic satire. Cynthia's demand that Mellefont prove
his wit by outsmarting Lady Touchwood "unless the Devil assist her
in *propria persona*" (IV.i.53–54) is ultimately ignored, and, at least in
their relationship, the "manners" requirements of social preeminence
take second place to the moral standards enforced by the presence of
"the Devil" in their midst.

   "The Devil," then, represents, in matter and manner, a moral challenge to the conventions of social satire. The deliberate and emphatic
discrepancy between Maskwell's characterization and that of the general
population of the comedy makes him its formal center. The implicit
juxtaposition of moral villainy and social corruption, though it brings
the play dangerously close to blatant inconsistency, allows Congreve
the benefits of both formal worlds. In fact, Congreve's choice of an evil
character rather than a virtuous paragon enables him to maintain an
environment of social corruption together with the specific depiction
of moral transgression. The general sense of depravity and cynicism
that is produced both by Maskwell's impenetrable malice and by the
inane, corrupt society of the Froths and Plyants reconciles the formally disparate aspects of the play. In effect, Congreve uses the social
context of the backdrop to avoid a melodramatically simple and op-
timistic conclusion. When the play ends and Maskwell's plots are exposed,
the Froths and Plyants go off unpunished to continue their affairs
elsewhere: the ejection of the villain, like the triumph of virtue in *The
Relapse*, does not carry with it all the final implications of the form.
The play achieves a wider reference as a consequence of its unique kind
of transitional experimentation. *The Double-Dealer*'s balance of social
and moral effect forces Congreve to find a means of characterizing a
superficially inscrutable villain. His resultant challenge to the conventional stereotypes of social comedy represents the first stage in his
movement toward a true fusion of moral assessment and social context.
The allusion to Shakespeare's Iago in Lord Touchwood's demand for
"Ocular Proof" (IV.i.562–63), as well as the more general resemblance
between Maskwell and that tragic villain, are signs of the implications
that Congreve saw in his experiments with soliloquy and with a new
kind of characterization.[25]

   Congreve continues and concludes his challenge to the transparent
characterization of dramatic satire in his best experimental comedy,
The Way of the World. This play is in many respects a mature reworking
of *The Double-Dealer*. After the respite from comic innovation represented by *Love for Love* (1695) and *The Mourning Bride* (1697), Congreve returns to the characters, the basic plot relationships, and, most
important, the fundamental formal concerns of his first, ill-appreciated

experimental play. Maskwell's duplicity and disturbing villainy are reproduced, with greater restraint, in the character of Fainall, and Lady
Touchwood's related violent malice is echoed by the more calculating
viciousness of Mrs. Marwood. These two characters, like their earlier
counterparts, are linked by an illicit sexual relationship that lends an
air of lewdness to their evil intentions. Lady Wishfort, like Lady Touchwood, blocks the central marriage because of an abortive affair with
the witty protagonist. And Mirabell and Millamant are greatly expanded
versions of the witty true lovers, Mellefont and Cynthia. In addition,
the plots of the two plays are superficially parallel, and notably distinct
from the more diffuse actions of *The Old Bachelor* and *Love for Love.*
Both *The Double-Dealer* and *The Way of the World* begin sometime
after an improper and disastrous sexual exchange between the protagonist and the aggressive older woman. Both nominally describe the witty
protagonist's attempts to outsmart the angry aunt and get the girl. And
both represent the schemes of a matched pair of evil characters, who
combine jealousy and monetary interest in their explicit motives and
come disturbingly close to achieving their ends.

The main mechanical change that Congreve makes in *The Way of the
World*, which is symptomatic of the significant differences between the
two plays, is his transference of the attention and activity of the plot
from the morally evil villain to the morally complex hero. In *The Double-
Dealer*, Congreve defies social stereotype by asserting the inscrutability
of extraordinary evil. In *The Way of the World* he attempts the much
more difficult depiction of the inner lives of essentially positive characters. Depth in the former play is restricted to the hidden motives of
the villainous hypocrite. In the latter, it is extended to a representation
of the problematic possibilities of individual happiness in a social world.

As we have seen, Congreve's defense of his last play resembles his
answer to the criticisms directed against the characterization in *The
Double-Dealer*, and reveals the important parallels in intention between
the two plays. The dramatist who was condemned in his first experimental comedy for making his hero a gull and for putting his villain
beyond the reach of external assessment again tampers with the straightforward terms of evaluation so strongly integral to Restoration comic
convention:

> Those Characters which are meant to be ridiculous in most of our Comedies,
> are of Fools so gross, that in my humble Opinion, they should rather disturb
> than divert the well-natur'd and reflecting part of an Audience; they are
> rather Objects of Charity than Contempt; and instead of moving our Mirth,
> they ought very often to excite our Compassion.
>   This Reflection mov'd me to design some Characters, which should appear
> ridiculous not so much thro' a natural Folly (which is incorrigible, and there-
> fore not proper for the Stage) as thro' an affected Wit; a Wit, which at the

same time that it is affected, is also false. As there is some Difficulty in the
formation of a Character of this Nature, so there is some Hazard which
attends the progress of its Success, upon the Stage: For many come to a Play,
so overcharg'd with Criticism, that they very often let fly their Censure,
when through their rashness they have mistaken their Aim. This I had occasion lately to observe: For this Play had been Acted two or three Days,
before some of these hasty Judges cou'd find the leisure to distinguish betwixt
the Character of a *Witwoud* and a *Truewit*. [p. 390]

In this passage, Congreve proposes a method of characterization that he
defines in explicit contrast to the manner of "most of our Comedies." It
requires a different sort of judgment on the part of the audience, it does
not submit to "hasty" or immediate interpretation, and it is not dependent upon a simple distinction between wits and fools. In fact, it deliberately avoids the depiction of the social fool and consequently the
instantaneous evaluative mechanism of dramatic satire. As Congreve implies, all the important characters in *The Way of the World* are witty,
and the presence of wit does not in itself permit us to distinguish frivolous from serious, violent from benevolent, contemptible from admirable, or even villain from hero. In place of the stereotypical distinction
essential to social satire between wit and fool, Congreve seeks, with
admitted "Hazard," to distinguish wit from wit by a means necessarily
more complicated and indirect. This entails the replacement of the
unsuccessful and limited self-revelatory soliloquy of *The Double-Dealer*
with an ethical standard derived from the tension between inner values
and the witty, social world. The inscrutability of the villain in that
earlier play is thus supplanted by the positive depiction of a full inner
life that generates the genuine complexity of characterization as well
as the particular form of *The Way of the World*.

Like *The Relapse* and *The Double-Dealer*, this comedy depends upon
a strongly represented social environment, to which the main terms of
its characterization and action are attached. The play's subordinate
characters are all designed to flesh out "the way of the world" with
comic manners and local ridicule, and to provide a context for the
protagonists' emblematic relationship and their opponents' schemes.
Taken together, characters like Petulant, Witwoud, Sir Wilfull, and
Lady Wishfort represent a world very much like that of conventional
social satire, but even the simple ridicule directed against them is qualified by the undermining of stereotypes, pervasive in this comedy. Petulant and Witwoud are not simple fools, but impudent and malicious
wits. Sir Wilfull is neither devoid of wit (III.i.497–501) nor lacking in
genuine and effective benevolence (V.i.577–87). And Lady Wishfort,
unlike Lady Touchwood, is a victim, not an agent, of the hypocritical
schemes.

This satiric background also provides the play with the fundamental concerns that are explored in the course of the action. Marriage is consistently ridiculed and denigrated, in the conventional satiric manner, by one witty commentator after another (e.g., II.i.103-07 and II.i.254-66).[26] The related issue of honest friendship receives similar harsh treatment. In fact, social exchange is characterized throughout the action as the hypocritical sparring of false friends: Fainall and Mirabell, Mrs. Marwood and Mrs. Fainall, Mrs. Marwood and Millamant, and Mrs. Marwood and Lady Wishfort. In effect, the social context pronounces its conventional cynical judgment upon the possibilities of meaningful human contact, either in marriage or friendship. But once again, that judgment is complicated and qualified, specifically, as we shall see, by the genuine emotional commitment implied in the relationship between Mirabell and Millamant.

The social world also dictates the terms of the play's main action. Mirabell and Millamant are the most adept and successful members of their society. Both of them are apparently possessed of unrivaled sexual attractiveness, and Mirabell is not only able to win the hearts of all the major female characters in the play, but even the loyal aid of his cast mistress, Mrs. Fainall. This conventional framework is reinforced by the incessant repartee that dominates the comedy. The first two acts open with conventional set pieces that display the prospective antagonists of the plot in witty and probing debate. In Act I, Mirabell and Fainall, just getting up from cards, exchange charged comments upon Mirabell's affairs, each attempting to ascertain the proximity of the other's relationship with Mrs. Marwood. In the parallel scene at the beginning of Act II, Mrs. Marwood and Mrs. Fainall engage in a similar tense verbal parlay in which they trade vituperative condemnations of "those Vipers Men" (II.i.43-44), each subtly seeking to discover the extent of the other's interest in Mirabell. By means of these matched manners debates, the central characters are immediately incorporated into the world of Petulant and Witwoud, and their schemes, unlike Maskwell's extraterrestrial plots, appear to emerge directly from "the way of the world."

But once again Congreve deliberately differentiates between the special, problematical world of his comedy and the stereotypical material of dramatic satire. The debates do not in themselves serve to distinguish fool from wit, or even villain from hero.[27] All four characters are socially adept, all appear to have virtually equal control of themselves and the situation, and all conceal their motives behind the equivalent dexterity of their tongues. In effect, the inscrutability which in *The Double-Dealer* is simply the product of hypocritical villainy is in this play the consequence of those very conventions upon which the action

is based. We are introduced to a world that proposes a kind of comprehensibility essentially like that of dramatic satire, but simultaneously
subverts the simple judgments that it invites the audience to apply.

Congreve's provocative use of the materials of social comedy is symptomatic of the particular form of *The Way of the World*. His qualifica-
tions and complications of this conventional social material constitute
an attempt to make moral and ethical values genuinely dependent upon
the social world with which they are at odds. Whereas *The Double-
Dealer* or even *The Relapse* poses its moral dimension in blatant opposition to the typical terms of social evaluation, in his most mature comedy Congreve makes the ethical values of an inner life the product of a
deepened exploration of "the way of the world." The result of this
merging of social and moral judgment is a unity of tone unique among
the transitional comedies of this period.

The core of the ethical assessment that emerges from the social context of this comedy is embodied in the formally central relationship
between the witty lovers. In keeping with the terms of their environment, they speak the language, strike the poses, and fight the battles
of dramatic satire. Mirabell's pragmatic scheming throughout the play
is designed to procure him Millamant's fortune. Millamant, in turn,
treats her admirer with the wanton cruelty of a social opponent (e.g.,
II.i.377-82). But their relationship reveals depths strangely out of
keeping with the superficial manner of their exchanges, and suggestive
of an inner life inaccessible to the normal means of social assessment.
Mirabell himself voices the surprising contrast in his own character between pragmatism and passion:

> *Fainall.* For a passionate Lover, methinks you are a Man somewhat too dis-
> cerning in the Failings of your Mistress.
> *Mirabell.* And for a discerning Man, somewhat too passionate a Lover; for I
> like her with all her Faults; nay, like her for her Faults. [I.i.156-60]

He is, in fact, a genuine lover, whose emotion actually gets in the way
of his wit (II.i.456-61). His final statement flatly contradicts the play's
concluding warning against "mutual falsehood" in marriage: "Well,
heav'n grant I love you not too well, that's all my fear" (V.i.597-98).
Similarly, Millamant breaks the surface control of her sharp repartee
with the sudden admission:

> Well, If *Mirabell* shou'd not make a good Husband, I am a lost thing;—for I
> find I love him violently. [IV.i.315-16]

All of the implications of these emotional depths, which are shown
to coexist with the external constraints of social exchange, are focused
and explored in the proviso scene. This scene represents Congreve's
most conscious and explicit recourse to comic convention,[28] and simul-

taneously his most concentrated and subtle revelation of the psychologies of his disputant lovers. Millamant explicitly seeks a relationship fully and elegantly conformable to the manners and "ways of the world," but in addition she requires, within that studied conformity, an assurance of continued affection and the space for a private existence. She seeks to prevent their being "asham'd of one another for ever After" (IV.i.205–06), and she demands the specific and limited independence available to her as a married woman (IV.i.212–25). Mirabell's provisos reflect similar concerns with the working details of a meaningful private relationship. He forbids the eccentricities and excesses that would endanger the genuine emotional commitment required of sexual partners, urging Millamant, in effect, not to trifle with their love (IV.i.234–43). He also covenants for the health and safety of his prospective offspring, for which we can already discern a fatherly affection extraordinary in the conventional rake (IV.i.260–63). The lovers negotiate in this scene for a mutual private happiness within the confines of a rigid and demanding social context, and they establish their relationship upon the possibility of such a reconciliation. Thus, Congreve presents the most conventional device of the manners tradition in all its studied satiric elegance, but makes it include a psychological verisimilitude that can suggest a separate inner standard of evaluation.

A common trope of Congreve criticism is the evocation of the graceful and polished social "dance" of the characters.[29] The elegance and artificiality of "the way of the world" depicted in this play certainly lend credence to the dance metaphor, and the manner of Mirabell and Millamant's exchanges is nothing if not polished and controlled. The matter of their relationship, however, completely escapes from the mode of decorous dance, as it does from the social form to which that metaphor refers. Congreve uses the pervasive social context of *The Way of the World* to the same ends as Maskwell's hypocritical inscrutability in *The Double-Dealer:* to suggest the possibility of a different kind of characterization and assessment based upon a sense of the insufficiency of social stereotype.

The perspective provided by this complex relationship between Mirabell and Millamant confers an ethical standard upon the whole social action of the comedy. From the moment of their opening repartee, Mirabell and Fainall are indistinguishable. Both are witty rakes. The contrasting critical interpretations of Mirabell, one finding him to be a representative of the ideal gentleman of Congreve's time[30] and the other claiming that he is an object of satire,[31] testify to this deliberate complexity of characterization. It is only by means of the gradual revelation of their inner natures that we are eventually able to tell villain from hero. Mirabell's genuine love for Millamant and his attempt to establish a meaningful marital relationship are contrasted with Fainall's vicious, manipulative, and unsympathetic attitude toward both his wife and his mistress, Mrs. Marwood. The distinction between Mrs. Marwood and Mrs. Fainall is similarly indirect. The initial apparent inscrutability of their characters is the product of the social context, according to which they are shown to be equivalent in wit and vituperation. But they are subsequently separated by the revelation of motives which that initial context obscured.

These characters are finally defined not so much by their social actions and manners as by the inner motives and meanings of those actions, gradually revealed by reference to the values of Mirabell and Millamant's love. In this context, the issues of friendship and marriage, initially introduced as conventional objects of social satire, succumb to an ethical assessment that the earlier convention cannot explicitly supply. We are provided with a means of distinguishing Fainall's reprehensible attitude toward marriage from Mirabell's admirable and ethical one, just as we declare against Mrs. Marwood's denigration of the values of friendship and honesty. Without subverting the social context of "the way of the world," Congreve gives it a moral valence that reconciles the rival forces of transitional form. The unprecedented, and unduplicated, complexity of characterization in *The Way of the World* is a consequence of Congreve's application of other, extrasocial standards of assessment to the characters of a social comedy. The resultant tension between social judgments and ethical commitments creates a vital inner world, defined in other terms than the context to which it must accommodate itself. And this inner world in turn deepens, complicates, and challenges the stereotypical judgments of dramatic satire.

Congreve's last play, then, is the formal culmination of the warring assumptions of transitional comedy. In this respect, like the other transitional dramatic forms of the period, it contains both aristocratic and bourgeois elements. Congreve's complex and original blending of social and moral is a successful attempt to rejuvenate an essentially aristocratic form through the integration of selected aspects of bourgeois ideology.[32] *The Way of the World* represents in effect the fusion of two forms that are simply contrasted in *The Double-Dealer* and *The Relapse*, and incoherently juxtaposed in the mixed drama of Durfey, Southerne, Cibber, Farquhar, Steele, and others. But Congreve's brilliant experiment in formal reconciliation is a casualty as well as a consequence of its particular time and place. His own accurate estimate of *The Double-Dealer* and especially *The Way of the World* was not shared by the theatrical consensus of the period, and these two plays were misunderstood, misevaluated, and surprisingly unsuccessful on the stage, especially in comparison with the great popularity of his formally conservative comedies, *The Old Bachelor* and *Love for Love*.

With *The Way of the World*, Congreve ceased original dramatic composition. The brief freedom afforded to the best dramatists of the period by the instability inherent in this formal transition did not extend to a blanket acceptance of the innovations which that freedom produced, and Congreve's comedies are fundamentally at odds with the prevailing conventions of the time. An audience accustomed to the stereotypical characterization of social satire and mixed transitional comedy was vehemently unappreciative of the soliloquies and complexities of *The Double-Dealer* and *The Way of the World*. A drama that was dominated by the constraints of a powerful prior convention could not utilize the experiments of its greatest innovator.

V

Despite the late date of his last work (1707), George Farquhar clearly belongs to the period of formal transition. His early comedies consistently display the mixed intentions of Durfey, Southerne, and Cibber and attest to the pervasiveness of the simple, incoherent juxtaposition of social and moral in this drama.[33] His works progress, like Cibber's, toward greater moralization, though his last and best two plays avoid serious moral *sententiae* in favor of lively, though chaste, good humor. Like Shadwell's, his most coherent moral comedy appropriately contains the most explicit expression of the ideology that he obviously associated with the full moral form. In short, his brief, closely continuous corpus, clustered around the turn of the century, provides a series of examples of the common mixed comedy of the period, and also an anticipation of the shape of comic works to come.

Farquhar's first play, *Love and a Bottle* (1698), resembles in its representative inconsistency Durfey's and Cibber's transitional forms. Its protagonist, Roebuck, exhibits both the rakish, amoral behavior typical in the heroes of social satire and the inner worth and generosity common to the protagonists of moralized comedy. These contrasting attributes are symptomatic of the contradictory intentions that dominate the action. Farquhar includes a conventional, affected foppish beau, Mockmode, with all the satiric trimmings, but makes his eligible young ladies moral paragons. The two kinds of representation, which coexist through the body of the comedy, collide in the last scene, when Roebuck is tricked into marriage with his abandoned true love, Leanthe. Roebuck believes himself to be seducing another woman, and emerges from the bedroom extolling her physical attractions in the licentious manner of the rake. But his rakish claims to physical prowess are transformed into assertions of virtuous true love, since his sexual language is attached to the only woman who should properly evoke such effusions. Like Loveless's, Roebuck's final reformation results from this simple trick and is expressed with all the characteristic sententiousness of moral form.[34] The dramatic sleight of hand effected by the final device in this comedy permits Farquhar to have his rake and his moral lesson toc, and to make the blatant incoherence palatable in the cleverest manner of transitional contradiction.[35]

Farquhar's first successful play, *The Constant Couple* (1699), provides another example of his ingenuity in constructing the typical incoherent transitional action. Here, instead of mingling social and moral, Farquhar neatly divides one from the other, consigning satire to the early stages of the plot and moral effect to the later. Because the moral force is relatively unadulterated in the second half of the drama, *The Constant Couple* is closer to a moral form than is *Love and a Bottle.* The play begins as an apparent social comedy, which focuses on the amoral affairs of Lurewell, a disillusioned female libertine, and the freedoms of a pair of gay rakes, Standard and the famous Sir Harry Wildair. It ends with an affirmation of morality and exemplary virtue, a tribute to true love, and a chain of aphoristic sententiae extolling the efficacy and attractiveness of those qualities.[36]

The comedy falls into two pieces, in fact, and the point of its formal transformation can be located precisely in midaction (III.iv). Up to that point, Lurewell appears to be a lecherous seductress, engaged in openly displayed sexual relationships with most of the men in the play. In that central scene she reveals the completely unanticipated moral motives behind her behavior, and thereafter she is defined as a kind of eccentric moral paragon. We learn that she is technically chaste, that she only flirts with dishonorable men, that she never trifles with those who honestly offer marriage, that in fact she is not a libertine at all, but almost a scourge of God.[37] Similarly, her unrecognized long-lost lover, Standard, appears up to that point to be one of Lurewell's lecherous hangers-on. Thereafter, however, his rakishness is turned to moral advantage, since his attraction to Lurewell is explained as the legitimate irresistible power of true love. By a series of subtle tricks and mistaken identities, Standard is transformed from a roving rake into an exemplary hero.

An identical transformation occurs in the rest of the characterization and representation of the play. After the turning point, strong moral statements and emblematic moral behavior, studiously avoided in the first, licentious half, dominate the action. Once again, Farquhar seeks to have it both ways. This time he makes the whole form of *The Constant Couple* out of the concluding trick of his previous, less successful play, and the implicit contradictions are justified in part by the elaborate rationalizations of Lurewell's earlier behavior and in part by a convenient series of mistaken identities. Significantly, the action of *The*

Constant Couple depends on the complications of the social portion of the form, whereas its resolution depends on the assertion of moral values. In this respect Farquhar, like Cibber before and Steele after him, uses the social segment of his transitional drama to motivate the dynamic plot that the moral action cannot produce. This particular functional recourse to social material is a symptom of the inherent problems presented by even a partially moralized form.

The *Twin-Rivals* (1702) is Farquhar's most coherently moral play[38] as well as his most explicitly ideological one. It addresses itself directly to contemporary attacks on the theater, and presents itself as an answer to Collier's criticisms (preface, p. 286). The minor debate that this comedy has occasioned suggests that modern critics find its moral claims somehow problematic.[39] The play is hard to place mainly because of its vigorous ideological adoption of a full moral form at a relatively early date and also because of its appearance in the midcareer of a dramatist best known for his late "laughing" comedy. Our notion of transitional form, however, permits us to see the moral propensities in Farquhar's earlier mixed plays and to anticipate the direction of his dramatic development.

The *Twin-Rivals* depicts a serious, generous, honest paragon protagonist, the Elder Wouldbee, who is rewarded with the hand and fortune of his virtuous and constant lover, and the defeat of his spendthrift, treacherous, hunchbacked younger brother, in a context replete with sententiae, with defiance and refutation of class judgments, and with grave claims to a "high" seriousness beyond the reach of conventional comedy (preface, p. 287). The play exemplifies the conjunction between the collapse of classical notions of decorum in characterization and separation of styles, and the advocacy of middle-class ideology. Farquhar admits to an attempt to mix comic and tragic, and to produce a new and morally serious kind of comedy. The moral paragon of this new form demands a higher tone and a blurring of the generic distinctions between serious and comic, and the values he represents are specifically dissociated from issues of social performance or status and produce an inversion of the traditional aristocratic hierarchies in characterization.[40]

In *The Twin-Rivals* these details of moral form are inextricable from their ideological context, and the play is a virtual catalogue of bourgeois sentiments. It recommends charity to the poor (III.ii, p. 322). It praises trade and advocates prompt payment for goods and services (III.i, p. 318), insisting that a generous tradesman is more noble and better deserving of a coat of arms than a lord (III.ii, p. 323). It claims that the upright but plain citizen should justly despise the immoral aristocrat (IV.i, p. 332). It celebrates the political consequences of the Glorious Revolution (V.iv,

p. 347). It supports imperial expansion in its glowing treatment of the military. And it espouses the causes of female chastity, wedded love and constancy, benevolism, generosity, and innate goodness. In short this play, like *The Squire of Alsatia*, reveals the necessary intimacy of moral form and bourgeois ideology, and it illustrates again the crucial role of strong partisan sentiment in the development of a fully moral action.

Farquhar's career, through his first moral play, provides an object lesson in the evolution of comic form from the end of the period of transition to the beginning of the hegemony of the moral action. But his two last and most mature comedies, *The Recruiting Officer* (1706) and *The Beaux' Stratagem* (1707), represent an attempt to double back, with greater dramatic sensitivity and technical expertise, to the transitional drama of his early career. With the altered perspective of the benevolence and geniality assumed by the moral action, Farquhar effects in these plays a subtler, smoother conjunction of social and moral than in any of his earlier works. Both plays illustrate the endeavors of an astute dramatist to produce a theatrically viable action in a period of increasing formal difficulty.

The Beaux' Stratagem exemplifies the significant characteristics common to the two plays. It simultaneously avoids the incoherence of *Love and a Bottle* or *The Constant Couple* and the sententious stasis of the unsuccessful play *The Twin-Rivals*. Its plot revolves around a fortune-hunting escapade, resolved by the protagonist's renunciation of his unscrupulous intentions on the verge of a lucrative marriage. Though it ends on a moral pitch,[41] the action is not consistently moral, but rather pragmatically amoral, in the manner of social comedy, and thus more dynamic and varied than that of *The Twin-Rivals*. Charles O. McDonald, like many other critics of the late comedy of manners, conflates this play with the major drama of the 1670s and finds Aimwell and Archer to be consistent objects of satire.[42] His reading responds to the play's proximity to social comic form, but without taking account of the signs of transition in its structure. Significantly, the energy of *The Beaux' Stratagem* does not strongly resemble that of *The Man of Mode* or even that of Farquhar's early transitional actions; this play deliberately avoids the satiric material of *Love and a Bottle* and *The Constant Couple*. In place of the conventionally affected urban and aristocratic fop of *Love and a Bottle*, Farquhar's last work includes instead an entertaining Irish priest and a pretentious French prisoner of war, both simple foreign and Catholic butts. And for the cynical sexual titillation of *The Constant Couple*, *The Beaux' Stratagem* substitutes the healthy flirtatiousness of Cherry, the landlord's daughter. Thus, though the plot of this lively play is social, not moral, it consistently replaces the satiric urban context with energetic and good-humored rural stage business,[43] which makes the moral lesson, when it comes, less incoherent and more congruent with the rest of the action than in any of Farquhar's early, mixed plays.

Farquhar further softens the moral blow by restricting its explicit expression to only one, though the central one, of the play's pair of matched protagonists. Archer's pursuit of Mrs. Sullen contains much of the material of the conventional sex-chase, and his attempts to persuade her to surrender recall the pragmatic eloquence of social satire. But even here the sympathetic portrayal of Mrs. Sullen's painful marital plight,[44] especially in the good-humored and partially moralized context of the rest of the action, reflects a slight alteration in the premise of the form. This serious treatment of the problems of matrimony is a sign of the transitional times. Southerne, Vanbrugh, and Farquhar all seem drawn to the beleaguered and injured wife, whose situation is defined primarily in conventional social terms but whose response is in some degree imbued with a new and explicitly moral consciousness of personal virtue. Such a figure is a potential locus for both sympathy and sexual pragmatism. Mrs. Sullen, by this means, achieves a depth faintly reminiscent of the complex characters of Vanbrugh and Congreve.[45] Significantly, she is Farquhar's only such creation, apparently only possible in a transitional form, and only when the blatant contradictions of mixed comedy are somehow reconciled. The frailty and brevity of Farquhar's exploration of character suggest the important link between successful major innovation and the forces of formal transition. Vanbrugh and Congreve, writing at the height of the major change in comedy, produced plays substantially more interesting and enterprising than the most talented young dramatist of the next decade could achieve. *The Beaux' Stratagem* represents a deliberate and futile attempt to turn back the evolutionary clock to that elusive earlier freedom, but, even in Farquhar's career itself, the tensions of transition had already given way to the assumptions of moral form.

In general, Farquhar's corpus illustrates the attempts of an astute and accomplished dramatist to locate a viable comic form. The difficulties that he encounters are indicative of the problems inherent in the mixed transitional drama common to this period, as well as of the weaknesses of the moral comedy that emerges out of that mixture. Most important, to the extent that he transcends these difficulties, Farquhar reverts to transitional form and attempts a new reconciliation of social and moral, more like that of Vangrugh and Congreve than like the simple mixed and divided actions of his early drama. In this respect, Farquhar's best plays represent an interruption of the straightforward evolution in his career from transitional to moral comedy. Thus they suggest, on the one hand, the potential freedom available to transitional form and,

on the other, the inherent and ultimately stifling constraints of the full
moral action.

VI

Like affective tragedy, transitional comedy stands between the aristocratic social drama of the Restoration and the bourgeois moral drama
of the eighteenth century. The act of mediation in itself suggests that
the parts played in this generic evolution by the affective action and by
the various sorts of transitional comedy are essentially parallel. Effect
in the absence of assessment has the same significance as contradictory
evaluation; both intercede between irreconcilable forms, and both
establish a strong historical continuity between the Restoration and
the eighteenth century. The period between social and moral form is
thus characterized by a general rejection of straightforward assessment: Jaffeir and Maskwell are equivalent consequences of the same
evolutionary process. Ideologically, affective drama and transitional
comedy represent different phases of the turn away from aristocratic
standards, and the evaluative emptiness and concurrent disillusionment of the former is an earlier version of the contradictory assumptions and divided intentions of the latter.

The significant differences between affective tragedy and transitional
comedy are in part consequences of the differing rates of evolution
between serious and comic forms throughout the Restoration. The
major heroic action predates the major dramatic social satire, as the
major affective tragedy predates the most important transitional comedy. In each case, the later form is characterized by a stronger and
more explicit sense of the forces of change that generate this generic
evolution. The contradictions that define the best social satire reflect
an admission of the irrecoverable loss of aristocratic social values much
more desperate and accurate than the simple celebration of epic standards in the early heroic action, or even the elegant conciliatory tour de
force of *The Conquest of Granada.* Similarly, the assumption of moral
judgment in transitional comedy, however chaotic the consequences,
attests to the growing strength of an ideology that two decades earlier
was felt formally only as a disillusionment with heroic assessment that
could put nothing except pathos in its place. In this sense, the later
social form resembles the earlier transitional form in its pessimistic attitude toward the viability of aristocratic values, though dramatic social
satire expresses that pessimism from the perspective of aristocratic ideology, whereas the evaluative limbo of affective tragedy places the transitional form altogether outside that perspective.

The social satire's criticism of the status quo not only accords with
its chronological lateness in comparison to the heroic action, but also

gives it a longer life, in this changing dramatic world, than the heroic action's blanket approbation could earn. For this reason, transitional comedy consists of a meeting of two incompatible forms, while affective tragedy arises out of the heroic action as a separate form of its own that is finally dissociated from its antiquated predecessor. The persistence of social satire as a formal force through the period of transition in the comedy produces a tension, unduplicated in the affective tragedy, that accounts for the greater formal variety of the comic drama as well as for the surprising range in its achievement—from untenable incoherence to unprecedented excellence.

The fate of an experimental dramatist like Congreve, however, is partly a product of the bifurcated nature of standard transitional comedy, which never achieves a formal coherence of its own and which passes on, in the necessary intimacy of a mixed action, all the restrictive conventions of the prior form and none of the assumptions that once gave those conventions meaning. Again like the affective tragedy, then, though in a different manner, transitional comedy serves as a conduit that transfers the constraints of characterization and scope to the new dramatic form of the eighteenth century. Mixed comedy like Southerne's, Cibber's, and Farquhar's enforces the substitution of moral for social stereotypes, even though the moral action does not by nature depend upon the immediate, superficial evaluation required by dramatic satire. The extraordinary lack of influence of the two best and most innovative dramatists of this period demonstrates the strength of Restoration convention and suggests the sources of the dramatic moral action's incalculable inferiority to the eighteenth-century novel. Vanbrugh's and Congreve's experiments with complex characterization are fatally tied to the transitional period of which they are a product. They result from the tensions of that period, and from the juxtaposition or reconciliation of two standards of evaluation, and thus the logic of their being passes with the change to moral drama. They are neither entirely social, nor purely moral, nor social and moral, like the easily adaptable mixed comedy, but rather separate, synthetic forms of their own, significantly different from the moral action to come. Vanbrugh's emphatic moral lesson earns him considerable popularity, but his elegant evaluative juxtaposition and his unprecedented exploration of character and motive are unrepeated and uninfluential. Congreve suffers an identical fate, with the added, historically significant ignominy of theatrical "failure," which resulted from his more radical and therefore less obviously moral experimentation.

Thus, ironically, the formal uniqueness and superiority of Vanbrugh's and Congreve's transitional comedy make it inaccessible to a dramatic posterity. The long, continuous tradition of Restoration convention reaches the moral action by way of the inferior mixed comedy of this period, and the experiments that arise outside of that tradition do not abate its strength. Those very resources which account for the excellence of the early novelistic moral action are here specifically denied to the drama. The sterility inevitably attendant upon Congreve's explorations of psychological complexity is the period's most eloquent signal of the predicament bequeathed to dramatic moral form.

PART III
MORAL FORMS, 1700–1760

Dramatic Moral Action

Moral form is based upon the direct representation of inner worth. It presents us with an action that proposes, by means of explicit aphorism, exemplary incident, and especially paragon protagonist, a coherent internal moral code that determines our expectations for its characters and our understanding of their world. We judge Rowe's Jane Shore not by her social status—as a private woman she has none—and not by her simple victimization—though pathos figures largely in her fate—but by her tested virtue, which is defined and applauded in her action and substantiated in her martyrdom. We understand Steele's Bevil Junior not by his witty social preeminence or his sexual mastery, but by his exemplary morality, his chastity, his filial dutifulness, his financial economy, his true love, and even his refusal to duel. The strong internal ethical hierarchy of this drama requires the designation of an exemplary or eminently reformable central character, whose representative merit is confirmed and codified in every incident of the plot. The form is thus implicitly, and often explicitly, didactic, and the morality that it extolls is proposed as an absolute standard, universally accepted and immediately accessible.

Unlike the heroic action or social satire, then, the moral action presumes to speak directly for its audience. While any willing auditor can temporarily share the aristocratic values of a social form, those values are never displayed as a universal and inclusive norm. In fact, a significant part of their effect and meaning, for the aristocratic as well as the bourgeois members of the audience, lies in their exclusivity. The protagonist of a heroic action embodies an epic or chivalric ideal that is largely defined by its distance not only from the recognizable behavior of the common man but also from the realities of the everyday world. Dramatic social satire may present a familiar urban social context, but not as an object of admiration, imitation, or even acceptance. It is precisely this disjunction and distance that the moral drama of the eighteenth century deliberately denies.

Thus, the moral action, unlike those earlier forms, can make a direct association between the standards of judgment it applies to its characters and the sympathetic emotional response of its audience, which duplicates those standards in the everyday apprehension of the real world. Consequently, in terms of its formal assumptions, the moral drama of the eighteenth century, like its novelistic equivalent, is predominantly sentimental and realistic. Viewed formally, sentimentalism in the drama is a direct, though not a necessary, function of the moral action. In this restricted sense, the notion of sentimentalism, at least for the purposes of generic history, is less significant than the formal changes of which it is merely a specific consequence.[1] The designation of a sentimental character, scene, or tone does not in itself explain the special nature of the play, nor its relation to the drama of the period. A virtuous character in an early play by Durfey has a historical significance distinct from that of such a character in *The Relapse* or *The Conscious Lovers*, and the apparent seriousness in one of the plots of *The Comical Revenge* is fundamentally different from the seriousness of *Love's Last Shift*, *The Way of the World*, or *The Lying Lover*. The "problem" of sentimentalism encountered by students of this drama arises from the failure to make precisely these kinds of discriminations.[2] The nature and historical limits of sentimentalism in the literature of this period can be clearly defined only from a perspective that defers first to a full account of the structure and effects of moral form.

Realism can also be seen as a component of the unique representational immediacy and evaluative universality assumed by bourgeois moral form, and in this special sense it too is common to both generic representatives of the moral action in the eighteenth century: drama and novel. In fact, the specific attributes typically designated as realistic in this period—the depiction of everyday life, the portrayal of the diverse workings of society, the enumeration of domestic detail, the concentration upon private experience, the elevation of individual concerns, the cultivation of a natural or plain style—are the essential local materials of moral form. Realism too, then, is a category that can be understood and clarified by reference to the particular effects of the moral action, though the various manifestations of the early realist mode are not limited to that form, or even to imaginative literature proper. In this respect, the novel is distinguishable from the drama not as a unique repository of fictional realism in the eighteenth century, but rather as the genre that finds the most successful means of representing a fundamentally realist form.

The moral action thus entails a major revision of Restoration dramatic practice and reflects a concurrent breakdown of the neoclassical rules that codify the social assumptions of the earlier drama. Its attention to individual worth disrupts classical notions of decorum in characterization, just as its concern with the seriousness and moral significance of private affairs deliberately disregards traditional generic distinctions and levels of style. It replaces elevation and elegance with involvement and domesticity, social status with moral worth, wit with sentiment, and verse with prose. In this respect, serious and comic form, which undergo distinct but parallel evolutions in the social and transitional segments of this generic history, converge in the moral action of the eighteenth century. The "low" protagonist of the tragedy and the exemplary hero of the comedy evoke the same direct internal moral standard as the arbiter of their merits, though one dies a paradigmatic death and the other wins the chaste mate of his choice. The generically leveling effect of moral assessment is perhaps even more obvious in the novel than in the drama. The formal similarity between *Pamela* and *Clarissa*, for example, is more significant than their distinction as comedy and tragedy. This similarity, in both genres, is a consequence of the special nature of the moral action and a sign of the times to which that form belongs. [3]

In effect, moral drama specifically rejects the class judgments of social form in favor of classless and universal values. The most significant feature of the new form is its insistence on its own transcendence of class distinction. But although these moral ideals are felt by the dramatist and presented in the action as universally applicable, their content, and even their claim of classlessness, is specifically bourgeois. In *The London Merchant* (1731), for instance, Lillo replaces the class judgments of traditional tragedy with an exemplary moral standard that levels all other distinctions, but the specific repository of that avowedly universal and absolute standard is the responsible London merchant. The moral action thus embodies the dominant ideology of eighteenth-century English society, and even the details of the form reflect the minutiae of bourgeois values—from chastity, marital fidelity, financial economy, charity, civic responsibility, benevolence, and natural goodness to individualism, constitutionalism, nationalism, and mercantile expansionism. [4]

Ideologically and formally, the moral action is the destination of dramatic evolution from the Restoration to the eighteenth century. It occurs at the end of the smoothly continuous development from heroic to affective to bourgeois tragedy, and from satiric to mixed to moral comedy. The radical divergence between the beginning and the end of this generic history, however, is as significant as its continuity, and the special conjuncture of divergence and continuity in the evolution of dramatic form determines the nature of eighteenth-century drama. The definition of the moral action, then, in itself and in the context of the history of the genre, provides a means of assessing its continuity with and divergence from its successful predecessors, and ultimately of explaining the pervasive inherent weaknesses in plotting and motivation that signal the decline of the genre.

In the serious drama, the double domesticity of Rowe's historical she-tragedies links the statusless affective forms of Otway and Banks to the bourgeois moral forms of Hill and Lillo. But Rowe, like those later dramatists, is unable in his moral plays to represent exemplary virtue in the context of a consistent dramatic action. Addison's *Cato* eludes the problem by nominally detaching the Stoic hero from the mechanism of the plot. Hill and Lillo, however, must sacrifice consistency to the virtue of their paragons.

The same inherent and insoluble problems plague the comic moral action, though that form is able to escape into intrigue and farce. Centlivre's intrigues illustrate the most effective, and inevitably trivial, avoidance of the issue, while Steele's early plays reveal the heroic and ineffectual efforts of a moral dramatist to invent a lively comic action. Fielding's full-length comedies constitute a group display of the symptomatic weaknesses of the form in their inveterately inconsistent and inadequate plotting and characterization. Surprisingly, and significantly, his dramatic moral actions are unsuccessful in precisely the respect in which his novelistic moral actions excel. Though these writers will supply our main models, less prominent dramatists are equally assimilable to this formal category. The faint inconsistency of a character like Lady Traffick in *The Lady's Revenge* (William Popple, 1734) is a commonplace in this period. And the bourgeois sententiae of Robert Dodsley's Lopesque *The King and the Miller of Mansfield* (1737) rival the ideological explicitness of *The London Merchant*. Thus, the dramatic moral action, both tragic and comic, voices the standards and ideals of its time, but with a collective difficulty that reveals the inherited inadequacy of the genre to the effective expression of its form.

I

Nicholas Rowe's early plays illustrate the close relationship between affective and moral drama, just as his mature she-tragedy provides the essential link between domestic and bourgeois form. His career constitutes a perfect formal spectrum, spanning the transitional and moral periods of this generic history. *The Ambitious Step-Mother* (1700), his first play, is an affective tragedy in the old near-heroic style, with the familiar Persian princes and violent, ambitious queen whose evil machinations eventually bring about the distressingly tearful deaths of the play's two true lovers, along with a general carnage that intensifies the unabashed evocation of pity. Like Titus and Teraminta in *Lucius Junius Brutus*, Rowe's happy pair have just married and felt the customary forebodings of pathetic doom when their lengthy torture begins. Like Otway's unfortunate protagonists, they spend their stage time bemoaning their fates, pledging their love, and reciting their dying farewells. Significantly, Rowe calls upon the authority of the age's preeminent affective tragedian to define and defend the form of his first play. He argues in his dedication that the end of a tragedy should leave its audience with the predominant response of pity, "a sort of regret proceeding from good nature, which, tho' an uneasiness is not always disagreeable, to the person who feels it."[5] And he cites Otway's technique as the decisive precedent. His prologue lists with admirable precision the essential features of the form: its emotionalism, its requirement for compassion, its dependence upon the female victim (specifically Monimia), and its implication of the magnanimous capacities of the audience (sig. A4[r]).

The Ambitious Step-Mother thus sets up the essential affective foundation upon which Rowe builds his major moral she-tragedy. *The Fair Penitent* (1703) makes the easy transition from an exotic to a domestic setting, from a subsidiary to a central female victim,[6] and from pathetic innocence to moral virtue. Its prologue once again extolls formal pathos, but it locates these pleasurable sorrows not in "the fate of kings and empires," but in private life, which it proposes as a more immediate, familiar, and therefore effective basis of pity:

> Therefore an humbler theme our author chose,
> A melancholy tale of private woes;
> No princes here lost royalty bemoan,
> But you shall meet with sorrows like your own.[7]

Rowe's "private woes" here reproduce the affective premises of *The Orphan*; *The Fair Penitent*, though explicitly indebted to an earlier, Renaissance play,[8] is in effect a moralized version of Otway's most domestic affective tragedy. It describes the fatal consequences of the familiar love triangle, in which the central marriage has been dishonored by covert intercourse between the penitent wife, Calista, and the libertine villain, Lothario. The plot contains the requisite pathetic duels and reconciliations of honorable friends, the passionate recriminations, and the ultimate chain of confession and forgiveness, in which Calista blames herself and is repeatedly forgiven by Altamont, her injured husband, and Sciolto, her dying father, until she finally commits exemplary suicide.

Rowe's version of the pathetic domestic triangle differs from Otway's, however, in its pervasive subordination of simple effect to moral intention. Thus Calista is not an unwitting victim of an elaborate nighttime sexual trick, but the erring lover of the false Lothario, who first sought to marry and then abandoned her. For the same reason, Lothario, unlike Otway's inconsistent Polydore, remains an unredeemed villain, and the duels and misunderstandings are enacted by Altamont and Horatio, his noble friend, who usurps part of Polydore's role and brings the incredulous and pugnacious Altamont news of his wife's falseness. Thus, Rowe sets up a more rigorously defined series of moral acts that preserve much of the pathos of Otway's play, but subtly transform the evaluative vacuum of *The Orphan* into the didactic ethical world of the moral action.

Most important to Rowe's reworking of Otway's form is the ultimate penitence of the erring Calista. Monimia's simple innocence in *The Orphan* is essentially amoral. Calista's last lines, however, give rise to an explicit moral lesson and transform her, for the purpose of the poignant conclusion, into an innocent heroine. Though she is portrayed through the first four acts as a rather lustful and defiant illicit lover, and though she begins Act V in desperate mourning over Lothario's corpse, in her final minutes she admits her error and expresses a rather sudden and incongruous love for Altamont (V.258-64). Her repentant death produces the didactic lesson of the tragedy:

> By such examples are we taught to prove
> The sorrows that attend unlawful love;
> Death or some worse misfortunes soon divide
> The injured bridegroom from his guilty bride;
> If you would have the nuptial union last,
> Let virtue be the bond that ties it fast. [V.288-93]

The general moral tenor of the whole play prepares us for this sententious conclusion, though the final pathos of Calista's innocent death contradicts her earlier characterization.

In effect, Rowe exchanges the affective inconsistency of the libertine villain Polydore, upon which Otway builds his form, for the arbitrary and unprepared moralization of the passive female protagonist. Calista's inconsistency, like Polydore's or Alexander's, provides another example of the significance of formal discrimination in generic history. Frank J. Kearful, in a useful and sensitive essay, finds in Calista's realization of guilt an example of complex characterization.[9] The priorities of the action, however, suggest that for Rowe both moralization and affect, in that order, rank above deliberate subtleties of character development. In *The Orphan* Polydore's characterization serves to keep all the tragic victims innocent. Calista's, at the climactic moment, makes her moral. Formally, virtue in *The Fair Penitent* takes the place of innocence in *The Orphan*. Both provoke the same emotional response, and the close similarity of the plays reveals the near equivalence of these two attributes. Moral form in its representation in Rowe's career is directly derived from affective tragedy, by the simple imposition of explicit moral meaning upon the innocence essential to pathetic drama. That innocence, and its unexplored suggestion of virtue, leaves an opening for explicit didacticism in tragedy, which the moral dramatists of the eighteenth century eagerly fill. Rowe's moral actions thus remain strongly affective, as do those of Lillo, Hill, Charles Johnson, and Moore after him. In this special sense, the evaluative vacuum left by Otway's rejection of aristocratic standards is the necessary ideological and formal precursor to bourgeois moral drama.

Rowe's tragedy displays its ideology in the most general shape of its dramatic world. Its attention to private woes, statusless women, exemplary virtue, didactic morality, domestic history, natural effect, and shared emotional experience all assume a hierarchy of values explictly affective and implicitly antiaristocratic. The full ideological significance of Rowe's moral form, however, is most obvious in his early tragedy, *Tamerlane* (1701), which offers a thoroughgoing bourgeois refutation of the erratic Herculean hero. Rowe's protagonist, unlike Marlowe's,[10] is a paragon of civic responsibility and generous virtue, in an action that has all the appropriate components of moral form, including exemplary lovers, tearful partings, virtuous self-sacrifice, and moralistic sententiae. Bajazet, the villain of this drama, embodies the qualities of the Herculean hero. This vicious rapist claims, like Marlowe's Tamburlaine, to be a demigod: he defies death, he attempts to revive his dead wife (in order to prevent her escape from him), he asserts the physical power and substance of his own words, and he pursues his violent course in the name of radical individualism and insatiable ambition. Rowe evokes the Herculean ideal in Bajazet in order to redefine it as villainy, and this ranting demigod, unlike Marlowe's natural man, is nothing more than depraved and repulsive. He separates two sympathetic lovers, eventually raping one and killing both. He rejects and attempts to murder his own virtuous and generous daughter, though she has undertaken to save him. And he deceitfully conspires against the magnanimous Tamerlane, to whom he owes his own life.

The responsible virtue of Rowe's paragon is defined in explicit contrast to the qualities of the Herculean demigod. Thus, in a symptomatic reversal of the heroic vehemence that Marlowe's Tamburlaine displays, Rowe's orderly hero counters Bajazet's threat to use him as a footstool and imprison him in a cage until he begs for death[11] with a moralistic and self-congratulatory announcement of magnanimous pardon (II.ii, pp. 86–87). This Tamerlane is the direct embodiment of the bourgeois ideals of the Glorious Revolution. He stands explicitly for civic virtue, constitutional monarchy, and religious toleration. He is himself an arm of divine Providence. He will end tyranny, establish prosperity, and bring imperial peace to the world. In short, he is William of Orange, with all the ideological accoutrements of that representative monarch.[12]

Tamerlane illustrates the intimacy of the relationship between bourgeois ideology and the moral action. Rowe's substitution of a sententious and exemplary hero for the Herculean demigod and his extensive evocation of the minutiae of that hero's moral code coincide with the largest formal intentions of the play. The same relationship is apparent in his last historical she-tragedy, *Lady Jane Gray* (1715), which resembles *Tamerlane* in its unusually explicit ideological detail. The play is a moral action with a paragon protagonist, several parting scenes, occasional sententiae, and a specific internal ethical hierarchy that advocates liberty, law, and Parliamentary rule and rejects tyranny and Catholicism.[13]

Significantly, Rowe's least ideological serious plays are also his least problematic, his least successful, and his least moral. The failed tragedies of his midcareer, *Ulysses* (1705) and *The Royal Convert* (1707), though they contain an occasional virtuous claim and a smattering of pathetic effect, are not full moral actions. The relative facility and consistency of their plotting and characterization, compared with the instability of Rowe's best, moral plays, is indicative of the inherent weakness of the form that Rowe derived from Otway. It is a revealing sign of the times that Rowe's consistent plays are trivial and uninteresting, while his best plays are moral and inconsistent. The exemplary virtue required by the fully pitiable and therefore flawless tragic moral protagonist cannot motivate an active and consistent plot of the sort available to the dramatists of Rowe's age. The problems attendant upon the period's primary form are clearly evident in Rowe's most popular and effective she-tragedy, *Jane Shore* (1714).

Rowe's historical drama, like Banks's before him, combines domestic passions with domestic history, and to the same formal ends. *Jane Shore* resembles *The Fair Penitent* in its selection of an injured and ultimately virtuous female as the affecting center of its action, but Jane Shore's story, unlike Calista's, is a segment of national history, with a tangible local setting and a cast rendered familiar in literature and ballad.[14] In this sense, historical she-tragedy is the logical extension of the moralized affective form that Rowe advocates in *The Fair Penitent*. Domestic history makes the fate of the virtuous heroine even more immediate and "homely" and therefore, as Rowe argues in his prologue, more affecting[15] than that of the Genoese Calista, just as domestic passions and female characters make the action more moving and emotional. Banks's defiant nationalism in his affective tragedy is thus the transitional precedent for the bourgeois nationalism of Rowe's moral form, which specifically links domestic material to "homely," "private," and implicitly classless virtues, though all the while, like Banks's, retaining the name of royalty.

Jane Shore makes a strong and consistent affective appeal, although, as in *The Fair Penitent*, its pathos is ultimately supplied with a moral and located in the exemplary virtue of the beset protagonist. The action is replete with disaster, self-recrimination, and forgiveness. From her opening scene, the weeping heroine details the anguish of her situation and anticipates the pathos of her fate (I.ii.98–105). As she valiantly protects her virtue from the assaults of the temporarily lascivious Hastings, she is treacherously betrayed by her best friend Alicia, Hastings's mistress, whose jealousy ruins both her rival and her lover. Hastings's execution is subsequently heralded by a heartrending mutual repentance, forgiveness, and farewell between the doomed patriot and Alicia, and the pathos of this scene prepares for the sustained emotionalism of the final act, in which Jane is discovered starving and wandering in the streets with disheveled hair and bleeding feet, patiently enduring her agony, praying for mercy on her enemies, and repenting her sins. She dies a tortured paragon in the arms of her long-lost husband, who breaks from the guard that carries him off to his own death to receive her final pleas for forgiveness.

Rowe thus fully exploits the seemingly infinite affective resources of the action, but he makes that pathos moral. Jane's fate is particularly pitiable because, in the context of the play, she is not only innocent but perfectly virtuous. And she is particularly exemplary because she is not only perfectly virtuous, but perfectly pitiable. She gamely defends her chastity against Hastings, loyally refuses to aid Gloster in his attempt to alter the succession, and graphically demonstrates her patience, charity, and true love. Her action is fully moral, and it generates the determining ethical hierarchy of the form.

But Rowe's designation of Jane as a moral paragon is obviously out of keeping with the facts of her ill-fated history. We know that she abandoned her husband for King Edward, whose charms she vividly recounts in the opening scenes of the play (I.ii.81–87). Her reiterated repentance and requests for forgiveness at the climax of the action also suggest something other than passive, virtuous victimization. These aspersions of guilt or misconduct, however, are carefully eliminated in time for the pathetic paroxysm of Act V.[16] In a clumsily intrusive piece of exposition, which immediately precedes Jane's most pathetic appearance, "*her hair hanging loose on her shoulders, and barefooted*" (V.142 *s.d.*), the royal whore's lengthy affair with Edward is summarily dismissed as a kind of rape at which her suffering equaled that of her abandoned husband (V.85–105). Rowe seeks to absolve Jane of guilt here in order to secure the full effect at which his best moral action aims. Jane's initial error is necessary to the motivation of the tragedy, but her virtue is essential to its form, and the slight inconsistency in Rowe's characterization of his protagonist is the simple consequence of his attempt to find a plot for a full moral action.

Hastings's character is manipulated for similar purposes. The exemplary and heroic nationalism of his defiance of Gloster contrasts strangely with his attempted rape of Jane and his betrayal of Alicia. He serves both as a villain, to test Jane's virtue, and as an English paragon in his own right, whose unjust death is rendered supremely pathetic by his tearful farewell to his mistress. The action of the tragedy, then, consists of a delicate balance of injured, innocent virtue and the necessary processes of the plot. Without *Jane Shore*'s inconsistency, Rowe's particular kind of moral action is plotless. *Lady Jane Gray*, for example, presents a perfectly virtuous, perfectly innocent, and perfectly dull heroine. The play is flawless in the integrity of its characterization of a passive paragon, and its action is consequently static. Jane Gray is made queen and then executed by Mary without a moment of suspense or conflict. Jane Shore, on the other hand, is both the erring center of a tragic process that produces her death and her redemption, and the moral paragon who gives that process meaning. In Rowe's corpus, the best moral action is not the most consistent, and that fact is a signal of the special problems posed by the new dramatic form.

J. Douglas Canfield has thoroughly documented the moral nature—and specifically the Christian content—of Rowe's drama, but he assumes that this morality is incompatible with pathetic effect.[17] The proximity of Rowe's moral plays to affective tragedy, however, is borne out in the telling similarity between the innocent and the virtuous protagonist. Both characters must be passive, and thus both quickly succumb to inconsistency in the motivation of a dramatic plot. Affective and moral incoherence are close formal cousins, just as affective and moral tragedy are ideologically related. But the difficulties arising from this incoherence are inevitably more apparent in a vehemently didactic form than in a meaningless one, and the sleight of hand that Otway can almost conceal becomes a crippling formal impediment to Rowe, Lillo, Hill, and others of this period. The continuity in the evolution of serious drama, then, brings old problems to the new forms of the eighteenth century, where every microscopic defect is magnified.

II

Joseph Addison's popular moral tragedy, *Cato* (1713), demonstrates the problems inherent in this recalcitrant form by its unique, roundabout solution to them. The premises of the play are moral, exemplary, and affective, in the tried manner of the period. Pope's prologue draws out, with the conventional epithets, the implications of this moral intention and illustrates, in comparison to Rowe's earlier, similar statements, the increasingly self-conscious didacticism of the form. Pope begins by defining the congruence of pathetic effect and moral form, of "tears" and "conscious virtue."[18] And he proceeds to make the moral paragon the object of patriotic imitation and affective identification for the audience (ll. 15-26). Pope describes the general effect of Addison's moral action, but not the specific ingenuity by which that effect is derived from a static, Stoic protagonist. *Cato* contains none of the inconsistencies that the other major moral tragedians of the period use as an excuse for the motivation of the plot. Instead Addison separates the generative forces of the action from the person of the exemplary hero, thus dividing the play in order to give it a dynamic plot, while still maintaining the spiritual centrality of the static protagonist.

Cato's character dominates the tragedy, and his virtue constitutes its ethical core. The primary expectation aroused by the play is that of his exemplary suicide, which is conditioned not only by history, but also by the frequent comments of his companions on the inevitability of his defeat and death (e.g., I.i.4–6, I.vi.11–13). The tragic end of his action thus represents the culminating expression of Cato's Stoical virtue, which remains from the beginning unqualified and unflinching. It is repeatedly defined by his admirers and by his own exemplary statements, which accompany each of his appearances on stage. Throughout the play, he instructs the other characters in this exemplary conduct, and thus provides the moral standard against which his whole world is measured. The villains of the tragedy, who conspire to betray him to Caesar, are simply anti-Catos, advocating point by point the exact opposite of his moral tenets (e.g., II.v.38–55), and the subsidiary positive characters are smaller replicas of the central moral model.

Cato's unstinting virtue is specifically public. His dry-eyed reception of the news of his son's death in battle is thus approvingly juxtaposed with his subsequent tears for the fate of his country (IV.iv.88–97). This brief moment of explicit emotion is, strangely enough, the consequence of Cato's exemplary Stoic detachment from personal concerns or affections. In fact, it is an emblem of Addison's particular moral form, which combines cold Stoic virtue and emotional effect. The tragedy as a whole, then, attempts to give affective power and dynamic motivation to a static, passionless paragon whose Stoic perfection would seem to stifle both.

Cato's action is supplied by proxy, through the intrigues and exploits of the subsidiary positive characters, little Catos split off from the passive paragon, who act independently of him but retain intimate familial and moral ties that designate them as his agents in the form (e.g., I.i.72–73, I.i.80–82). These characters, unlike Cato, endure the pains of the conventional love triangle, rush eagerly into battle, hear the temptations of treasonous conspirators, suffer near-rape, duel on stage with the enemy, and stab him through the heart. They are Cato's action. The first dynamic conflict is supplied by the love rivalry of Cato's two sons, Portius and Marcus, for the hand of the exemplary Lucia. Portius and Lucia are shown to be Cato's active representatives of virtuous self-denial, while Marcus is Cato's son in military honor. His death in battle resolves the love triangle, which is consistently associated with the civil war and the "sorrows" of the times (e.g., I.ii.26–27, III.1.15–20). In the second subplot the Numidian Juba, whose admiring imitation of Cato causes the dying hero to note that in such times all virtuous men are Romans (V.iv.91), defies the dishonorable conspirators, falls in love with Cato's daughter, Marcia, and simultaneously takes vengeance on the political villain of the tragedy and saves his mistress from rape. The domestic passions and fates of these characters are thus made to appear necessary to and dependent upon Cato's tragic situation.

This concerted conversion of political into domestic experience is further elaborated in the references to pastoral convention that link this play with the affective drama of the transitional period. Cato, the public hero, like Otway's Acasto, urges his family to retire to the countryside where "all our frugal ancestors were blessed / In humble virtues and a rural life" (IV.iv.138–39). Such obscurity, according to Cato, is the necessary consequence of his tragic situation: "When vice prevails, and impious men bear sway, / The post of honor is a private station" (IV.iv. 142–43). It is also the necessary resort of Addison's moral form. At the end of the play, Cato's reiterated concern for his friends and family, and his paternal blessings of the double marriage, represent Addison's final attempt to bind private to public and pathetic effect to Stoic virtue.

In short, the subplots of *Cato* are not incidental to its form. They are not in fact subplots at all, but rather Cato's action, once removed, and embodied in the active concerns of his spiritual and physical offspring. Faced with the problem of a consistent, infallible, and theoretically emotionless protagonist, Addison motivates an affecting and dynamic plot by leaving him out of the tragedy, and thus by giving him the credit of a tragic action without any of the normally attendant flaws. In this manner, Addison finds a mechanical solution to the challenge presented by the moral action's exemplary hero, and he simultaneously reconciles Stoic virtue with moral form. Cato does nothing but die, and yet his action is energetic and well motivated. He is a public hero, and yet the center of a domestic intrigue. He is reserved, remote, and even unfeeling, and yet his story is gauged to produce the sympathetic emotional response that proves the corresponding moral magnanimity of the audience. In this special formal sense, *Cato* reflects contemporary concerns with the validity of Stoical ideals, and Addison's clever reconciliation represents the first major effort of a sentimental age to incorporate the Stoic hero into an anti-Stoic sensibility.[19]

More important to the fate of the dramatic moral action, however, is the fact that Addison's immensely successful tragedy achieves adequate motivation and consistent characterization only through formal trickery. Addison's talent apparently resided in compromise. He makes a Stoic ethic the source of domestic tears; he plays simultaneously upon Whig and Tory partisan sentiments while voicing the major aesthetic and ideological attitudes of his age;[20] and he tames the dramatic moral action by pretending to give it a coherent tragic plot. His achievement in this respect is unique and virtually unrepeatable. The other major serious dramatists of the period, like Rowe, can place a moral paragon in a dynamic tragic situation only by tampering with the integrity of characterization, chronology, or effect. Addison's ingenious solution, however, since it depends upon a formal trick, does not produce a memorable tragedy. Richardson's, in another genre, does, and the comparison suggests the inherent limitations of the dramatic moral action, even when the playwright manages to make its form coherent and its troublesome paragon consistent.

III

The affective and didactic premises of the early moral action provide the formal foundation for full bourgeois tragedy, and the pathetic middle-class paragon of this important, flawed drama is the logical consequence of the statusless and female protagonists of earlier plays. Mitchell, Hill, Lillo, Fielding, Charles Johnson, and Moore, in their discussions and defenses of these tragedies, all reiterate the increasingly familiar adages of private woes, homely emotions, and concurrently greater pathetic and moral effect. Joseph Mitchell's preface to *The Fatal Extravagance* (1721), by Aaron Hill, argues defensively for the instructive value of drama,[21] and Hill in his prologue links that instruction to "private Sorrows":

> To Ills, remote from our Domestic Fears,
> We lend our Wonder, but with-hold our Tears.
>   Not so, when, from such Passions, as our own,
> Some Favourite Folly's, dreadful Fate is shown;
> There the Soul bleeds, for what it feels within;
> And conscious Pity shakes, at suffering Sin. [sig. a3^r]

George Lillo's dedication to *The London Merchant* (1731) makes the leap from domestic to bourgeois material, maintaining that "tragedy is . . . far from losing its dignity by being accommodated to the circumstances of the generality of mankind."[22] The prologue provides the usual comparison between aristocratic and statusless moral drama:

> The Tragic Muse, sublime, delights to show
> Princes distrest, and scenes of royal woe;
> In awful pomp, majestic, to relate
> The fall of nations, or some hero's fate. . . .
> Upon our stage, indeed, with wish'd success,
> You've sometimes seen her in a humbler dress,
> Great only in distress. When she complains
> In Southerne's, Rowe's, or Otway's moving strains,
> The brilliant drops that fall from each bright eye

> The absent pomp, with brighter gems, supply.
> Forgive us then, if we attempt to show,
> In artless strains, a tale of private woe.   [p. 8, ll. 1–20]

Lillo here reveals, like Rowe before him, an awareness of the connection between earlier affective drama and his own bourgeois play. Fielding's prologue to Lillo's later *Fatal Curiosity* (1736), like Charles Johnson's to *Caelia* (1732),[23] runs through it all again:

> No fustian hero rages here tonight;
> No armies fall to fix a tyrant's right.
> From lower life we draw our scene's distress;
> Let not your equals move your pity less!
> Virtue distressed in humble state support,
> Nor think she never lives without the Court.[24]

And Moore's preface to *The Gamester* (1753) reminds us, in the same formulaic language:

> The play of the *Gamester* was intended to be a natural picture of that kind of life, of which all men are judges; and as it struck at a vice so universally prevailing, it was thought proper to adapt its language to the capacities and feelings of every part of the audience.[25]

All of these didactic writers, then, implicitly or explicitly, trace the ancestry of this form back through the she-tragedy and moralized affective plays of Rowe and Southerne to the statusless, purely affective drama of Otway. All of them define the moral import of this tragedy specifically in terms of its pathetic effect. And ultimately, all of these bourgeois tragedians, in their attempt to create a flawless protagonist whose innocence and virtue are essential to their moral form, encounter the same fundamental problems that trouble Addison, Rowe, and, with less disturbing consequences, Otway. The symptomatic inconsistency of the best, most popular, and most strictly bourgeois of these plays, *The London Merchant*, illustrates the inherent weakness of even the successful versions of the dramatic moral action. George Lillo handles the formal problem more boldly, but less elegantly, than Addison, and perpetrates a central ambivalence in the characterization and chronology that extends even to the theological and philosophical dimension of the tragedy.

The shape of *The London Merchant*, as Lillo susggests in his dedication, is moral, affective, and deliberately didactic. Its utility, in the pragmatic terms of Lillo's moral marketplace, is directly proportional "to the extent of its influence and the numbers that are properly affected by it" (p. 3, ll. 21–23). Like *Jane Shore*, this play claims a local and homely ballad origin, but it differs from Rowe's tragedy in its celebration of the merchant class, and the details of its ideology supply a rich context for Lillo's particular version of moral form. The play contains two set disquisitions, voiced by Thorowgood, on the social responsibility and infinite merits of the London merchant (I.i.31–43 and III.i. 1–28). These claims establish the moral assumptions of the action, and all the material of the drama's local context serves to flesh out this ethical world. The play concurrently advocates indulgent treatment of children, voluntary choice in marriage, wedded love, the intermarriage of merchant and aristocratic families, the appropriateness of bourgeois merit at court, the prompt payment of tradesmen, and a general anti-Spanish nationalism and imperialism in keeping with contemporary political concerns. [26] These virtues are by definition ideally inherent in the bourgeoisie, and all the main characters of the tragedy, except Millwood, are bourgeois paragons.

Barnwell's character is derived directly from this ideology. In fact, Thorowgood's standards are set up to define Barnwell's merit and to give him the exemplary status of a member of an exemplary class. He is, according to universal testimony as well as his own behavior, the direct embodiment of the values that his action celebrates (e.g., II.ii.60 and III.iii.19–23). Lillo's problem, then, like Rowe's and Addison's, is that of motivating a workable tragic plot with a static, flawless, and supremely pathetic central figure. His solution is ingenious inconsistency. Barnwell is a criminal, represented in the commission of robbery and murder. But the manner of Lillo's depiction of his crimes is calculated to erase the blame and leave only the pathos of his tragic fate. Lillo's most evident extenuation of Barnwell is in the characterization of the evil villainess Millwood. Several critics have noticed the inordinate strength of her presence in the play, [27] and indeed her power is almost supernaturally irresistible. She is a "sorceress" (IV.xvi.22) whose infinite talents are directed solely toward the ruin of men. Even Thorowgood, the play's repository of virtue, testifies to her attractions, and thus implicitly excuses the innocent Barnwell (IV.xvi.79–85).

In clearing Barnwell, Millwood serves simultaneously as a negative advocate for the values represented in his action. Her speech of vindication and defiance after her capture extends the source of evil to which our exemplary hero succumbs from the wiles of a single angry woman to the inequities of a whole society. We learn that Millwood is the product of a pervasive institutional corruption, in the courts, the government, and the church. She convincingly attributes her crimes to her poverty and to her situation in an unjust world (IV.xviii.60–68). This further displacement of Barnwell's guilt makes his fall appear to be the inevitable consequence of the kind of social corruption that would have been specifically opposed by the progressive and reformist bourgeoisie. Appropriately, then, Thorowgood eagerly assents to Millwood's challenges: "Truth is truth, though from an enemy and spoke in malice.

You bloody, blind, and superstitious bigots, how will you answer this?" (IV.xviii.57–59). Equally appropriate is Millwood's final diatribe, in which she attributes her ruin and consequent criminal course to that aristocratic vice most frequently cited by the bourgeois moralists of the eighteenth century, sexual libertinism (IV.xviii.69–78). Millwood's characterization, then, is both a means to Barnwell's innocence and an ideological end in itself, which reinforces the bourgeois values of the form.

A slightly more subtle maneuver is necessary to justify the criminal acts consequent upon Barnwell's passion for his wily seductress. First, Millwood convinces him that she will be ruined without his aid. Thus, the benevolent hero finds himself caught in what he believes to be a genuine moral dilemma (II.xiii.1–5), and he steals from his master to save a helpless woman from "want and misery" (II.xiv.16). From this perspective, his crime is the accidental consequence of his characteristic virtue—an admirable capacity for pity like that of Alexander, Antony, Monimia, and Jaffeir—which is betrayed to destruction by unexampled villainy and misfortune. Though at other points in the play Barnwell takes responsibility for his acts, confesses the appeals of the passions, and describes the necessary exercise of reason and conscience in the battle for human virtue, here he is the innocent victim of circumstance and sorcery.

The delicacy required in the handling of the murder, of course, exceeds that demanded by the robbery. Unlike the ballad source, which gives the fallen apprentice full responsibility for the crime,[28] Lillo's version tends to exonerate Barnwell from the beginning by crediting Millwood with a remorseless demand for blood and by depicting Barnwell's heartrending response to her scheme (III.iv.52–103). The uncle's innocence and benevolence increase the pathos of the scene, but Barnwell's actions once again almost excuse him of the crime. While his unsuspecting victim meditates upon the meaning of death, Barnwell, concealed, "*sometimes presents the pistol, and draws it back again*" (III.vii.8 *s.d.*) in graphic, conscience-stricken indecision. Conscience wins the battle, Barnwell drops the gun exclaiming, "Oh, 'tis impossible!" (III.vii.9), and at this "*his uncle starts and draws his sword*" (III.vii.8 *s.d.*) in order to defend himself against a supposed assailant. In self-defense, then, Barnwell commits the murder. The predominant portion of the scene is occupied by the pathetic consequences of this accident. Barnwell's histrionic guilt and vehement self-accusation help to anticipate and thus dismiss much of the horror and blame that inevitably accrue to his deed. The purpose of the scene, then, is to represent Barnwell in the commission of a heinous crime, but simultaneously to absolve him of blame so that he can remain, in one formally essential sense, a moral paragon, and so that his fate, much like that of the self-flagellating Jaffeir of *Venice Preserved*, can be supremely pathetic.

The most notable of Lillo's necessary devices in *The London Merchant*, however, is his deliberate disruption of the play's chronology. The unspoken, predominant presumption of the first four acts, represented in the dialogue and behavior of Thorowgood, Maria, and Trueman, as well as in the consecutive process of the scenes and incidents, is that only a single day has passed. Barnwell is absent overnight and the next morning commits the theft, writes a note confessing his crime, then flees his master's house forever; he takes refuge with Millwood, immediately agrees to commit the murder, and stabs his uncle to death. According to Millwood's servants, Lucy and Blunt, however, Barnwell has continued to visit his mistress over several weeks or more, has stolen repeatedly from his master, and has pursued a lengthy course of inveterate crime (III.iv.22–60 and IV.iii.9–10). The subsidiary version of the duration of Barnwell's alliance with Millwood corresponds with that of the ballad source, in which Barnwell not only spends a length of time in Millwood's company and numerous gifts of money in her support, but even passes a fortnight with his wealthy uncle before he commits the murder.

This deliberate chronological ambiguity, again, serves to make Barnwell both the guilty, flawed instigator of his own destruction and an innocent, generous youth who lodged one brief night away from home. The weeks of dalliance are essential to the motivation of the tragedy, since they make Barnwell's agreement to murder his uncle seem at least plausible. Appropriately, then, Blunt and Lucy's description of Barnwell's course of crime is placed immediately before their exposition of the agreement for the murder. Lillo inserts the documentation of Barnwell's guilt in an allusion to the much more probable chronology of the ballad, but does not permit that incriminating chronology to dominate the representation. In short, he seeks to supply motivation and the subsequent pathetic effects of inevitable punishment without the accompanying blame. He keeps his paragon as pure as possible by means of the dominant, mercifully brief chronology that reigns throughout most of the plot and that makes Barnwell's indiscretion a matter of hours and his role one of essential innocence.

The functional chronological inconsistency in this tragedy serves the same purpose as the deliberate contradiction in Rowe's characterization of Jane Shore and the domestic intrigues of Cato's various offspring. It motivates a plausible tragic plot while maintaining the exemplary moral status of its protagonist. Significantly, the fundamental inconsistency in Lillo's treatment of Barnwell's action is reproduced in the serious theological and ethical material of the play. Thus we find assertions of innate goodness and natural benevolence juxtaposed with disquisitions upon the weakness of the will and the continuous battle between reason and passion. Barnwell's character, for example, is defined by his possession of a large portion of "the general love we owe to mankind" (I.v.33–34). It is this love, we are asked to infer, that causes his peculiar vulnerability to Millwood. Innate and natural feeling, for Barnwell, is more powerful than the external applications of reason: "Reason may convince, but gratitude [to the merciful Thorowgood] compels" (II.v.4–5). And Thorowgood himself effectually absolves his virtuous mercantile protégé from responsibility by emphasizing his natural innocence and neglecting the failure of his will (IV.xvi.21–49). Concurrently, a rigorous contrary doctrine finds Barnwell responsible, and traces his sin to the failed vigilance of his controlling reason. Barnwell himself cites "the law of Heaven . . . that requires us to govern our passions" (I.viii.9–10), alludes to the ethical notion that describes the progressive narrowing of moral choice consequent upon an initial immoral act (II.i.3–13), and subsequently compares his irresolution to the psychomachiac battle between reason and passion, where reason represents virtue and passion stands only for sin (III.v.24–29).

These contradictions have been the cause of significant critical disagreements over the play's ethical content and Lillo's metaphysical beliefs. Ernest Bernbaum documented the evocation of "boundless sympathy" for Barnwell and concluded that Lillo's intention is to "[free] his hero from responsibility" and to make the tragedy "an accident to virtue."[29] George Bush Rodman, challenging Bernbaum's view, demonstrated Barnwell's self-confessed sinfulness and inferred that Lillo distrusts human nature and notions of innate goodness.[30] Raymond D. Havens, answering Rodman, emphasized the sympathy evoked for Barnwell and the elevation of feeling over action in the play.[31] And William H. McBurney has described the problem as a collision of Calvinist predestination and classical responsibility.[32] In effect, the ethical and theological inconsistency disputed here is simply the counterpart of the formal inconsistencies that we have discovered in the action of the tragedy. The reprehensible victory of passion over reason, which produces Barnwell's rigorous punishment, motivates the plot. The benevolist insistence on Barnwell's innate goodness and on the supremacy of natural feeling, on the other hand, sustains the necessary virtue of the exemplary protagonist. To the extent that Barnwell is blamed for the crime, human nature is inherently sinful, and to the extent that he is innocent, human nature is naturally virtuous.

The play ends with the supreme pathos contingent upon the tragic victim's innocence and consequently upon his innate goodness, though his punishment, which is approved by Thorowgood and assented to in his own exemplary repentance, belongs to an ethic of vice and retributive justice. The final effect of the tragedy, then, is the exemplary moralized pathos specified by Lillo's utilitarian dedication and produced by the careful inconsistencies of the action. Barnwell's perfect bourgeois virtue defines the moral form of the play, and his perfect innocence elicits the emotional response necessary to its universal appeal. The two are simultaneous effects of the drama's particular structure, which requires the tragic death of a sympathetic bourgeois paragon in an action that unreservedly celebrates bourgeois virtue. The eternal reward that Barnwell earns at the end of his brief but affecting career corresponds with the merit that his virtue and innocence denote, and supplies the justice that such paragons are denied on earth. Thus, his Christian manner of dying, like his characterization in general, is morally exemplary. The weaknesses of Lillo's tragedy arise directly from the attempt to create a dramatic action capable of bearing the full didactic and emotional import of moral form. The other bourgeois plays of the period closely resemble *The London Merchant* in their approach to this problem, though they produce much less memorable results.

Lillo's later *Fatal Curiosity* (1736) depicts a particularly horrible version of the innocent victim's tragic end. The story, like Barnwell's, has a "homely" local source,[33] strong bourgeois values, and a pervasive affective intention. The noble, loyal, and generous Young Wilmot, another perfect exemplar of commercial "science," has traveled abroad accumulating wealth "by care and honest commerce" (I.iii.67) in the most laudable manner of merchant morality, and returns home where, with patriotic enthusiasm and proper bourgeois nationalism, he intends to invest his fortune in his native land, restore his destitute parents to financial felicity, and marry his loyal and patient Charlot. The result is grotesque, unadulterated misfortune. Wilmot's long absence has convinced his parents that he is dead, and their demeaning poverty has sunk them into moral degradation. After a reunion with Charlot, Wilmot, succumbing to a "fatal curiosity," visits his parents incognito in order to savor their surprise later when he will announce his identity, reveal their change of fortune, and be joined by his fiancée and friends. Needless to say, during his nap the evil Wilmots, discovering his immense wealth, murder their son in his sleep, and the play ends in a crescendo of horror, distraction, and suicide.

The effect of this short, unsuccessful tragedy is that of *The London Merchant* without its essential inconsistencies. Wilmot's "fatal curiosity" hardly justifies his depressing demise, and his innocence effectually excludes him from the motivation of the action. His parents receive some interesting attention in Lillo's attempt to provide a bourgeois version of Macbeth's murder of Duncan, but the focus of the play is Wilmot's horrible end and not the developing criminal psychologies of his assailants. *Fatal Curiosity* is primarily Wilmot's action, and without the vital inconsistencies of Lillo's earlier tragedy, the play succumbs to meaningless, almost absurdist disaster, as if the central character of *Macbeth* were the innocent, generous Duncan, and the duration of the play its first two acts. In this case the formal exigencies of the moral action force Lillo to exclude any generative relationship between the central character and his unfortunate fate. [34]

Edward Moore's popular drama, *The Gamester* (1753), is a lengthier reworking of the early bourgeois tragedy, *The Fatal Extravagance* (1721), [35] by Aaron Hill. Both plays resemble *The London Merchant* and *Fatal Curiosity* in their attempt to keep their tragic protagonists innocent and virtuous, [36] and both thus provide still further substantiation of the weakness of dramatic moral form. Hill's Bellmour and Moore's Beverley are essentially virtuous, loving husbands who are tricked by Machiavellian villains into gambling away their fortunes and reducing their beloved families to poverty. The depressing consequence in each case is suicide, minutes before a happy revelation and the death of a wealthy relative make such desperate expedients doubly ironic. Bellmour is an explicit paragon, who is lured to destruction by the malicious Bargrave, forced to sign the crucial bond while drunk, and finally ruined by his investment in the South Sea Bubble. His murder of Bargrave and subsequent suicide are thus, like Barnwell's transgressions, as innocent as such acts can be made to appear. Beverley is less explicitly moralized, since the predominant repository of sententious virtue in his longer action is his patient wife. But like Bellmour he owes his ruin to an irresistible villain, in this case Stukely, who has at his disposal a whole regiment of evil agents to assist in the nefarious plot. Moore, however, avoids the challenge of virtuous murder, which Lillo and Hill so eagerly take up, and instead Stukely conspires to murder Beverley's friend and blame the truly innocent Beverley for the deed.

These dramatists both attempt, like Lillo, to find a tragic plot for a moral paragon. Both turn to the irresistible villain for the motivation for their actions, and both plays ignore the character of the static hero, divert the plot from any direct relationship with his merit, and produce a depressing and apparently irrelevant disaster much like the gruesome conclusion of *Fatal Curiosity*. Thus, though he is merely a device to excuse the innocent Beverley, Stukely dominates the stage time with his complicated orders to servants and stooges and his elaborate, endless schemes to ruin the hero. Moore's dramatic energy is engaged primarily by the affecting scenes of Mrs. Beverley's perils and lamentations, and by the grotesquely pathetic final suicide with its conventional, hysterical reiterated repentance, forgiveness, and parting. In general, then, Moore and Hill seek a moral and emotional effect that requires them to sacrifice either the integrity of their plot or the consistency of their characterization to the all-important innocence and virtue of their protagonists. The resultant weakness of their plays is symptomatic of the inherent and apparently insoluble problems of dramatic moral tragedy.

IV

In the course of this period, the tragic moral action becomes increasingly didactic and explicitly bourgeois. Rowe's move from affective to moral drama corresponds immediately to his selection of the suffering, statusless woman—the perfect early bourgeois repository of inner moral worth—as the formal center of his tragedy. Addison's Cato is a protobourgeois protagonist whose formal path to inner worth is smoothed by his republican political allegiances and whose exemplary Stoicism is clearly directly didactic. The fully bourgeois paragon of Hill, Lillo, and Moore is the most direct expression and logical conclusion of the moral action's formal premises. In terms of the evolution of serious drama, he is a kind of institutionalized woman, whose lack of status is, by class definition, a social virtue, and whose sole defining characteristic is his morality. Significantly, however, the formal premises that assume the preeminence of inner worth precede the period's generally recognized and explicitly bourgeois tragedy. Hill and Lillo merely supply local, didactic detail to an established form that is in its most fundamental conception bourgeois. Hence, the significance of their plays, both in themselves and in the context of this dramatic history, transcends a superficial accumulation of middle-class epithets. It resides instead in the prior formal premise, already clearly evident in tragedies like *Jane Shore* and *Cato*, that determines not only those numerous dramatic details but the fate of the genre as well.

The attempt in all these tragedies to present an exemplary and therefore innocent protagonist whose virtue supplies the essential moral apparatus of the form produces a collection of suspiciously similar, recurrent inconsistencies and weaknesses. Collectively, these dramatists propose two related kinds of evasions of the problem that they all confront. Rowe in *Jane Shore*, Lillo in *The London Merchant*, and Hill in *The Fatal Extravagance*, for instance, resort to a simple functional inconsistency—in characterization, chronology, or effect—that permits them to assert the exemplary and sympathetic virtue of their paragons while simultaneously displaying a crucial flaw or cardinal error by which the tragic protagonist brings about her or his own destruction. Lillo in *Fatal Curiosity*, Moore in *The Gamester*, and even Addison in *Cato*, on the other hand, use a kind of formal irrelevance to protect their paragon's virtue, by separating him from the action and by omitting any meaningful relationship between his obvious merit and his tragic fate. This tactic produces, in *Cato*, an elaborate and finally trivial

dramatic trick and, in *Fatal Curiosity* or *The Gamester*, an ineffectual
and unintentional absurdity. Similarly, the injured, innocent heroine of
Charles Johnson's *Caelia* is necessarily static, passive, flat, and thus
effectually excluded from the plot of her own tragedy. In a form that
appears particularly suited, through its attention to inner worth, to
the examination of character, the stereotyped paragons of this drama
are subjected alternatively to inconsistency or irrelevance. And frequently, in either case, these exemplary protagonists are accompanied
and often overshadowed by the shocking, irresistible villain, who serves
as another means of deflecting blame from the hero, except, in the inconsistent action, when such blame is momentarily intended. Thus, in
the venerable tradition of melodrama, we can trace the moral form back
through its villains, from Glanville (Dodsley, *Cleone*, 1758) and Stukely
(*The Gamester*) to Agnes (*Fatal Curiosity*), Wronglove *(Caelia)*, Millwood (*The London Merchant*), Bargrave (*The Fatal Extravagance*),
Bloody Mary (*Lady Jane Gray*), Alicia (*Jane Shore*), Lothario (*The Fair
Penitent*), and ultimately Pierre (*Venice Preserved*), Polydore (*The
Orphan*), and even the "other Cleopatra" (*All for Love*).

The didactic last lines of these plays, which invariably claim a strict
poetic justice out of keeping with the predominant effect of the form,
provide a further example of the concerted attempt by these playwrights to give coherent internal motivation to their tragedies. Addison
incongruously attributes Cato's death to the evils of civil war without
acknowledging his hero's active participation in that war (V.iv.107–12).
Rowe claims that Jane Shore's martyrdom is a strictly just result of
her sexual crimes, even though she is in fact punished for her admirable
patriotic defiance of Gloster's illegal usurpation (V.435–40). Lillo warns
his audience to derive the proper lesson from Barnwell's deserved end:
that we weep in vain at "others' woe, / Unless we mark what drew their
ruin on, / And, by avoiding that, prevent our own" (V.xi.13–15). And,
most disturbingly, the conclusion drawn from Young Wilmot's death in
Fatal Curiosity is a tribute to "Heaven's mysterious ways":

> Though youthful Wilmot's sun be set ere noon,
> The ripe in virtue never die too soon.   [III.i.306–07]

In *Jane Shore* and *The London Merchant*, these claims reflect the
inconsistencies that motivate the actions. According to the brief view
of Jane as Edward's whore, her punishment is just. And according to
the occasional version of Barnwell's action that makes him the victim
of his passions, he can be said to deserve execution. But both characters, of course, are primarily innocent, static, and sympathetic, and in
this sense the final adages contradict the predominant effect of their
exemplary deaths. In the case of the irrelevant protagonists, Cato and
Young Wilmot, the final pronouncements are merely an attempt to

bring them into their actions, as if there were some genuine internal motivation and formal justice for their fates. In short, the claim for poetic justice in this drama represents the assertion of an aesthetic coherence and inevitability that these writers could not realize in the unfolding processes of their plays.

V

The moralized comedy of this period operates under the same premises as the tragedy, and encounters the same impediments. Its exemplary protagonist supplies the serious ethical standard of the form and advocates the values by which he is judged and rewarded. He must be both virtuous and efficacious, and the interaction between his merit and his fate must provide the substance of the plot. The dramatic careers of the major comic playwrights, Steele and Fielding, testify to the recalcitrance of the form. Minor writers, when they venture beyond faintly moralized intrigue to more serious comedy, surrender to rampant, ruinous inconsistency. Simple intrigues like those of Susanna Centlivre, for instance, present the practiced playwright with no problems of consistency or motivation. Two of Centlivre's most popular and best comedies, *The Busie Body* (1709) and *A Bold Stroke for a Wife* (1718), turn upon farcical Spanish outwitting tricks. *The Wonder: A Woman Keeps a Secret* (1714) is another Spanish intrigue of mistaken identities and intentions, multiple closet scenes, and the standard jealous blocking figure of this form.[37] These plays are revealingly straightforward in their characterization and motivation. In *The Gamester* (1705), Centlivre's only significant moral comedy, however, the central, reformable gambler, Valere, seems to alternate between inveterate rakishness and genuine love for Angelica. Centlivre's attempt to make a lively action out of his reformation forces her to confuse and even rescind his conversion, though the moral lesson that it inculcates is the primary intention of the form. These familiar inadequacies, attributable in the minor drama to lack of talent or experience,[38] are duplicated in the plays of the best comic writers of the period.

The recognized master of moral comedy, Richard Steele, begins his career with a pair of confused and inconsistent plays and ends it with a rigorously homogeneous, spectacularly successful one. *The Funeral* (1701) and *The Lying Lover* (1703), Steele's first two works, are both inconsistently moralized comedies in the manner of the contemporary mixed transitional drama of Cibber and Farquhar. In *The Tender Husband* (1705), however, Steele temporarily abandons his campaign to introduce serious moral content into comedy and writes a lively, influential intrigue without strong sentimental assumptions.[39] The development in his abilities from those early, inconsistent plays to his last,

uniformly moral comedy, *The Conscious Lovers* (1722), reveals, first, the
recurrent problem that he was forced to confront and second, the related
weakness of his solution. In this sense Steele's corpus provides perhaps the
clearest example of the maturation of moral form in comedy and, simultaneously, the best documentation of its inherent inadequacies.

The Funeral begins as an apparent social satire with all the "unnatural" vigor that Steele can muster, including the mock-death of Lord
Brumpton, the hypocritical and lascivious activities of his joyful new
widow, and the grotesque funeral preparations of the self-interested
undertaker, Sable. The undertaker's observations upon death and
mourning constitute a satiric indictment of hypocrisy, avarice, gossip,
slander, vanity, and sexual license. But these characteristic criticisms,
and Sable himself, immediately disappear from the play. The happy
widow, who is made to seem from these initial discussions of female
hypocrisy the central character of a satiric plot, becomes the melodra-
matic blocking figure for a sentimental moral action in which Lord
Brumpton's son, Hardy, is tearfully reunited with his estranged father
and wins the virtuous Sharlot.

Symptomatically, the moral attributes and consequent sentimental
potential of the characters are withheld from the first few scenes of
the play. We learn only in Act II of Hardy's perfect virtue, his generosity, his loyalty, his filial duty, and his true love. After his entrance,
however, the moral implications of the action increase, and the exemplary hero comes to dictate the nature of our expectations and the
shape of the plot. Hardy's role makes *The Funeral* a moral action, and
the body of the play emphasizes exemplary character, tearful inter-
ludes, filial loyalty, generous forgiveness, and rewarded virtue. But all
of these aspects of its moral form, and the relationships and events
that produce them, arise from a decidedly farcical and amoral situation
in which Hardy steals his father's coffin as it is brought to burial and
Sharlot leaps out of it into the arms of her surprised lover, who greets
her in the "Exalted Rapture" of lyrical blank verse.[40] In its juxtaposition of grotesque irony and sentimental effect, this scene captures the
formal ambivalence of the whole drama. Steele deliberately initiates
and sustains his plot with the ultimately irrelevant and potentially discordant evocation of an amoral comic tradition. The very obvious inconsistency in the tone of this play[41] is the immediate consequence of
Steele's recourse to social comedy and satiric farce in motivating a
moral drama, and the ridiculous funeral with its energetic apparatus
provides a lively plot for a set of generous, dutiful, chaste, and tender
characters who are, by definition, excluded from the initiation of any
action of their own. This kind of reliance upon an incongruous farcical episode or subplot is typical of many of the sententious moral
actions of the age and indicative of their common formal requirements.

Lillo's *Silvia* (1730) or *The Country Lasses* (1715), by Charles Johnson, for instance, both *Pamela*-like comedies, incongruously mix the vicissitudes of the female paragon with lively antics equivalent in ridiculousness to those of *The Funeral.*

In its explicit advocacy of serious content in comedy, *The Lying Lover* provides an even clearer example of Steele's difficulty in motivating a moral form. The preface indicates the play's formal proximity to the moral tragedy of the period, and Steele's self-conscious rejection of generic distinctions resembles, from the other side of the fence, the didactic assertions of Hill, Lillo, Fielding, and others. He hopes with mock modesty that the play "might be no improper Entertainment in a Christian Commonwealth" (p. 115, ll. 8-9), and justifies the moving evocation of its rash protagonist's repentance in jail after a drunken duel with a friend as "perhaps, an Injury to the Rules of Comedy" but "a Justice to those of Morality" (p. 115, ll. 23-25). The familiar tender emotion that Steele sets out to arouse is named and defended in the epilogue:

> Our too advent'rous Author soar'd to Night
> Above the little Praise, Mirth to excite,
> And chose with Pity to chastise Delight. [p. 189, ll. 1-3]

But, significantly, *The Lying Lover* does not begin with visible serious intentions, virtuous characters, moral standards, or even sentimental potential. Its first four acts proceed as an intrigue in which the protagonist, Bookwit, competes with his friend Lovemore for a beautiful unknown woman. The conflict is complicated by mistaken identity, comic cross-purposes, and other elaborate misunderstandings essential to the plot. Bookwit shows no symptoms of "true love," and in a resolution typical of intrigue form, is finally matched with a different lady from the one whom he has pursued throughout the play. In the early acts, he and his ally Latine are nowhere subject to moral assessment, and in fact such judgment is implicitly denied by the wholly amoral relationships among the characters. Suddenly, in the middle of Act IV, Bookwit duels with Lovemore and apparently runs him through. This misfortune, however, does not alter the tone of the play, or Bookwit's characterization, until the beginning of Act V. Two comic scenes intervene, one with the over-zealous constables who eventually arrest Bookwit, the other in Newgate, where Bookwit is robbed by the knowing prisoners.[42] Thus, the transformation of the action that occurs at the opening of Act V is arbitrary not only in its juxtaposition with the earlier intrigue effects, but also in the intervening delay between its presumable cause and its manifestation. Bookwit wakes up sober, realizes what he has done, and in lofty language pronounces a moral indictment of dueling (V.i.81-90). An entirely different set of formal assumptions supplants the intrigue interests of the first four acts. The reigning effects of these final scenes include weeping, swooning, benevolent filial and paternal sentiment, moral instruction, and selfless last-minute heroics. In short, Bookwit and Latine are metamorphosed into exemplary heroes whose virtues become the primary dynamic force of the drama.

Presumably, Bookwit reforms because of his apparent murder of his friend. Latine has no such excuse, nor do the other characters who engage in these final effusions. In fact, the emotions and values produced by this sentimental scene bear no relationship to the earlier intrigue action of the play. The expectations aroused by the first four acts are quickly dispensed with in the final neat pairing of the lovers appended, almost as an afterthought, to the predominant pity of the conclusion. In effect, Steele simply changes forms in midstream, and attempts to justify the exchange under the guise of reformation.[43] Again, he finds a means entirely outside the moral intentions of the form by which to motivate his plot, and this time he sustains the entertaining machinations of the necessary formal substitute for four full acts. In general, the reformed protagonists in the comedy of this period, like Bookwit or Cibber's earlier Loveless, are not the products of a continuous exploration of character that makes their change internally probable, but the victims of arbitrary formal shift. These playwrights use reformation as a device to construct an engaging moral action, rather than as a means to the examination of character. This accounts, first, for the pervasive absence of character complexity in the moral forms of the period, and second, for the seamlessness of the evolution from mixed to moral comedy. In effect, the flat characterization attendant upon the opportunistic formal mixture of the transitional plays merges with the inherent motivational inconsistency of the comic moral action, and the propensity for stereotyping is translated from the earlier drama to the later. In *The Lying Lover*, that inconsistency is caused by the amoral intrigue material that stands in for the plot motivation that the moral action could not supply.

In *The Conscious Lovers* Steele eliminates the telltale inconsistencies that were his first resort in *The Funeral* and *The Lying Lover*. The play is the final, mature expression of his reformist efforts in the drama;[44] it embodies his famous affective misinterpretation of Terence in its moralistic and sentimental revision of *Andria*;[45] and it is religiously homogeneous in tone, characterization, and action. Like its tragic counterpart, *The London Merchant, The Conscious Lovers* is one of the period's preeminent expressions of bourgeois ideology,[46] primarily in the character of the noble merchant Sealand, who defends his wealth as a sign of his virtue and expounds upon the worth and, implicitly, the marriageability, of the bourgeoisie: "We Merchants are a Species of Gentry, that have grown into the World this last Century, and are as honourable, and almost as useful, as you landed Folks, that have always thought

your selves so much above us" (IV.ii.50–53). As in Lillo's later play,
those values are epitomized in the character of the admirable protagonist. Bevil Junior is law-abiding, economical, obedient, chaste, generous,
modest, unaffected in his dress, opposed to property marriage, and,
most important, hostile to dueling.[47] His exemplary virtue is the cause
of the dilemma that produces his action. His filial duty to "the best of
Fathers" (I.ii.147 and passim) collides with his chaste, true love for
Indiana, "a Woman of Honour and Virtue" (I.ii.134–35). His respect
for his father prevents him from marrying without permission and
seems to require that he wed the wealthy merchant's daughter, Lucinda.
His own generous true love, however, dictates loyalty to Indiana,
though his rigorous sexual propriety has forbidden him from declaring
his honorable purposes to her and even from visiting her in the absence
of her chaperone.

Implicit in our paragon's conflict is the issue of property marriage,
a custom contrary to the bourgeois values that inform the whole action
of the play. Steele's reliance upon inner worth, particularly manifested
in a celebration of true love, issues specifically in a rejection of mercenary marital arrangements. Bevil Junior, happily possessed of an adequate fortune of his own, proves his virtue in his determination to
marry the penniless, orphaned Indiana. Appropriately, Sealand voices
Steele's approbation of these views: "How laudable is Love, when
born of Virtue!" (V.iii.208). Sir John Bevil, on the other hand, would
marry his son to increase the estate, and Steele represents his attitude
—the cause of the play's central conflict—as unambiguously avaricious
(IV.ii.115–62). Steele's formally central distaste for property marriage pervades the play, and surfaces continually in the minutiae of the
representation. Lucinda's comical encounters with the mercenary Cim-
berton, for instance, display with admirable satiric vigor the consequences
of the reduction of a woman to a piece of purchasable horseflesh (III.
252–96).

Sir John is in effect the blocking figure of Bevil Junior's action and
the repository of a rival and reprehensible mercenary attitude toward
marital relationships. Some of the sting of his position is removed by
the description of his own youthful love match, however, and Steele
attempts to conceal his culpability while maintaining the substance of
his son's dilemma. In fact, despite his reprehensible views, Sir John
must remain without debate "the best of Fathers," since the conflict
between Bevil Junior's loyalties depends upon the presumably equal
virtue and desert of the two "best of" rivals for his allegiance. And,
most important, Bevil Junior's own exemplary character is demonstrated in the process of the action by his impeccably virtuous behavior
toward both. For this reason, the presumably perfect Sir John cannot
be shown to "reform," and the action predicated on Bevil Junior's

virtue begins in unbreakable stalemate. The plot generated from this dilemma is calculated primarily to display Bevil Junior's merits. Consequently, scenes of compliance with his father alternate with scenes of generosity toward Indiana or his friend Myrtle. Central to these, of course, is the issue of the duel, which allows the hero to exhibit his rational self-control and to produce the moral conversion of his friend, who confesses himself "beholden to that Superior Spirit you have subdu'd me with" (IV.i.203–04).

All of this material gives Bevil Junior an action that is an immediate consequence of the specific virtues of his character. It is governed by the values he represents, it proceeds to exercise his merit in terms of those values, and it populates a dramatic world with characters whose morality complements his own. But it cannot reach a resolution that derives from these moral premises. In fact the conclusion of *The Conscious Lovers* bears no relation to Bevil Junior's character or to the issues that arise from his dilemma. We are induced to expect a vindication of Bevil Junior's choice of true love and consequently of the virtue that determines his characterization as well as the process of his whole action. But since both he and Sir John are defined as perfect, the latter at the service of the former's merit, no resolution can be struck between them. Instead, in a scene from romance that generates the requisite tears of sentimental reunion, Sealand discovers that Indiana is his long-lost daughter and thus the heiress to half his wealth. She consequently becomes not only a suitable, propertied mate, but virtually the identical merchant's daughter for whom Sir John had originally contracted. The contradiction between true love and filial duty at last simply vanishes, leaving merely an assertion of the inevitable reward of virtue (V.iii.285–89).

Steele provides Bevil Junior with a genuine moral action, then, but not with a moral fate that evolves from the internal logic of that action. The serious issue of property marriage disappears along with Bevil Junior's dilemma, though throughout the plot it is presented as a primary tenet of the play's moral hierarchy. Sir John's apparent avarice is rewarded along with his son's virtue. To the extent that it contradicts the standards upon which Steele's moral action is founded, this conclusion violates the premises of the comedy. But Steele is apparently unable to supply a resolution that derives directly from the moral virtues of his paragon. Without the aid of the romantic device that brings it to a fortunate finish when no internal end is in sight, Bevil Junior's perfection renders him impotent and his plot static. Steele's best moral effort, then, while it does not resort to the functional inconsistency that characterizes his first two plays, reveals, in the ultimate formal irrelevance of the exemplary virtue of its protagonist, a confrontation with the same fundamental problem.

In the course of his career, Steele changes his dramatic tactics toward a more coherent, less internally discordant comic action. Initially, in *The Funeral* and *The Lying Lover*, he resorts to simple, openly visible inconsistency. Ultimately, in *The Conscious Lovers*, he chooses to separate his paragon's merit from his fate, and to make that moral virtue irrelevant to the outcome of the plot. In this respect, his movement from inconsistency to irrelevance parallels the evolution of Lillo's tragic career from *The London Merchant* to *Fatal Curiosity*, though in Lillo's case the earlier, inconsistent play is the more successful one. Irrelevance in comedy is perhaps inevitably more viable and less disturbing than in tragedy, since notions of responsibility are more significant in a drama that concludes with destruction. In a very general sense the irrelevant action can be seen as a maturer manifestation of dramatic moral form, since it deals in a less superficial, less evident, and perhaps less simplistic evasion—an evasion that appears at times to emanate from the internal contradictions of bourgeois ideology itself. Inconsistent plays, in both comedy and tragedy, are comparatively more frequent in the early years of this period, and more common among the minor writers throughout. For the major comic dramatist of the time, inconsistency and irrelevance serve the same purpose as they do in the contemporary tragedy. The pervasiveness and fundamental similarity of the attempted solutions, from comedy to tragedy and from play to play, suggest the magnitude and universality of the problem presented by their common form.

VI

Henry Fielding produces seven original full-length comedies, all of which exhibit the same symptomatic inconsistencies and irrelevancies that weaken the other major drama of the eighteenth century. He resorts repeatedly to a random diffuseness in characterization and plot, designed to conceal, with simple stage activity, the absence of a coherent comic motivation. Most important, though these problems are virtually ubiquitous in his standard comedy, they are not repeated in his farces, his unconventional dramatic forms, or his novels. The particular difficulties in Fielding's full-length plays appear to be specific to their genre, and even his best comedy, *The Modern Husband* (1732), which gives him the plot of *Amelia*, does not entirely escape these inherent defects.

Fielding's standard drama constitutes a collection of more or less moral actions in various states of necessary disarray. Their explicit sententiousness diminishes as the reliance upon local satire or humors characterization increases, so that the most satiric comedies, *Rape upon Rape* (1730) and *The Universal Gallant* (1735), display the least interest in true love, inherent benevolence, and exemplary virtue. Even these

plays, however, are predicated upon directly evident, internal moral
assumptions. Thus the corrupt magistrate of *Rape upon Rape*, Justice
Squeezum, who is the butt of the play's central satire, is eloquently
denounced by the contrasting, just, incorruptible, and benevolent Justice Worthy, who provides general educative commentary upon English society and ultimately pronounces the proper, inevitable sentence
on the evil Squeezum. Similarly, in *The Universal Gallant*, though the
focus is on the consequence of the ridiculous marital humors of a pair
of brothers, one overly jealous, the other overly lenient with his wife,
the injured and virtuous wife of the first voices, at least for a time, the
underlying ethic of female chastity. The rest of Fielding's full-length
comedies are much more obviously, conventionally moral, with sensible, worthy country lovers, chaste or exemplary women, true and
virtuous passion, instantaneous moral conversion, benevolent parents,
and generous, grateful children. These effects are sustained, in the
context of diverse and often farcical plots, by arbitrary final reforma-
tions, inconsistent characterization, irrelevant intrigues, and incongruous, providential conclusions.

Fielding's first play, *Love in Several Masques* (1728), while it illustrates the marked superiority of his style, demonstrates also the typical
consequences of the dramatic attempt to manufacture a comic action
with a moral component. Though the central values of the play reside
in a single virtuous couple from the country who are genuinely in love,
Fielding surrounds them with a flurry of alternate activity that conceals the stasis of their relationship. The play is artificially motivated by
a sequence of plots, disguises, and double crosses, promoting a series of
lively exchanges for the collection of characters who sustain the action.
Some of these intrigues, for instance, are created out of thin air by the
convenient servant Catchit, whose lies to her mistress's lover instigate a
conflict without substance for one of the subsidiary couples, which is
subsequently resolved as easily and instantaneously as it was conjured
up. By juggling the lovers and throwing in an irrelevant test, an unnecessary and ultimately inexplicable disguise, and a third marriageable pair
from intrigue convention, Fielding transforms a moral action with a
central, sensible country couple whose relationship can only provide
sententious criticism of amoral London manners, into a diverse, lively,
lengthy, unmotivated, and intriguelike comedy.

The Temple Beau (1730), Fielding's second comedy, represents a
less extreme version of the formal tactic of his first. Fielding seeks again
to subordinate, as much as possible, the morally central country couple
to a diverse collection of subsidiary characters. But here he allows somewhat greater prominence, and some explicit sententiae and tears, to
his virtuous pair, and he adds to the simple diffuseness of his first play
an arbitrary moral conversion and an accidental conclusion. The virtu-

ous, sensible, antilibertine male paragon reforms his rakish friend, Valentine, who has conceived a passion for our paragon's chaste beloved, in a sentimental and pervasively sententious scene where a simple citation of morality, honor, friendship, and love causes the young cynic to renounce his former ways. Comic convention has made this conversion acceptable, if not believable, but Fielding adds inconsistency to inconsistency by allowing his arbitrarily and, to all appearances, permanently reformed rake to suffer an arbitrary relapse for the purpose of the plot, and then to be re-reformed for the conclusion. The slender action, which is further bolstered by a collection of strictly irrelevant and occasionally contradictory incidents, is concluded by the accidental and again arbitrary discovery of a defrauded fortune, which, like the magic parentage of *The Conscious Lovers*, permits the virtuous couple to marry peacefully.[48]

Rape upon Rape (1730) achieves its energy from a strong local satire, which promotes a genuine action, since the corrupt Justice Squeezum effectually separates and threatens the comic lovers of the play. Significantly, however, the comedy ends in arbitrary morality, offered as an alternative to and commentary upon the corrupt social scenes that make up the substance of the action. The careless rake is suddenly transformed into a virtuous, sentimental true lover, to match the merits of his restored wife, the sister of the benevolent justice whose moral pronouncements give the drama its form. The same kind of arbitrary reformation becomes the central tenet of *The Wedding-Day* (1743),[49] in which the rakish protagonist, Millamour, undergoes a conversion and reconversion parallel to that of Valentine in *The Temple Beau*. In a similar manner, his mistress, who appears throughout to be a coy whore, is transformed into a virtuous, self-denying paragon, and even more arbitrarily, her aged husband of a few hours is discovered by great good fortune to be her father, thus permitting the reformed Millamour to take her as his wife.

The Universal Gallant (1735) juggles overt didacticism and satiric humors characterization in a manner similar to that of *Rape upon Rape*, and with similarly incoherent consequences. Again, the satire dominates the body of the action at the expense of the subsidiary exemplary couple, who marry at the end. But most important, Fielding's desultory attempt to moralize the comedy creates a continual confusion typical of the form. The wives of the humors husbands are used as an explicit, internal source of moral value, and consequently their occasional laudable virtue conflicts with their otherwise active roles in the diffuse plot. Lady Raffler, for instance, the wife of the ridiculously jealous Sir Simon, alternates without warning between virtuous injury and hypocritical prudery, and we are never provided with a means of reconciling or even comprehending these two aspects of her representation. Fielding's inconsistent exploitation of character for moral profit effectively sabotages the evaluative premises and thus ultimately the consistency and comprehensibility of the play.

Fielding's last, late comedy, *The Fathers* (1778, posthumously), suffers from a similar, injurious formal confusion. In fact, the comparative failure of the play—composed in the 1740s during Fielding's novelistic period[50]—shows that the pervasive weakness of his standard comedy does not result primarily from inexperience or immaturity.[51] It is his least diffuse and most fully moralized, openly didactic drama, celebrating benevolence, generosity, filial duty, and true love. But typically, the depiction of the good characters is so weak that it confers no sense of the probability of the conclusion and thus no anticipation of the plot's direction. The young Boncours, who are revealed in the end to be generous, dutiful, perfect children, are at first, for the purposes of a viable action, undifferentiated from the evil young Valences, whose hypocritical self-interest surfaces in a final schematic moral contrast. Fielding's flat characterization of the good children provides him no means of suggesting the presence of inner worth and at the same time maintaining the apparent plot conflict that arises from their initial alliance with the evil Valences. He can only make them superficially ungrateful and frivolous at one point, then superficially generous and moral at another; he can serve either plot or consistent characterization, but not both.

Thus, Fielding's standard comedy evolves from the simple diversity of his first play to the increasingly single-plotted and increasingly inconsistent or irrelevant actions of his later drama. In every play, however, plot and characterization are confused or undermined by the imposition of moral values, which defy the dramatist to construct an engaging and coherent action.[52] The instantaneous transformations of character permit a moral form to sustain itself by means of an intrigue plot. The irrelevantly fortunate conclusions serve to bring a static moral action to an end by ignoring the internal standards upon which it is founded and by imposing upon a realistic form the arbitrary outcome of intrigue or romance. These lively plays are weakened by diffuseness, inconsistency, irrelevance, and in general by a consequent diminution of formal probability and thus of comic expectation. We are constantly forced, up to the last act, to revise our understanding of the characters and our anticipation of their fates, though the form posits a consistent moral standard that is immediate, intuitively valid, and universal.

From the perspective of formal coherence, *The Modern Husband* (1732) is the best of Fielding's comedies, and it escapes many of the characteristic repeated weaknesses of its contemporaries in his canon. In effect, Fielding brings meaningful order to the diffuseness typical of his comic form. Its prologue claims an unprecedented loftiness of intention, which distinguishes it from the "Frolick Flights of Youth" and declares its attempt to "restore the sinking Honour of the Stage!"[53] The seriousness asserted here apparently differs from the moral assumptions and benevolent sentiments that are combined with light entertainment in the earlier comedies. And Fielding appears, for the time at least, to find his previous works, specifically the burlesque *Tom Thumb* (1730), excessively frivolous.

This play, in its repudiation of farce and its explicit recourse "to Nature, and to Truth" (prologue), finds its serious subject in the examination of "modern" vice and the depravities of contemporary society. Its range of subject matter and concerns greatly exceeds that of any of Fielding's previous or subsequent comedies. Most important, the particular seriousness of the play's depiction of modern society reduces the centrality of the moral paragon, Mrs. Bellamant, though not the significance of her virtue. Fielding's emphasis is upon the harshness of the social world and the pervasiveness of modern vice, and not the comic love relationships that dominate most of his other plays.[54] In addition, Mrs. Bellamant is not depicted as the marriageable young virgin of conventional comedy, but as an injured and endangered wife, the innocent victim of the evils of modern society. By this means, Fielding incorporates her special moral position into the play's examination of vice, but without permitting her passive virtue to dominate and damage the action. The morality of the form is directly evident in her character, then, but the vital source of the plot resides in the depraved realities of the world.

Mrs. Bellamant's force is exerted, in her absence, by the moral errors of her unfaithful husband, whose deplorable concession to Mrs. Modern's sexual and financial appetite arouses explicit allusions to the trusting virtue of his injured wife (II.i, p. 22, and III.xii, p. 48). Mr. Bellamant's capitulation to vice thus provides his portion of the play with a plot, while maintaining the moral values that define his reprehensibility. Accordingly, Mrs. Modern's seduction of the erring hero, and Mr. Modern's subsequent attempt to expose them and bring suit for adultery, supply the primary motivation for the action. By restricting Mrs. Bellaamant's role, by permitting her flawed spouse a genuine moral transgression, and more important, by subordinating both of them to the pervasive and depraved machinations of the Moderns and Lord Richly, Fielding creates his most consistent, most effective, and best dramatic moral action. The social range of the play, which attempts to implicate the general evil of genteel society, enables Fielding to sustain a coherent moral plot by deflecting the essential motivation from the source of virtue to that of vice.

But though *The Modern Husband* contains none of the disturbing inconsistencies that mark Fielding's other standard comedies, the play's unique solution to the problem of the moral action is at best incomplete. The evocation and generalization of modern vice force Fielding to complicate the plot and multiply the characters and their schemes to the limit of viable dramatic representation, and perhaps beyond. Even this conscious and perilous attempt to generalize the evil motivation of the action, however, is ultimately unsatisfying, since modern society must finally be represented by only an unscrupulous lord and a fashionable London couple. Fielding's attempt at social inclusiveness in *The Modern Husband* does not rival the parallel effort in *Tom Jones* or even *Amelia*. Perhaps more immediately pertinent is the instantaneous conversion that Mr. Bellamant undergoes upon his exposure with Mrs. Modern. The arbitrary suddenness of this reformation is better prepared for in *The Modern Husband* than in any of Fielding's other comedies, but even here its startling speed signals the inherent difficulty of making the passively virtuous heroine efficacious in a realistic, moral form.

The conclusion that follows Mr. Bellamant's reformation is similarly problematic, not because of the routine fortuitous dispensation of poetic justice to the good characters, since Fielding, unlike Steele, does not insist upon the providential inevitability of their happy fates, but because of the arbitrary elimination of the bad, as if the hypocrisy and depravity of modern society could be dispelled by a simple public confession. In general, then, the strength of *The Modern Husband* is in its evocation of a larger world that provides not only the motivation for the action, but also a broader backdrop which makes the morality of that action less simplistically sanguine than it appears in its typical dramatic manifestation. The play's weaknesses arise from its inability to complete or to sustain the depiction of that world, and from its consequent occasional turn to the inconsistent and irrelevant commonplaces of dramatic moral form. Significantly, the source of this play's unprecedented integrity is the same as the fundamental formal recourse of Fielding's novelistic moral actions: an attempted representation of social scope.

Fielding's characteristic full-length comedies, from *Love in Several Masques* to *The Fathers*, differ in formal unity not only from *The Modern Husband* but also from his numerous farces. Those short forms rely upon the same moral assumptions, the same reigning benevolence, and the same virtuous true love as the longer comedies, but their brevity protects them from the problems of motivation and characterization that plague the standard drama. For example, *The Intriguing Chambermaid* (1734) tells the brief, sentimental story of a profligate son whose angry father is reconciled to him when his generous and true love offers him her hand and tiny portion even though he has been disinherited. The slight plot serves only to prepare for that benevolent act and its consequences by introducing the lovers, their predicament, and the father's entrance upon the scene. It requires no development and only the most rapid distinction of character. The same is true of *An Old Man Taught Wisdom* (1735). *Don Quixote in England* (1734) also follows this pattern, but provides an example of the potential subtlety of the form. Don Quixote's madness is transformed in the process of the farce into a special kind of sanity, which is contrasted with the behavior of the "normal" British country characters and which ultimately represents the triumph of genuine human feeling and sensibility. Don Quixote is not himself romanticized, and remains essentially a figure of fun—smashing the inn, frightening off the coachman, and falling on his knees to the maid—but becomes concurrently a respected hero of sensibility whose madness has a value of its own. The delicate and effective balance of sentiment and satire in this play suggests that, for Fielding, farce was not simply a trivial last resort, but rather a genuine alternative.

Since this shorter form effectually eliminates motive and since its depiction of character is necessarily minimal, it is a natural recourse when those particular constituents of the dramatic moral action become insolubly problematic. David Garrick's successful farces fit this formal category. The slight action of *The Lying Valet* (1741), for example, sustains its moralization with no injury to the energy of its plot or the consistency of its characterization. Fielding's and Garrick's achievements in this mode are not, of course, without precedent. The popularity of Edward Ravenscroft's plays attests to the presence of the farce tradition in the first decades of the Restoration and to the early influence of French farce and of the commedia dell'arte. But as the century continues farce becomes increasingly frequent and significant in relation to the standard drama of the age,[55] partly because it represents a comparatively constant and completely unproblematic locus of dramatic vitality and energy. In this respect, the prominence of farce in the eighteenth century is itself a sign of the inherent inadequacies of the standard drama, not, as Nicoll claims, because farce is necessarily an illegitimate or degenerate mode,[56] but rather because in its very nature it evades the central representational problems posed by bourgeois realism. Fielding's resort to rehearsal satire, burlesque, and other unconventional dramatic forms seems to reflect a parallel discontent with the capacities of standard comedy. Not surprisingly, then, his farces, farcical operas, and burlesques outnumber his full-length comedies, and also exceed them in popularity and perhaps even in merit.[57] Significantly, all the experimentation and, except for *The Modern Husband*, all the memorable accomplishments of Fielding's dramatic career occur outside the domain of established drama.

The comparative superiority of Fielding's farce and burlesque, on the

one hand, and the unquestionable preeminence of his novelistic moral
actions, on the other, suggest that the weakness of his moral comedy
is more than accidental. Its striking inferiority is not simply a product
of the physical capacities of the drama, since dramatic farce surpasses
it in consistency and formal integrity. Its defects are certainly not
solely the inevitable consequences of its moral assumptions or the ethical prescriptiveness of bourgeois ideology, since Fielding's novels
expound with even greater rigor a virtually identical doctrine. The
problems of dramatic moral form are inherent in the capacities of
the standard comedy to embody the shape that Fielding and the other
dramatists of his time and place sought to give to their understanding
of reality. The genre is specifically excluded, as farce and novel are not,
from the means necessary to the successful representation of moral
form. Its liability is the self-conscious continuity of dramatic evolution,
which limits the conventional resources of the genre at that very point
in its history when the advent of a radically distinct set of formal and
ideological assumptions imposes extraordinary pressures upon literary
composition. Fielding's novels are free to respond to these pressures
in a manner that is forbidden to the standard drama.

VII

The decline of the drama, then, is attributable to the particular nature
of its formal history, or, more precisely, to the crucial interaction
between the continuity of its evolution and the radical divergence in
ideological and formal assumptions from the beginning of that evolution to the end. In the serious drama, the development from an aristocratic to a bourgeois form entails a fundamental change in evaluative
assumptions that is reflected in every detail of the play's representation, in the tenor of its whole fictional world, and in the essential terms
of its comprehensibility. But affective tragedy serves, in effect, to
bridge the gap between these intrinsically irreconcilable forms. It emerges
directly from the fragmentation of the aristocratic hierarchies of the
heroic action, and it comes to repudiate the most essential premises of
that drama not by breaking with the straightforward judgmental assertions of social form, but by allowing them to lapse into an evaluative
vacuum. The affecting innocence of its central character is subsequently
translated, with equal seamlessness, into the perfect virtue of the moral
paragon. And concurrently, the sympathetic identification between the
pitying audience and the beset protagonist, whose own "soft pity to
th'oppressed" provides the affective model of the form, becomes the
universal evaluative approbation of bourgeois realism. Throughout this
evolution, then, though the fundamental formal and ideological premises
of the plays are radically transformed, the conventions of dramatic

representation are passed unchallenged from hand to hand. The limited scope and flat characterization integral to the artificiality of the heroic action find a new justification in the requirements of pathetic effect. And the essential domesticity and intrinsic inattention to character of that later form are conveyed, with all their inconsistencies intact, into the moral action.

The strong resemblance between affective and moral drama thus extends even to the duplication of characteristic defects. Though their materials and purposes differ, the flatness of the innocent and virtuous stereotypes in these two forms produces an essentially similar functional inconsistency. For the dramatists of the eighteenth century, however, that inconsistency is not the simple unintended consequence of an action that treats character as entirely subordinate to effect, but a fundamental, necessary defect in a form that regards the moralized paragon as the primary vehicle of comprehensibility. Barnwell embodies the meaningful standards of his action, but Jaffeir is only a means to Otway's pathos. For this reason, Otway's resort to inconsistency is practically invisible, while Lillo's adoption of the same functional trick appears as a blatant defect. Schematically, the increasing obtrusiveness of the device illustrates the increasing weakness and inadequacy of stereotyped characterization in the new form.

The disjunctive premise of Restoration dramatic satire, like the remote, baroque mode of the heroic action, is diametrically opposed to the immediacy, the sympathy, and the unimpeded evaluative identification of bourgeois realism. From the largest perspective, then, the movement from social to moral comedy is identical to the change that takes place in the serious drama, and in this sense the histories of comedy and tragedy in the period are formally analogous. The transitional comedy, like the affective tragedy, connects the social and moral extremes of this evolution, but by mixture rather than by mediation, because questions of status are traditionally less significant in a "low" form. The change in comedy is inevitably less pacific than that in the serious drama, and therefore the experimentation of playwrights like Vanbrugh and Congreve, whose innovations arise directly from the tensions of this transition, is unduplicated in the serious form. But the mixed drama, in its own incoherent manner, ultimately welds social to moral with equal firmness. Like the tragic moral action, the comic adopts the dramatic conventions of its predecessor; the social stereotypes and restricted scope essential to Restoration dramatic satire become, by way of the confused or opportunistic premises of mixed drama, the moral stereotypes and narrow material of the later comedy.

Flat characterization, as it appears in mixed comedy, is simply the necessary attribute of an incoherent form and is thus invariably accompanied by an inconsistent representation. As the moral member of the mixture emerges to dominate and eventually usurp the form, the opportunistic incoherence of the mixed drama and the functional inconsistency of the new moral drama merge. For this reason, it becomes difficult, except with the aid of external criteria, to distinguish the mixed plays of Farquhar or middle Cibber from the early inconsistent moral plays of Steele; inconsistency serves as a means of plot motivation for transitional and moral alike. Stereotyped characters and their accompanying inconsistency are passed along together from the mixed to the moral form, but in the first the phenomenon is an essential concomitant to formal incoherence, while in the second stereotyping is a fatal liability that itself necessitates the formal evasions of inconsistency or irrelevance. For example, the instant reformation of Cibber's Loveless is understandable and necessary, if not admirable, as the consequence of a divided formal intention. The same reformation in Steele's early comedy, *The Lying Lover* (or in Centlivre's or Fielding's plays) represents the last desperate attempt of an endangered form to wring a lively plot out of a flat moral protagonist. Both Cibber and Steele can be said to use the device to gain plot interest, but in Steele's case it is occasioned by a crucial conventional constraint that injures the form, rather than by an inherent formal necessity.

The close continuity of this evolution has grave consequences for the radically new dramatic forms of the eighteenth century, both tragic and comic. The inconsistency and irrelevance that damage this drama are the direct result of its attempt to embody a new form in the conventions of an old. The constraints of characterization and scope inherent in dramatic convention preclude those very innovations that produce the successful novelistic moral actions of Richardson and Fielding. In novel or drama, the moral action presents significant difficulties of motivation. The exemplary protagonist of this problematic form is static by definition, and thus an impediment to the construction of an energetic plot. Because the dramatists are denied an intense exploration of inner character, they are forced to rely upon simple plot activity for their representation of moral values. This results almost inevitably in the prevalent inconsistency and irrelevance that signal the genre's inability to make a flat moral paragon the center of a lively, external action. Even the most mechanical means for the dramatic representation of character complexity is denied to the genre; the contemporary criticism of Congreve's use of soliloquy illustrates the irrevocable distance between Restoration and Renaissance forms.

Because these dramatists are similarly unequipped to represent a broad range of social experience, they are committed to a narrow segment of society and ultimately to the exemplary character of the paragon himself for the motivation, conclusion, and meaning of their action. They are prevented from giving their realistic form a context in which moral virtue could be endangered by its inevitable, ordinary interaction with society, and in which the sanguine conclusions that reduce the dramatic moral action's sensitivity to serious human problems could be placed in the perspective of a larger and less simplistic reality. Dramatic moral form is again forced to make its whole action and interest out of the simple and unassailable virtue of the solitary and self-enclosed paragon.

Inevitably, then, the dramatic moral action can embody only the most trivial and simplistic versions of the ideology that it attempts to express. The inherent limitations upon the drama's representative capacity in this period in turn limit the plays' potential sophistication or subtlety. Steele, for instance, for all of his proselytizing intentions, can say in his drama no more than what the genre permits him to say, and thus, to this extent, his defective and intractable form dictates the triviality, opportunism, and irresponsibility of his meaning, much as Lillo's insoluble formal problems allow him nothing more than metaphysical fence-sitting. The self-congratulatory, irrelevant conclusion of *The Conscious Lovers* and the falsified providential claims of the tragedy reveal, then, not that those writers were morally trivial, simplistic, and opportunistic individuals—though perhaps they were—but that their genre permitted them nothing better.

The conclusion of this generic evolution suggests, from a more general perspective, the nature of the crucial relationship between large forces of formal change and the specific operations of convention in literary history. Formal change, as we have seen, is the aesthetic corollary of ideological change, representing the inevitable and continual alteration of the shape that men and women give to their understanding of reality in the course of history. The plays of the eighteenth century are products of their historical time in respect to the shapes of the stories that they attempt to tell. But they are also products of their own generic past, which dictates the specific ways in which those stories can be told. Literary convention, at least in this case, determines the inherent capacities of a genre to embody its form, though it does not determine the form itself, which is the consequence of those larger conditions of the artist's relationship to the forces of his time and place. History tells these writers what they *must* do, and convention tells them what they *can* do, by dictating the means that they can use. The power of convention is inexorable, but subordinate—it determines only the specific realization of aesthetic form. The role of history, however, is fundamental, necessary, and dominant, but insufficient in itself to explain the course of generic evolution.

The failure of the drama is thus not primarily the consequence of Collier's campaign or of the contemporary criticisms directed against the theater at the turn of the century. Those events are merely specific expressions of the larger ideological change that begins to take place decades earlier, and that eventually affects all the literary forms of the period. It is only partially and locally a result of the inhibiting effects of the Stage Licensing Act of 1737,[58] since the fundamental problems of the drama, as we have seen, are formal rather than political, and the inherent defects of the form are visible well before that time, in the period of comparative theatrical activity and freedom. The failure is not attributable to weaknesses inherent in drama as a genre, since the complex characterization and social scope that eighteenth-century drama lacks are eminently within the capacities of dramatists of the Renaissance or of the nineteenth and twentieth centuries. Nor is it simply due to the specific nature of eighteenth-century bourgeois ideology,[59] although the set of formal assumptions that accompany that ideology produce the fatal divergence of dramatic history, since novelists of the period turn the same ideology to better use. In the end, the eighteenth-century moral action simply could not find adequate expression in drama. The novel made it famous, and the success of the rising genre depends upon precisely those means that the declining genre was denied. The crucial discrepancy between drama and novel, then, provides the final key to this formal history. The rise of the novel defines the decline of the drama. In this sense, the fates of the two genres are inextricably joined.

SIX
Novelistic Moral Action

The history of the drama over this century can be told in isolation, but a final assessment of its trajectory depends upon a comparison with the successful moral actions of another genre. The fundamental formal similarity of drama and novel makes such a comparison possible and provides the basis for a discrimination of the crucial differences that indicate the sources of these genres' separate fortunes. The novels of Richardson and Fielding, like the drama of the same period, are predicated upon the direct and formally generative depiction of inner moral worth, conceived and comprehensible in terms of an overt internal ethical system that supplies character, action, and assessment at once. As in the drama, the immediate approbation assumed by these novelistic moral actions produces a "realist" form that offers its moral norms, and thus its fictional world, as the direct equivalent of its reader's daily experience and ethical ideals. This essential premise of universality is manifested in the particular qualities of tone, technique, material, setting, and language that constitute the concrete attributes of bourgeois realism in its various novelistic guises. Significantly, Richardson's and Fielding's narratives are both recognized as realistic, though one depicts the complex operations of individual psychology and the other the multiple detail of a panoramic social experience; and though Richardson presents his fiction as an unmediated collection of letters setting forth the spontaneous and intimate workings of his characters' minds, while Fielding deliberately intervenes and, with a persistent, self-conscious address to the reader, calls attention to the fictiveness of his "history."

Realism, in this special formal context, is adequately characterized neither by the specific technical device of psychological complexity nor by that of social breadth, since these devices are only the particular consequences of more fundamental assumptions shared by the moral actions of Richardson and Fielding as well as by those of the major contemporary dramatists. Like sentimentalism, then, realism can be greatly illuminated by a consciousness of literary form, even though it may ultimately be found to cross formal boundaries. A rigorously formal account of realism, for instance, can help to resolve some of the problems that recent critics have found in Ian Watt's description of the phenomenon.[1] It accounts fully for E. M. W. Tillyard's objection that eighteenth-century literature in general, rather than the novel in particular, is characterized by the growth of realism.[2] It answers Diana Spearman's attempted refutation of the social and historical basis of literary realism by showing why the verisimilar descriptions of earlier writers are not strictly comparable with the formal assumptions of the major novelists and dramatists of the eighteenth century.[3] And it can handle the general complaints about Watt's preference for Richardson by providing a balanced account of both Richardson and Fielding as early novelistic realists who simply use different means to the same formal end. Such an account has the added benefit of explaining the rise of the novel as a single coherent event and thus obviating the necessity of positing a separate self-conscious tradition like that outlined by Robert Alter.[4]

As we have seen, the moral action, by its very nature, poses a crucial problem for the storytellers of the eighteenth century. Its virtuous protagonist is excluded from the commission of an error that could motivate the plot, since a genuine flaw would undermine the moral standards which that paragon represents and confers to his or her fictional world. The heroes and heroines of these stories are reduced to inactivity or victimization, and their stasis inhibits the energy and engagement of the action, just as their flawless virtue hinders its motivation. The inherent difficulty is that of achieving a generative relationship between the moral merit of the exemplary protagonist and the process of a dynamic action that produces his or her fate. In the drama, this difficulty is the direct cause of the inconsistency and irrelevance that weaken the genre. In the novel, the means by which the same problem is overcome represent the sources of that genre's excellence, separate it qualitatively from its inferior literary precedents, and account formally for its rise. Richardson and Fielding successfully exploit the very solutions denied to the drama in its time of trial: psychological complexity and social scope. As the drama's decline suggests, these innovations are essential to the consistently successful embodiment of moral form. They have consequently become synonymous with realism, though they are in effect the ingenious means by which the best realistic form of this period is figured forth.

Although the novel is not without literary precedent in the prose fiction, indigenous and imported, of the seventeenth and early eighteenth centuries, it is clearly distinguishable from the drama in its lack of a strong prior formal history. The early heritage of prose narrative includes the fiction of Elizabethan writers like Sidney, Greene, Lodge, Nashe, and Deloney, and the general influence of French heroic romance. The English "novel" of the seventeenth century consists mainly of translated French *nouvelles* (which in midcentury take the place of the full-length prose romance) like those of Madame de Lafayette, whose *La Princesse de Clèves* (1678, translated 1679) exerted an enduring influence on English narrative fiction. The most important of these translations is the *Lettres portugaises* (1668, translated as *Five Love-Letters from a Nun to a Cavalier,* 1678), which represents a primary predecessor of the minor tradition of epistolary fiction that runs through the eighteenth century. Behn's prose narratives resemble these translations in their reliance upon romantic material, transformed and domesticated by the influence of *vraisemblance.* Congreve's stylized *Incognita* (1692) takes up the same sexual subject matter, but gives it a slightly antiromantic tinge and a closely knit plot from neoclassical drama. Congreve's technical innovation, however, had no influence on the diffuse prose fiction of the early eighteenth century. This literature, a popular commodity, is written primarily by and for women, and reproduces the romantic material of the earlier French imports, often in epistolary and semiepistolary form. It consists of secret histories or scandal chronicles, erotic and pious novellas, and pathetic tales, by hack writers and translators like Manley, Haywood, Aubin, Barker, and Rowe. The general movement, then, after 1660 is from the translation and imitation of the French romantic *nouvelle,* with its focus on aristocratic domestic sexual dilemmas and its increasing attention to internal emotion and motivation, to the popular female fiction of the early eighteenth century, which exploited the sexual material of the earlier romance for pornographic, pious, scandalous, or escapist purposes.[5]

The popular tradition of the seventeenth century remains distinct from these distant, altered successors of the early French prose romance, even though, by the eighteenth century, the differentiation between popular and literary fiction begins to disappear, and Defoe's criminal biographies as well as Richardson's female novels must be classified as both popular and literary. Popular narrative of the seventeenth century is derived from oral tradition, from ballad and legend, and from debased *chansons de geste, Märchen,* or abridged and altered romance. It includes the adventures of folk heroes, criminal biographies, rogues' tales, moral and religious stories, didactic works, and travel literature. Most important is the popular Puritan spiritual narrative, autobiographical and fictional, represented by Bunyan's influential works. Defoe is obviously the heir of this tradition, both in his subject matter—the rogues, whores, criminals, pirates, pilgrims, and travelers of the popular canon—and in his form—the autobiographical manner and vivid psychological and local detail of the Puritan narrative.[6]

The eighteenth-century novel also felt the influence of the antiromance, primarily Spanish in origin and represented by the picaresque adventures, journeys, burlesques, and protorealist stories of writers like Scarron, Le Sage, and, above all others, Cervantes. To complicate the account, this Spanish antiromance finds its way into English prose fiction twice, once through the romantic French *nouvelles* of the late

seventeenth century, which adopted the *vraisemblable* settings and
characters of Cervantes's *Novelas ejemplares* without their antiromantic
implications, and again through the direct and strongly antiromantic
influence of *Don Quixote*. [7] In short, English prose fiction, at the moment of the novel's emergence as a primary and clearly distinguishable
genre, provides a varied and wide, though perhaps not a rich, resource
for narrative experimentation.

Richardson's novels belong to the epistolary tradition traceable from
the *Lettres portugaises* and the narratives of Behn to the works of Manley and Haywood. The essential situation of *Pamela* and *Clarissa*, that of
persecuted female virtue, is an altered and extended version of the ama-
tory tale adapted from the old prose romance and constantly retold in
the hack fiction, essay, and drama of the age. [8] In Richardson's particular
case, the epistolary tradition is augmented by the increasing prominence
of the familiar letter as a kind of rudimentary fiction, which, in his creative mind, took the shape of an extended, unified action. [9] One recent
scholar of seventeenth-century prose, Charles C. Mish, has argued that,
with the numerous precedents available, the major novels of Richardson
and Fielding required "little more than the addition of the characteristic eighteenth-century ingredient, moralizing and sentimentality, to make
their appearance." [10] But significantly, a survey of seventeenth-century
prose works gives little evidence of such future promise. In fact, the addition of moralizing and sentimentality was made by several of the
early writers of popular female fiction like Aubin, Barker, and Rowe,
but none of these women was able, by that simple means, to produce
an equivalent of *Pamela*. Despite such precedents, Richardson's novels
are vitally, undeniably "new." As Robert Adams Day observes at the
conclusion of his survey of pre-Richardsonian epistolary fiction:

> To show that earlier fiction had anticipated Richardson's novels in all but
> their total effect is by no means to minimize his claims to be the father of
> the modern English novel; it is rather to elucidate them. . . . The excellence
> of Richardson's novels appears more to advantage in contrast with these
> early attempts than it does in a literary void. [11]

There is no smooth, continuous evolution that ends in *Pamela*. The
narrative tradition which precedes that novel is weak, diffuse, unself-
conscious, and consequently essentially powerless in formal history.
Richardson's work represents as much of a break with that tradition as
an adoption of the details of its matter and manner. Specific precedents, though not insignificant in the creation of an individual masterpiece, do not play the same role in literary history as a continuous,
self-conscious, generic development, and Richardson's radical originality
is not diminished by the presence of the *Lettres portugaises*, Manley's
New Atalantis, or even his own *Familiar Letters*.

The other main precursor to Richardson's fiction is the autobiographical Puritan tradition of Bunyan and Defoe. Richardson's relationship
to these writers is less evident, though perhaps more significant, than
his specific ties to the early epistolary novel. Defoe's attention to vivid
local detail and his exploitation of a full-length popular prose narrative
are essential to the basic premises of novelistic realism, and in this sense
his works are more like Richardson's than are the anticipatory seduction plots of Manley and Haywood. Defoe, too, confronts the problem
of reconciling an energetic story with an explicitly didactic intention:
he justifies his description of Moll's life of crime by claiming that its
whole purpose is to warn parents to keep their children safe at home,
or to advise travelers to look out for their luggage. In these and other
respects, Defoe's significance for the development of realism in the
period cannot be exaggerated. But again, the antecedent Puritan tradition he represents is formally quite distinct from Richardson's shaped
fictions. Defoe invents and perfects a fundamentally different kind of
narrative—one that imitates the randomness of real life and therefore
must be read and understood as a rendering of reality rather than as a
self-contained system of judgments and expectations. Unlike the novelistic or dramatic action, his pseudofactual tales permit a large degree
of incoherence, and hence he is not forced to find a resolution to the
major formal problem of the period; he produces instead an uneasy
stalemate of adventure and didacticism. Defoe fights some of the same
aesthetic battles as the major novelists and dramatists of the early
eighteenth century, but for a different cause, and therefore there is no
direct contact and no smooth formal evolution from his creative version of Puritan autobiography to Richardson's moral action.[12] To the
extent that Richardson's novels represent a triumphant surfacing, in
a bourgeois age, of the popular undercurrents of literary history, they
alter those undercurrents almost beyond recognition in transforming
them into a primary tradition.

In general, the examples of the anticipatory epistolary female fiction and the realistic popular Puritan narrative serve to emphasize
Richardson's originality and, more important, to illustrate the discontinuous nature of the evolution of prose narrative from the seventeenth
to the eighteenth century. The important similarities—in attention to
local detail, exploration of internal emotion, use of colloquial language,
and increasing interest in the particularities of time and place—among
all these narrative traditions, including that of Richardson, are the consequences of the larger forces of the period, which exert themselves,
in various ways, on the diverse heritage of narrative prose. The Richardsonian novel belongs fully to its age, but remains an original form, free
to utilize the materials and methods of prior narrative, but relatively
unconstrained by them.

As *Shamela* and *Joseph Andrews* testify, Fielding felt, perhaps before any other influence, that of the unprecedented success of Richardson's *Pamela.* But this single rival obviously acts more as a spur to the creation of an alternative kind of moral action than as a strong, continuous formal history. Antecedents of Fielding's comic epic include Homer, Virgil, Scarron, Le Sage, Marivaux, Fénelon, Cervantes, and the Augustan satire of Pope and Swift. These writers provide sources and parallels for Fielding's epic aspirations, his antiromantic premises, his authorial intrusions, his humorous chapter heads, his interpolated tales, his ironic commentary, his burlesque scenes and language, his picaresque plots, and his parodic intentions. Notably, though, whatever the important international and temporally scattered influences that link Homer, Virgil, Cervantes, and Scarron to Fielding, these precursors do not constitute a continuous, national, formal history. In addition, Fielding's novels differ fundamentally from those works that could be considered parallels, just as Richardson's epistolary fiction differs from the earlier English tradition. Fielding is free to draw upon the epic and antiromance, parody and burlesque, of the greatest Continental models, but he is also free to alter, to experiment, and to supply the particular requirements of his own moral form.

Unlike the drama, then, the eighteenth-century English novel is an innovative genre with a discontinuous literary history. It is consequently exempt from the constraints of a strong prior convention.[13] The comparative formal freedom that the novel enjoys as a result, however, is not absolute. It is a freedom from the pressures of convention, not from the forces of history. It is a freedom of means, not of ends: the dictates of convention are felt only in the means that the writers of a particular time can use to embody the shape that they give to their understanding of experience. Thus, confronting the same intractable moral form as that of the declining drama, Richardson and Fielding are able to discover the particular means by which that form can be coherently embodied. The paired and equivalent innovations of psychological complexity and social scope, which make possible the success of the genre by enabling it to tell a consistent and engaging moral story, owe their invention in part to the discontinuity in the evolution of prose fiction. To this limited extent, the genre itself owes its rise to the special nature of its history.

I

Richardson admits no inconsistencies in his moral action. The perfection of his paragons is rigorous and absolute. In this important respect, *Pamela* and *Clarissa* are more like *The Conscious Lovers* and *Cato* than like *The London Merchant,* whose hero, at least from one aspect of his presentation, actively enters into his plot by committing a morally and legally punishable transgression, murder. The physical passivity and avowed innocence of Richardson's heroines remain essentially undisturbed throughout their narratives. But this passivity is the integral precondition of the dynamic formal activity that constitutes their uniquely engaging actions. Richardson's moral form never succumbs to the dramatists' common evasions of inconsistency or irrelevance. Instead, Richardson embraces the stasis of the moral plot, and makes a virtue of that necessity. The energy and engagement of *Pamela* and *Clarissa* arise not from the external reversals of a lively action, but from the internal tensions of a complex psychology. With this single simple innovation, Richardson solves the fundamental problem of moral form and avoids the fatal weaknesses that destroy the drama. But the solution is at first accompanied by a subsidiary ambiguity of assessment, which is only fully overcome in Richardson's greatest work.

In *Pamela*, as later in *Clarissa*, Richardson, like Otway and Rowe, places an innocent and virtuous female at the center of his action. Pamela's sex, as a comparison with *Grandison* will show, permits Richardson to exploit the full potential of the static moral plot without compromising the character of his protagonist, since a woman is, by contemporary definition, naturally passive and defenseless and thus properly less in control of her fate than a man. Pamela is not only a woman, however, but, like Lillo's Barnwell, a member of the lower class as well. Richardson thus gives a double guarantee of the purely personal nature of her merit and makes inner worth the ideological and formal tenet of her story.

The process of Pamela's action serves simultaneously to demonstrate her virtue and to produce the happy fate which that virtue deserves. The passive, static, and eventually imprisoned heroine repeatedly refuses Mr. B's advances, under increasingly trying and perilous circumstances. The simple enactment of her merit generates the plot, and as her peril increases, so does the proof of her virtue and the probability and proximity of her reward.[14] In short, vigilant chastity is Pamela's defining characteristic, it is the motivation of her action, and it is the only means to her marriage with Mr. B. That marriage may carry with it an unintended taint of materialism, but those mercenary implications do not injure the perfect formal coherence in the conjunction of Pamela's moral desert and her fate. The vulgarity of Pamela's sexual and financial reward is the consequence of the happy conclusion that distinguishes this particular embodiment of Richardson's ideology. Pamela must triumph at last, and since her character, unlike that of Steele's Bevil Junior, is immediately generative of her happy fate, it must be shown to be directly efficacious in the carnal and material world. In this moral action, Richardson seeks to display "virtue rewarded" in the most

convincing earthly terms he can conceive. (Significantly, his moral tragedy, *Clarissa*, does not give rise to such objections.)

The action of Richardson's first novel, then, is defiantly, consistently
static in its physical representation, though its form is continuously
dynamic. Where Lillo contradicts the virtue of his protagonist with accusations of guilt, Richardson maintains for Pamela an absolute and
unwavering innocence. Where Steele in *The Conscious Lovers* resorts to
irrelevant stage business to sustain his plot, Richardson progressively
reduces Pamela's activity and even her physical freedom. The energy
and excellence of Pamela's action derive directly from this very inactivity. Richardson responds, without evasion, to the problem of moral
form by translating the single-minded assumption of passive virtue into
the demand for a particular scrutiny of the psychology and motivation
of that virtue. He makes Pamela's inner life both the formal center of
her moral action and the vital source of its interest and engagement.
Thus, he solves the problem of the form by confronting its full implications.

The solution that Richardson discovers in *Pamela*, however, itself
gives rise to an incidental difficulty in assessment that injures the fullness of that novel's success. Pamela's thoughts are disclosed to the
reader in such a way that she appears, despite her ingenuous claims, to
anticipate or even to design some future relationship with Mr. B. Her
seeming hypocrisy, or Richardson's seemingly ironic treatment of her
virtue, is the consequence of the particular formal boldness with which
Richardson encounters the problem of the comic moral action. In making
Pamela's merit fully efficacious, in granting her a reward commensurate
with her virtue, and in assuring his readers the pleasurable anticipation
of that reward—in other words, in shaping a coherent comic moral
form[15]—Richardson must give Mr. B the attractions of a desirable mate,
and he must show the permanently transfiguring effects of Pamela's
passive virtue upon that eligible libertine.[16] In this endeavor, Richardson
is partially betrayed by the epistolary technique which permits the
formally essential exploration of Pamela's inner life. The information
that prepares the way for Pamela's happy marital fate and that conveys the signals by which the reader is informed that Pamela's action is
a comic one must be transmitted by means of the innocent, loquacious
letter writer herself. Pamela's psychology, in all its detail, dominates
the form, dictates the technique, and even usurps the physical space of
the novel, and we receive no objective testimony upon Pamela's character—which might substantiate her integrity—and no internal account
of Mr. B's reformation—which might dismiss the charge of Pamela's
manipulative scheming. Furthermore, the psychological detail of Pamela's characterization calls special attention to motivation, and intensifies
the difficulty produced by the very technique that makes such detail

possible. When the thoughts and actions of a character are continuously scrutinized, any potential ambiguity inevitably invites suspicion, and since Fielding's *Shamela* (1741), Pamela has been a prime suspect.

In *Pamela*, then, Richardson chooses psychological complexity at the expense of clarity of assessment.[17] While solving the fundamental problem of the moral action, he creates a new and subsidiary difficulty directly attendant upon the nature of his solution. The psychological complexity that makes his moral action successful depends upon a technique that produces an unintended ambiguity in his presentation of character, and continuously reinforces that ambiguity through its evocation of a verisimilar inner life. *Pamela's* greatest virtue is also the source of its greatest defect, though the formal achievement of the novel outweighs its consequent weakness. Its defect, moreover, is the pardonable result of an initial experiment far beyond the generic capacities of the period's most talented dramatists. Richardson's second effort builds upon the virtues of his first, and eliminates its difficulties.

Clarissa's story, like Pamela's, is predicated upon a passive and exemplary female virtue that supplies the moral standard of the novel and generates its plot. The impeccable and imprisoned heroine is in every respect the formal center of her action, and consequently the plot, like that of *Pamela*, is physically static, although Clarissa's moral struggle is actively dynamic. In the whole lengthy process of her tragedy, Clarissa is shown only to endure, first the unjust dictates of her family, then the villainy of Lovelace, and finally, with Christian acceptance, the inevitability of her own death. Each of her uncompromising acts of rejection substantiates her virtue as it increases the present peril of her situation, and the reiterated proof of her merit is the direct cause of her tragic fate and ultimately of her transcendental reward.[18] Like its comic predecessor, Richardson's tragedy accepts the logical consequence of the consistent moral paragon, a consequence that the dramatists of the period tried desperately to avoid.

Because it is a tragedy, however, *Clarissa* differs from *Pamela* in its elimination of the potentially problematic earthly reward of virtue. Clarissa is already possessed of considerable wealth, and this significant change represents the first step in Richardson's elimination of the taint of crass materialism that is built into the fortunate outcome of Pamela's story. Furthermore, Clarissa finds her justice only in heaven, and thus the process of her action reproduces the comic reversal of Pamela's in a purely metaphysical dimension that of course is not represented in the narrative. Clarissa's virtuous behavior, like Pamela's, defines her merit and increases her peril as it simultaneously ensures an ultimate and definitive reward. But in the world of *Pamela*, the appropriate reward is envisaged in concrete terms and bestowed in this life. In the world of *Clarissa* it must await the life to come, and thus succeed the greatest possible earthly trial and the final earthly adversity. Christian tragedy, in this instance, is merely an extension and intensification of secular comedy.

Once more, the fundamental problem of the moral action is directly encountered and simply solved by the location of all the novel's formal energy in the inner life and motives of the static paragon and her exemplary, dynamic moral struggle with her satanic opponent. The unembellished outline of *Clarissa's* plot carries little interest in itself, as *Caelia*, the novel's close dramatic parallel, will testify. But Clarissa's tragedy, as Richardson shapes it, is powerful and absorbing. Its particular internal intensity is a consequence of the stasis of moral form, and guarantees that form's success. Thus the greatest virtue of Richardson's best work represents simply a repetition, with increased maturity and sophistication, of the formal solution invented in *Pamela*. In addition, Richardson avoids the subsidiary ambiguity of assessment attendant upon his exclusive concentration on Pamela's psychology by providing several letter writers and thus several controlling perspectives on his heroine's action. He eliminates any suspicions of the protagonist's hypocrisy not only by making Clarissa wealthy and her story tragic, but also by overcoming the technical difficulty that plagued his first experiment in psychological complexity. *Clarissa* does not sacrifice assessment to inner life. In *Pamela* Richardson's preoccupation with the primary formal problem seems to have obscured, with good reason, the subsidiary difficulties that the solution to that problem might produce. The resolution of those difficulties as well awaited only his second effort.

The significance of Richardson's formal achievement in *Clarissa*, while strongly evident in the intensity and the moral grandeur of the novel itself, is clearly discernible in a comparison with the best consistent moral tragedy that the drama of the period can offer. Addison's *Cato* closely resembles *Clarissa* in its barest moral premises, since it too presents the tragic career and inevitable death of a paragon whose particular virtue—Roman honor—disqualifies him from life in an imperfect world, "th'abode of guilt and sorrow" (V.iv.93). Unlike Rowe's Jane Shore or Lillo's Barnwell, both Cato and Clarissa are consistently, programmatically virtuous, and this virtue, in both instances, is the immediate cause of their deaths and of their subsequent—and, in the case of Cato, presumed—eternal rewards. Both writers, once they invent a viable action for a flawless character, find the full moral tragedy endurable only with the stipulation of a divine justice, which in part nullifies the blatant injustice of their protagonists' earthly fates. But at the level of concrete detail this resemblance dwindles. Clarissa is the center and agent of her own action, while Cato's tragedy is a formal trick, attached to him by Addison's ingenious conflation of domestic pathos and public honor. Clarissa is given a full psychology, while Cato is made the flat

representative of a simple moral category. Thus, though Cato's plot is
comparatively more lively and full of business and Clarissa's is claustrophobic and immobile, *Clarissa* is undeniably the more engaging work.
The superiority of the novel, its moral magnitude, and its unflinching
seriousness are the direct consequences of its solution to the problem
of the moral action. The inferiority and triviality of the play result from
its clever evasion of that problem. The psychological detail of Clarissa's
inner life produces the energy which Addison attempts to secure by
means of his lively pseudo subplot. Thus, the diffuseness of Cato's action
derives from Addison's inability to make a passive protagonist engaging, while the powerful focus of Clarissa's, which never deviates from
the moral choices and the consequent plight of its static heroine, is
made possible by the inner life that it is peculiarly suited to display.
These telling differences between Addison's and Richardson's moral
forms constitute a specific instance of the general and vitally significant
distinction between the drama and the novel of the eighteenth century.

More immediately relevant to this distinction is the comparison between *Clarissa* and its probable dramatic source, Charles Johnson's
Caelia (1732).[19] *Caelia* takes up the story of the injured heroine after
her arrival in town, and follows her to Mrs. Lupine's (Mrs. Sinclair's)
whorehouse and thence to prison where, on the floor of an ill-furnished
room, Caelia bemoans her fate and finally dies, apparently of a broken
heart, after receiving news of the death of her seducer, Wronglove (Lovelace), in a duel with her defender, Bellamy (Belford). Incidental differences and great foreshortening do not obscure the similarity between
Caelia's story and Clarissa's. The plot of the novel diverges mechanically from that of the play primarily in the order of the events, the
number of available dramatis personae, and the ingenuity in Richardson's account of the heroine's innocence. Unlike Caelia, whose action
begins after her flight to London, Clarissa appears first as a tormented
prisoner in her parents' house. And her reconciliation with her family
occurs triumphantly too late, while Caelia is visited by her father in
the moments before her death. Bellamy's role is divided between Belford and Morden, and the kind Keeper's Wife who befriends Caelia
in prison furnishes Richardson with both Mrs. Lovick, the widow who
befriends Clarissa in the weeks before her death, and the wife of Row-
land, the officer at whose house she is imprisoned. Caelia seems to have
committed a pardonable indiscretion in yielding, before the opening
of the plot, to the charms and promises of the unscrupulous Wronglove.
Clarissa, on the other hand, is betrayed, against her will, into flight
with Lovelace, and finally raped while unconscious. In addition, Richardson, unlike Johnson, fails to specify the precise consequence of
the sexual relations of heroine and villain; Clarissa's physical state after
the rape is a subject of debate. Caelia, however, is pathetically pregnant.

With the allowance of an approximately fifty-fold expansion, Richardson's novel, specifically in its last three-quarters, tells a story essentially identical in its mechanical details to that told in Johnson's play, though fundamentally different in effect and success. The resemblance of the two heroines' basic situations is augmented by numerous specific similarities, including among others the characters of Lovelace, Belford, and Sinclair and the situations in the whorehouse and the prison. *Caelia* also anticipates *Clarissa* in such incidents as the insolent background commentary of Sally and Polly, Sinclair's evil participation in the tragedy, Clarissa's "charming" defiance of her persecutors, her parents' final forgiveness, her pleas for release from "this house," her affecting scenes of innocence, her denial of friends and family, her prostration on the prison floor, her gift of a ring and request for a coffin, her generous forgiveness of Lovelace, his pretended negotiations of marriage, his moments of genuine contrition, his reported death in a duel with a "man of honor," and his desperate dying attempt at recompense. And finally, the resemblance extends to such sentiments as Belford's lectures to Lovelace on honor and justice, the generalization of Lovelace's act to implicate the largest tenets of morality, and the explicit connection of Lovelace with the devil.

Given these substantial similarities, the differences between *Clarissa* and *Caelia*, like those between *Clarissa* and *Cato*, are especially relevant to the fundamental and fatal divergence of the dramatic and the novelistic moral actions. Caelia is reservedly guilty, and some of the pathos of her story is a product of her admission of that guilt. Clarissa is defiantly innocent, and her impeccable virtue gives her tragedy a moral grandeur that transcends mere pathos. Furthermore, Caelia is a flat and undeveloped victim who makes no choices and plays no part in the formal process of her weak and essentially trivial action. In fact, her stage time amounts only to the necessary representation of her plight and eventual death, which has no resonance beyond its immediate didactic lesson. Clarissa's full and engaging inner life, on the other hand, makes her the primary formal agent of her action, as well as the vital center of its power, its interest, and its moral seriousness.

In general, *Caelia* is one of the closest approximations, in the drama of the period, to a consistent moral tragedy. But although Johnson was an experienced dramatist, it is not a good play, and its abject failure on the stage seems to have put an end to his career. It duplicates faintly the weaknesses typical of moral drama in its vaguely inconsistent characterization of Caelia as an innocent victim, on the one hand, and an indiscreet pregnant mistress on the other. And the unrelieved pathos of her dismal end, which gives no promise of an eternal reward, tends to produce a slight sense of irrelevance: it generates no functional relationship and no real tension between asserted merit and anticipated fate, and therefore arouses no strong expectations about the outcome of its characters' careers. But despite these small potential deviations, Johnson's pursuit of consistent moral form is unusually single-minded, and it is the comparative purity of his action that does the most damage. Because it largely avoids the necessary evasions of Rowe or Lillo, *Caelia* is a lifeless tragedy with no engaging center of interest. The relative consistency of Caelia's characterization, on the one hand, and Johnson's inability to make her a vital creature in her own right, on the other, reduce her to a cipher of virtue and stifle the tension and motivation of her tragedy.

The nature of *Clarissa's* success clearly illuminates the causes of *Caelia's* failure. Richardson's boldly moral scheme isolates and highlights the impeccable heroine. The consequent power of Clarissa's character and the fullness of her inner life simultaneously supply the energy and motivation of her action. Her psychological complexity makes her perfect virtue formally possible, and her virtue in turn produces the intimate exploration of motive that gives her a psychology and a central role in the process of her action. Richardson's indisputable originality is not in his invention of a plot—in their superficial material, the plots of both *Clarissa* and *Pamela* were commonplace in the period—but in the means by which he gives his plots their particular shape. The same story, told again by Richardson with the innovations available to the novelist, finds an afterlife in literary history. These essential innovations constitute the difference between *Clarissa* and *Caelia* and, more generally, between the novelistic and the dramatic moral action.

The fact that Johnson did not discover the means that guaranteed the success of Richardson's tragedy does not in itself prove that such means were unavailable to him, but only that they were eminently available to Richardson. A choice not taken cannot be proven in the same manner by which historical fact is verified. But though the state of our understanding of those things that failed to happen differs in nature from our reasoning about those things that demonstrably did occur, our inferences are not necessarily any less valid. The significance of Johnson's failure lies not in its reflection upon his particular creative talents (modest though they may have been), but rather in our interpretation of its relation to the failure of moral drama in general, from Rowe to Moore. Notably, Congreve's dramatic experiments with psychological complexity—fatally tied to transitional comedy rather than to moral form—result only in the early termination of a promising career. It is symptomatic of the divergent fates of the two genres that Congreve is an anomaly in the period, while Richardson is a landmark.[20]

The particular formal problems of *Sir Charles Grandison* afford an additional insight into the workings of Richardson's moral action. To

the extent that it fails, *Grandison* shows by negative example how
Richardson gives his successful static moral plots motivation and direction. The most obvious and therefore, not surprisingly, the most important difference between Richardson's last novel and his earlier two
works is its male protagonist. Richardson's choice of perfect male
rather than female virtue gives rise to a series of formal consequences
that largely account for the diffuse and episodic shape of the narrative and thus for its deviation from the earlier pattern of *Pamela* and
Clarissa. The static protagonists of these two works are formally
central to their actions, because their plots receive motivation and
energy from the tension we feel between their moral worth and the
undeserved dangers they face. Grandison's masculine virtue, however, precludes the victimization that makes Pamela's and Clarissa's passive merit the generative source of their actions. In fact Grandison's
moral nature, marked though it is by chastity, reticence, incomparable
modesty, and a delicate sexual innocence, consistently manifests itself
in extraordinary acts of physical prowess in which he is shown to overcome armed opponents without drawing his weapon and thus without
transgressing upon his virtuous interdiction against dueling. Since
Grandison is not a victim, but rather, despite his nominal class status,
an apparently omnipotent example of bourgeois virtue, Richardson
cannot manufacture the tension that gives Pamela's and Clarissa's stories
their energy, and he cannot design a plot in which Grandison's choices
figure as a primary formal motivation. In short, he cannot provide his
perfect paragon with an action, even a static one.

All of the actionlike incidents that occur in the novel arise from the
characters of the two "best of women," Harriet and Clementina, whose
problems and resultant epistles represent a series of variations upon the
exemplary female protagonist's plight. Harriet must maintain her innocence despite the attacks and antics of the immoral London gentry, and
she must exert her virtuous generosity in a willingness to relinquish the
love of "the best of men." Clementina faces a more exotic trial, in which
her devout virtue triumphs over her love for the hero. But inevitably,
the brief and temporary tensions that accompany the primacy of one or
the other of these characters in the narrative serve to increase the novel's
diffuseness and to emphasize the episodic nature of its structure. Despite the comparative interest that they generate, Harriet and Clementina are subsidiary characters, and their fragmentary actions are initiated
and interrupted in the service of the novel's central and omnipresent
figure of masculine virtue. In *Grandison*, then, Richardson is forced to
follow his hero from one emblematic enactment of his merit to another,
since that merit is defined in part by the paragon's invulnerability.

A comparison between the rambling and undirected plot of this novel and the rigorously unified and centrally motivated actions of *Pamela* and *Clarissa* suggests that Richardson's use of psychological complexity is necessary, but not sufficient, for a strong, successful moral action of this kind. As we have seen, in Richardson's first two novels psychological complexity provides energy and motivation to a plot centered on a static and endangered heroine by permitting an examination of her inner life that makes her moral choices the determining generator of her action. The psychological detail with which Grandison's exemplary acts are rendered cannot produce a dynamic and engaging plot, because Grandison is never endangered, and whatever moral choices he makes bear little relation to his fate. The represented inner lives of Grandison, Harriet, and Clementina give Richardson's last work a strong central preoccupation with the niceties of a rigorous and precisely defined virtue like that of *Pamela* and *Clarissa*, but such a preoccupation does not constitute the formally central motivation that those earlier novels achieve.

The unstinting depiction of inner life that characterizes Richardson's solution to the inherent problem of moral form is a means to that solution, and not a solution in itself, just as the same narrative device is only a means to a successful novelistic realism, though it has come to stand for the end that it is designed to serve. Such a device, then, is most accurately assessed in terms of its operation in a specific formal context. In these terms, the comparative inadequacies of *Grandison* are entirely reconcilable with the contrasting success of *Pamela* and *Clarissa.* And, perhaps equally important, the originality of Richardson's achievement in the two earlier works is not belied by the moments of intimate internal detail that occur in the prose narratives of Behn, Manley, Haywood, or Defoe, and that anticipate Richardson's particular fictional device without anticipating Richardson himself.

II

Since Fielding's moral universe differs significantly from Richardson's, his solution to the problem of the moral action differs as well. He turns not to the internal justification of rigorously regulated moral character, but rather to the confrontation between innate goodness and the corruptions of a vast and various society. He creates a dynamic action for his moral paragon by placing him in a fully detailed social context, and he gives his formal premise meaning and seriousness by defining the good nature of his hero in terms of the evil of the world. Social scope provides Fielding with a means equivalent to Richardson's psychological complexity for the successful representation of a consistent moral action. Fielding's means answers specifically to the assumptions of his

own particular moral and ethical system, but, like Richardson's, in
enabling the moral action to find effective expression it too ensures
the success of novelistic realism.

In *Joseph Andrews* Fielding achieves an engaging and sustained narrative with a central moral purpose by directing formal interest to a
panoramic social backdrop. But in this early work that simple interest
is largely episodic and diffuse. Notably, the novel has two active moral
paragons, Joseph and his mentor, Parson Adams, who are equally and
similarly exemplary. Adams is the errant representative of the latitudinarian good man, the patriarch of primitive Christianity, and the novel's
repository of charity, compassion, and genuine benevolence. Joseph
is the simple embodiment of innocent male chastity, with an equivalent
biblical resonance.[21] This divided focus is indicative of Fielding's ingenious attempt to bring together the energy of a lively social peregri-
nation and the coherence of a centrally motivated moral action.

Each of Fielding's two Christian heroes has a separate role. Joseph
is supplied with an action of sorts—his search for and defense of Fanny
—and an ultimate fate—his deserved union with her after the climax
of their seeming separation. Thus, formally as well as nominally, Joseph
is the primary figure in the plot. Since Fielding, like Richardson before
him, is never tempted to trifle with his protagonist's perfection, Joseph's
impeccability raises the familiar specter of stasis and threatens to dis-
qualify the paragon from the process of his action. The profusion of
energetic activity with which Fielding supplies his narrative by introducing his naïve protagonist to the innumerable perils and impediments of
society helps to obscure this difficulty. Those perils, however, are not
seen, even in part, as the consequence of Joseph's own acts, his character, or his moral choices, but rather as an external impingement of social
corruption and self-interest upon the purity of primitive Christianity.
They cannot give the passive paragon a determining role in the plot,
though they can give his plot a continual and thematically unified source
of interest.

Thus, a moral protagonist of Joseph's impeccability, whose special
virtue is defined in contrast to the ways of the verisimilar contemporary world, can be supplied with great episodic activity through his
engagement with society, but not with a continuous action.[22] Joseph's
formal situation, then, is essentially like that of Pamela. He is battered
and beleaguered by external forces against which he merely asserts a
static and unvarying virtue. But Joseph, of course, is not provided with
the inner life that makes Pamela's stasis generative of her fate. For this
reason Joseph's action, such as it is, appears relatively slight, subordinate, and strangely detached from the substance of the worldly battles
that, placed end to end, make up the narrative. Joseph may be nomi-

nally and formally central, but much of the activity of the novel arises from a separate source.

The task of sustaining this episodic activity falls upon the novel's other moral exemplar, Parson Adams, who unlike Joseph is never clearly envisaged as the center of a coherent action. Adams plays the part of the benevolent picaro in unceasing conflict with the self-interest and egotism of the characters he meets. He is the primary spokesman and physical butt for the confrontation of Christian virtue with the world, and maintains an energetic battle with society without completely obscuring the action of which Joseph is the passive hero. As the chaste youth's mentor, he is even tied to the central story, though only in the context of his own pilgrimage through a countryside of picaresque, isolated, and emblematic perils.

Thus, the journey through a diverse social world is of fundamental formal importance in the plot of *Joseph Andrews*, but it contributes activity, not an action, and that activity tends to attach itself mainly to the indomitable Adams rather than to his relatively insignificant protégé. It usually does not affect the weak action of that protégé himself, which is inevitably subordinated to the energy of the parson's escapades. The resultant aimlessness of the novel, and its comparative neglect of a dominant and evolving tension between merit and anticipated fate, is counterbalanced, as in the picaresque and antiromantic forms that provided Fielding with inspiration, by the vitality of its social dimension.

In general, Fielding's first attempt to solve the problem of the moral action by placing the perfect protagonist in an imperfect world results in an ingenious enlivening of a static plot. But like Richardson's, his early innovation becomes an end in itself, to the partial exclusion of the kind of formal achievement that distinguishes his subsequent, superior novel. *Joseph Andrews* differs significantly from *Tom Jones* in its inability to reconcile social scope with the plot of the nominal protagonist, and in its resultant separation of action from narrative vitality. By failing to provide the motivation for a coherent plot, Fielding's ingenious means fails to serve the immediate end of effective moral form. The solution in *Joseph Andrews* is therefore at best partial—the novel represents a successful picaresque moral adventure and not a successful coherent moral action—but only because Fielding's innovation is not fully reconciled with his protagonist's evolving career. In *Tom Jones* Fielding's social scope maintains, and even increases, its prominence, but without detracting from the action of the moral hero.

Tom Jones, Fielding's best and most successful novel, resembles *Joseph Andrews* in its ethical intention, but Fielding makes a major and crucial adjustment in the function of the panoramic social backdrop.

The diffuseness of *Joseph Andrews* is a consequence of that novel's divorce of social verisimilitude from the evolving tensions of a coherent action. In *Tom Jones*, however, the hero's special moral merit and his movement toward a fortunate fate are made to depend upon the diverse world in which he finds himself, and the unusual seriousness of Fielding's comic form arises directly from this conjunction. In altering the nature of the connection between his protagonist and society, Fielding alters the relationship between action and scope, and thus brings his particular innovation directly to bear upon the fundamental problem of moral form.

Tom differs from Joseph not in the tenor of his virtue, but in the terms of its representation. Like Fielding's earlier paragons, Tom fully embodies the latitudinarian notions of benevolence, charity, and natural goodness, and in this respect his merit is the center of the novel's moral form. But Tom's virtue is conceived not in isolation, as an abstract moral ideal whose juxtaposition with social reality reveals only the imperfections and falsities of the fallen world, but rather as an inevitable inhabitant of that world. Tom, like Joseph or Adams, is a good man, but unlike those impeccable figures, he is also defined by his earthly involvements. As the narrator and Allworthy tell us, Tom is injured by the inadequate regulation of his inherently benevolent passions. His problems, then, arise from his imprudence, which is only activated by the exposure of innate good nature to a world in which self-interest is the norm.[23] Tom's indiscretions are the product of the confrontations of warmhearted inexperience with a corrupt, conniving society, and consequently Tom's moral virtue remains unflawed, though his engagement with the world causes him to instigate and subsequently ensure his own ever-increasing peril.

Thus, to the extent that Tom functions formally as a defective character and as the consequent generator of his own plot, it is by means of Fielding's social scope. *Tom Jones* is motivated by the interaction of the perfect hero with the world. Fielding eliminates the problematic stasis of moral perfection by making Tom an actor whose every generous, though warm-blooded, action, because of the nature of his environment, seems to entangle him more inextricably in misfortune. The dangers and distresses that Tom must face do not qualify his masculine virtue, since they are not perpetrated by an individual opponent (whom Tom, like Grandison, is perfectly able to dispatch) but by the larger operations of society which invariably transform his virtues into defects. The process of Tom's story, like that of Clarissa's, emerges from his particular moral character as it moves through the world. Though Fielding's motivation is external rather than internal, it has the same end as Richardson's: effective moral form.

As Tom's peril increases, so does his proximity to a happy fate, though the sequence of events that brings about his reunion with Allworthy and marriage to Sophia is concealed until its fulfillment.[24] While his accumulating distresses are the product of his imprudence in the context of a malignant environment, his reward is the result of the conjunction of his own merit (which exhibits itself in his crucial relations with Mrs. Waters, Mrs. Miller, Nightingale, and many others) with the marvelous operations of Providence.[25] Tom's character is thus the formal touchstone of every aspect of the plot, from his temporary danger to his ultimate felicity, though the first can only occur in the social world that Fielding designs for it, and the second is only assured by the fortunate coincidences that reveal the hand of a just deity and the hope of a future reward.

In *Tom Jones*, then, Fielding's "great, useful, and uncommon doctrine" has two distinct components, both equally essential to the form and meaning of the novel. First, in order to motivate the moral action and to give it logic and coherence, Fielding must evoke, with considerable power and vividness, a vast, diverse, and comically corrupt society, and place the hero in its midst. But there is nothing in the nature of Tom's interaction with society that is likely to produce a happy ending, since the ways of the world that Tom confronts are necessarily random and frequently unjust. In order to reward his paragon, to fulfill his comic intention, and to provide the emblematic example of a higher justice that his moral assumptions require, Fielding must also evoke a beneficent Providence. These two aspects of the novel's form account for its two most striking characteristics: its unprecedented and engaging social scope and its lengthy, self-conscious, and deliberately disruptive authorial intrusions. The action depends upon the vitality of the social backdrop. The analogy to Providence that is asserted in the happy conclusion depends upon the narrator's suggestions of the fictionality of the plot, upon his reminders that all will be arranged to the benefit of the deserving, and upon his simple and persistent presence as a benevolent power above the world he describes.

In this special formal sense, the famous authorial intrusions of *Tom Jones* are a function of the particular innovation—social scope—that enables Fielding to represent a consistent and dynamic moral action. The social world that motivates the plot cannot resolve it, except by the means that seems to be promised throughout the comedy: hanging. In fact, in order to keep that comic peril constantly before us and thus to sustain the tension of the plot, the vicissitudes of life in a defective society cannot even be qualified. Only the natural intervention of a special Providence, conceived as such and thus distinguished from the random justice of the world, can bring Fielding's action to a close without some kind of irrelevance, either like that of *Fatal Curiosity*, where an innocent character is absurdly obliterated, or like that of *The*

Conscious Lovers, where instant good fortune simply violates the terms of the prior action. If the happy conclusion of *Tom Jones* is the comic analogue of providential justice, the intrusive narrator is the comic analogue of Providence itself,[26] and his presence is essential to our sense that Tom's fate represents the image of an ultimate order rather than the arbitrary and irrelevant contradiction of the nature of the social world.

Thus, the particular form of *Tom Jones* is a product of the meaningful conjunction of its two most striking components: providential patterning and social scope. Fielding not only motivates his plot, but also rescues it from the triviality typical of Steele's moral comedy by situating it in a corrupt world of random and uncertain justice. While Tom's happy fate enacts the ultimate reward of virtue and supplies the conclusion proper to Fielding's comic moral intention, Fielding never relinquishes his clear and critical assessment of society, and never suggests, as Steele must, that the victory of virtue is simple, inevitable, and automatic. In *Tom Jones*, then, through the integration of character and scope in a plot consciously shaped to imitate a higher justice, Fielding creates a comic moral action of extraordinary formal coherence and unprecedented seriousness. The novel's success, as well as the distinctive features that have become associated with that success, are the consequence of its particular answer to the challenge of moral form. In a sense, it is to that challenge that Fielding owes his greatest literary achievement.

Amelia bears a marked resemblance to *Tom Jones* in its moral assumptions as well as in its primary reliance upon a broad social context for the mechanical operations of its plot. The comparative failure of the novel arises from the intensification of the flaws of its hero and the consequent transference of the role of paragon from the active male protagonist, who like Tom is directly engaged with the world, to the passive heroine of the title. The result of this transference is an inevitable reduction in the novel's action and a parallel diminution in the significance of its providential conclusion. Fielding short-circuits the effectiveness of social scope by permitting a character whose moral nature is defined, not through her engagement with society, but through her absolute detachment from it, to assume a large share in the focus of the plot. The greater somberness in *Amelia* is centered in this alteration in the character of its protagonist and in the concurrent changes in Fielding's depiction of the social context.

Like Tom, Booth is an essentially generous and overly trusting soul, and many of his misfortunes occur as a result of his inability to assess the intentions of those innumerable other characters who make up his world and whose self-interested motives are invariably inscrutable to him. Significantly, however, Booth is characterized not by repeated acts of generosity, but by repeated failures of judgment, and he is consistently portrayed in terms of his defects, rather than in terms of the virtues of which those defects are presumably the consequence. Furthermore, his errors extend beyond those of judgment to a much more serious failure of faith, which represents a genuine character flaw, unattributable to any conceivable extrapolation from his moral merit. His "atheistic" rejection of the abstract notion of virtue, and his corollary assumption that all acts are based upon self-interest, contribute to those errors of judgment that arise from his good nature. These defects motivate Booth's action, but they are only partial consequences of his social context, and Booth is both less virtuous and less fully tied to the scope of his narrative than is his more famous predecessor.

The place of the paragon in this moral action is filled by Amelia. She is the necessary embodiment of the novel's evaluative standards and the center of its form. Therefore, though she does not entirely usurp the role of the protagonist, her position in the action differs significantly in extent and function from that of Fanny or Sophia. In fact, Fielding gives her a plot. As a victim of Booth's errors and indiscretions, and, more important, of the repeated attempts on her well-guarded chastity, Amelia serves as a center of interest in her own right. Her trials evoke the expectations proper to a primary character, and the hopes that Fielding arouses for the happy resolution of the action depend at least as much upon our desire to see Amelia's just deserts rewarded as they do upon our sense that Booth's mistakes do not outweigh the virtues of his good nature. In its designation of a heroine, then, Fielding's last novel resembles *Pamela* and *Clarissa*, and encounters the problems inevitably attendant upon innocence, passivity, and stasis.

Not surprisingly, the plot of *Amelia* is less lively, less continuous, and less engaging than that of *Tom Jones*. Though Booth's career gives the action a coherence that distinguishes it from *Joseph Andrews*, Fielding's last novel consists primarily of an accumulation of emblematic distresses, each somewhat worse than the last, but otherwise interchangeable in order and importance. Amelia's moral centrality endows her with a force disproportionate to her appearances in the plot, and to the extent that the female paragon dominates the form, it suffers all the liabilities of *Clarissa*'s stasis with none of the advantages of Richardson's psychological complexity. The social scope of the novel, since it does not impinge upon Amelia's character except as an indirect agent of her misfortune, cannot serve as the source of motivation for a dynamic plot. With respect to our interest in Amelia, the world becomes simply a malevolent external force that imposes suffering upon a paragon who is made its arbitrary victim.

Booth's serious flaws save the novel from a full Richardsonian stasis, but make Fielding's providential conclusion problematic. The instantaneous reversal that ultimately restores Booth to prosperity is not as formally pleasing as that which grants Tom Sophia, because Booth is not simply a sufferer from the generous and youthful excesses of his virtues. The nature of his defects prevents us from trusting completely in his reformation, and perhaps more important, the process of his action gives him no role in procuring his reward. Tom's generosity leads by natural means to the marvelous conclusion of his history. Booth merely errs, suffers, and errs again. His reward consequently appears more arbitrary than providential. Amelia, on the other hand, is a more satisfying recipient of instantaneous prosperity. Significantly, she is given a role like Tom's in the procurement of her just deserts, since it is her sale of the miniature, saved out of love for her by Atkinson, that prompts Robinson's crucial confession. But the weakness of Amelia's static share of the action precludes the evolving series of tightly controlled coincidences that characterize the plot of *Tom Jones*, and thus the providential reward can be effective only as a devout assertion of ultimate justice, and not as the pleasurably surprising and inevitable conclusion of a coherent process. In general, then, the particular form of *Amelia*, as well as its specific weaknesses, is manifested in the alteration in the character of the protagonists, their relationship to the novel's social backdrop, the shape and coherence of the action, and the nature of its providential conclusion.

A comparison of Fielding's least successful novel to the play that provided him with the outlines of a portion of its plot suggests that the mere presence of full novelistic social scope is not sufficient in itself to solve the problem posed by moral form. In *Amelia*, Fielding greatly expands and elaborates the corrupt setting that appears in *The Modern Husband* as the contrivances of three reprehensible characters—Lord Richly and Mr. and Mrs. Modern. This change transforms the action from one that focuses on the evil deeds and depraved marital relationship of the villains to one that centers upon the career of a hero and heroine pitted against a world, or at least a city, of random villainy. In this respect, the social scope of *Amelia* is potentially much more effective in the construction of a moral action than the gestures toward such a device exhibited in Fielding's anticipatory play. But Fielding also expands the character of Mrs. Bellamant, the drama's representative of virtue, and gives her and Mr. Bellamant, in their reincarnation as Amelia and Booth, a proportionally larger role in the action as the centrality of the Moderns is reduced. Consequently, the increased significance of the beleaguered heroine diminishes the formal relevance of the social context as a solution to the problems of the moral action, and Fielding effectively cancels out his greater control of social scope by designing a novelistic action which that specific innovation cannot serve. The heir of the conditional dramatic success of *The Modern Husband*, then, with its limited experiment in the direction of social scope, is not *Amelia* but *Tom Jones*, since Tom's story represents the realization of the full potential of Fielding's initial efforts toward formal innovation in the moral action. The example of *Amelia*, like that of *Grandison* in Richardson's career, illustrates the necessary relationship between the primary devices of novelistic realism and the formal ends that they are made to serve. The comparative failure of Fielding's last novel does not call into question the significance of social scope, but rather clarifies the nature of its role in the emergence of the genre.

III

The success of Richardson's and Fielding's most memorable works is the consequence of the particular innovations that distinguish the moral action in the novel from the same form as it is embodied in the drama. For Richardson, psychological complexity makes a viable static action with a passive female paragon not only possible but effective. Fielding uses social scope to motivate an active moral form with a consistent male protagonist. The two devices represent, respectively, the two possible approaches to the problem of the moral action: one assumes and builds upon the stasis of the paragon, the other assumes and justifies his activity. Because of the contemporary notions of ideal female passivity and the complementary attitudes toward active male virtue, these two formal extremes are sex-linked. Psychological complexity gives motivation and energy to a static action with a passive heroine, but it is largely irrelevant to the distinct problems created by the active virtue of Grandison. Similarly, Fielding's social scope is gauged to provide Tom with an energetic action in the world, but Amelia remains formally unaffected by the same device. In general and more schematically, the relationship between the particular kind of success achieved in the novel and the particular kind of failure exhibited in its dramatic counterpart suggests that psychological complexity is necessary but not sufficient to the viable representation of a moral form with a static protagonist, and that social scope is necessary but not sufficient to the consistent embodiment of a moral form with an active one.

In respect to their function in the moral action, psychological complexity and social scope are equivalent innovations. They serve the same end through the same kind of recourse to a verisimilar description of experience, though one prefers an internal and the other an external verisimilitude. Together they demonstrate the relative freedom of novelistic form and the potential benefits of generic underdevelopment in a period of major formal and historical change. Together they constitute the crucial and determining point of distinction between a genre with strong continuous ties to its past conventions and a genre eminently equipped to respond to the requirements of a new form. Together they represent the fundamental formal adjustment essential to the full and serious embodiment of the moral action and to the successful expression of eighteenth-century bourgeois realism. Appropriately, then, psychological complexity and social scope arise together at a time when the moral action has reached the most rigorous and most problematic point of its development. And also appropriately, these two devices continue together to play a primary role in the subsequent history of the genre.

Finally, if Richardson's and Fielding's equivalent innovations are necessary to successful formal realism, then the drama of the period is irrevocably excluded from a share in that success. Of course, an event as significant as the replacement of one major genre by another has a vast collection of causes. In the case of the rise of the novel and the decline of the drama, a single political circumstance—the Stage Licensing Act—can be cited as a major factor in the reduction of the range and fertility of theatrical experimentation in London. On the other hand, several critics have argued that the greater length of the novel makes it better able than the drama to fulfill some of the requirements of the moral action, specifically the sustained development of emotional effect.[27] Perhaps of greater importance is the privacy of novel reading, which is more suited, in differing ways, to the intimacy of Richardson's and Fielding's narrative devices, and which may also reflect a general cultural preference for individual, as opposed to public and communal, literary experience. The substantial expansion of the reading public, the spread of circulating libraries, the increase of genteel leisure among tradesmen's wives—these, too, help to explain the novel's relative advantage over the drama in the eighteenth century. But all of the preceding forces, even taken together, cannot account for the drama's decline. Drama has flowered in periods of more severe censorship and monopolization; it has been successful in regions of high literacy; it flourished as a bourgeois and sentimental form on the Continent during the eighteenth century; it has thrived even in competition with the novel in much of Europe from the late nineteenth century on.

The thesis offered here—that the specific nature of the genre's fate in eighteenth-century England is a consequence of the complex interaction of formal evolution and historical circumstance—is the only explanation that from a single perspective both defines the causes of generic decline and specifies its particular manifestations: the ambiguity of *Jane Shore*'s characterization, the centrality of *Cato*'s subplots, the chronological inconsistency of *The London Merchant*, the irrelevance of Steele's conclusion to *The Conscious Lovers*, or the prominence of the villain Stukely in *The Gamester*. This explanation, however, is fully compatible with those numerous other interpretations of the drama's decline. The arguments from political contingency, generic property, cultural preference, literacy, or theatrical history all ultimately acknowledge the larger historical process that this essay also recognizes as the fundamental fact behind eighteenth-century generic evolution. The Stage Licensing Act, the growth of the reading public, the prominence of "the ladies"—or their proxies—in the theatrical audience, the advent of economic individualism—each is ultimately a consequence of the increasing dominance of bourgeois ideology and of the practices and institutions of early British capitalism.

A total account of the drama would undoubtedly modify and enrich the findings of the present study, but without altering the basic contours of the argument. For instance, an emphasis on the operations of the theater—on audiences, actors, and managers—would reveal similar ideological trends and predilections and similar generic preferences to those we have discovered in the plays themselves.[28] In a sense, then, this history locates in dramatic form the workings of the largest forces that we can identify in generic evolution as well as in culture and society as a whole. In this respect, to the extent that the moral action generally contradicts, in form and ideology, the aristocratic social forms of the Restoration, its unique requirements inevitably constitute a specific contradiction of the conventions that the drama inherits from that earlier period. History presents this genre with precisely the task that it cannot perform. This is the cause of the drama's decline. The novel owes its rise and the drama its fall to the special stringency of eighteenth-century moral form, a form that for all its numerous and complex links with the past plays the key role in the major literary transformation from which the future derives its shape. This examination of its first failures and successes catches the rising form in the act of acquiring the conventions that are to become the dogma of bourgeois realism. The drama's fate is a sign of the irrevocable processes of history, in which we may trace, at last, the direction of formal evolution in a century of change.

NOTES

Introduction

1 For a recent critique of this fragmentation, see Brian Corman, "Toward a Generic Theory of Restoration Comedy: Some Preliminary Considerations," in *Studies in Eighteenth-Century Culture*, vol. 7, ed. Roseann Runte (Madison: Univ. of Wisconsin Press, 1978), pp. 423-32.

2 Robert D. Hume, *The Development of English Drama in the Late Seventeenth Century* (Oxford: Clarendon Press, 1976); A. H. Scouten, "Plays and Playwrights," in *The Revels History of Drama in English*, vol. 5: *1660-1750*, by John Loftis, Richard Southern, Marion Jones, and Scouten (London: Methuen, 1976), pp. 159-295.

3 For a more detailed discussion of modernist trends in Restoration drama criticism, see my "Restoration Drama Criticism: Revisions and Orthodoxies," *Themes in Drama* 3 (1980). This essay reviews Hume, *The Development of English Drama* and Peter Holland, *The Ornament of Action: Text and Performance in Restoration Comedy* (Cambridge: Cambridge Univ. Press, 1979). Holland's book appeared after the present study was complete. Its emphasis on theatrical performance provides a perspective on the drama complementary to my own.

4 My notion of formal history owes much to R. S. Crane, "Critical and Historical Principles of Literary History," in *The Idea of the Humanities and Other Essays Critical and Historical* (Chicago: Univ. of Chicago Press, 1967), vol. 2, pp. 45-156.

5 See Clifford Leech, "Restoration Comedy: The Earlier Phase," *Essays in Criticism* 1 (1951): 165-84; Rose A. Zimbardo, *Wycherley's Drama: A Link in the Development of English Satire* (New Haven: Yale Univ. Press, 1965), p. 2; Scouten, "Notes toward a History of Restoration Comedy," *Philological Quarterly* 45 (1966): 62-70, and "Plays and Playwrights," in *The Revels History;* and Hume, "Theory of Comedy in the Restoration," *Modern Philology* 70 (1973): 302-18, and *The Development of English Drama*, pp. 32-62.

6 In his discussion of the "ideology of the text," Terry Eagleton makes the same argument against a simple empirical treatment of literary objects:

> In this sense it is appropriate to speak of every author, and each text of every author, as yielding a "different" ideology. The ideology of Wycherley is not that of Etheredge [sic], nor is the ideology of *The Country Wife* that of *The Plain Dealer*. Yet there is nothing to be gained in the end by arguing that there are as many ideologies as there are texts—a claim as vacuous as the proposition that there are as many ideologies as there are individual subjects in class-society. . . . It is not a *reduction* of the works of Wycherley and Etheredge to situate them on the same ideological terrain: it is only by doing so that their differences, and so their unique identities, can be established. An empiricism of the literary text entails, inevitably, a nominalism of ideology.

See *Criticism and Ideology: A Study in Marxist Literary Theory* (London: NLB, 1976), pp. 99-100.

7 This is a venerable argument, and its power is demonstrated in its tendency to transcend conventional critical divisions. Two recent versions provide a good illustration. Fredric Jameson, from a Marxian perspective:

> The force of a work of art is directly proportional to its historicity. . . . There is indeed no contradiction between our present-day appreciation of a work and its concrete historical content. . . . The greatness of Corneille is not atemporal, but springs immediately from the force with which his plays reflect the struggles of an event like the Fronde—itself apparently a mere historical curiosity for us today. . . . The example of Corneille shows that such contradictions [the progressive and reactionary ideals of the Fronde] have a very special way of coexisting in the literary work, and that as a desperate and vital episode in the long class struggle of human history, it is precisely not in the history books that the Fronde lives on, but rather in the very bones and marrow of literary form itself.

See "Criticism in History," in *Weapons of Criticism: Marxism in America and the Literary Tradition*, ed. Norman Rudich (Palo Alto, Calif.: Ramparts Press, 1976), pp. 49–50. And Ralph W. Rader, from a neo-Aristotelian perspective:

> In our nostalgia for the grand faiths of traditional Western culture, for its spiritual splendors and the dignity, reflecting the Great Chain of Being, supposedly attached to its hierarchical social structure, we have been led too easily to conceive the experienced value of the literary work as if it were in fact identical with an external structure of value once vitally located—and now lost—in the past, whereas the view outlined here would emphasize value as inhering in the embodied cognitive act of the work itself and see in it our most vital means of access to whatever in the values of the past was truly valid and universal.

See "The Concept of Genre and Eighteenth-Century Studies," in *New Approaches to Eighteenth-Century Literature: Selected Papers from the English Institute*, ed. Phillip Harth (New York: Columbia Univ. Press, 1974), pp. 113–14.

8 Though my approach, particularly in the technical aspects of my analysis, is indebted to the modern neo-Aristotelian tradition, my inclusion of the local historical context, as well as my notion that shape confers meaning, distinguish my definition of form from those of Sheldon Sacks, *Fiction and the Shape of Belief: A Study of Henry Fielding With Glances at Swift, Johnson and Richardson* (Berkeley and Los Angeles: Univ. of California Press, 1964), ch. 1; and to a lesser extent R. S. Crane, "The Concept of Plot and the Plot of *Tom Jones*," in *Critics and Criticism: Ancient and Modern*, ed. Crane (Chicago: Univ. of Chicago Press, 1952), pp. 616–47.

9 My understanding of the action is derived from Crane, "The Concept of Plot and the Plot of *Tom Jones*"; Sacks, *Fiction and the Shape of Belief*, ch. 1; and especially Rader, "Defoe, Richardson, Joyce, and the Concept of Form in the Novel," in *Autobiography, Biography, and the Novel*, by William Matthews and Rader (Los Angeles: William Andrews Clark Memorial Library, UCLA, 1973), pp. 29–72.

10 I am indebted to Rader for my definition and understanding of this term in relation to the novel, as well as for much of my thinking about generic form. See his "Fact, Theory, and Literary Explanation," *Critical Inquiry* 1 (1974): 245–72, and "Defoe, Richardson, Joyce."

Chapter One

1 *Cavalier Drama: An Historical and Critical Supplement to the Study of the Elizabethan and Restoration Stage* (New York: Modern Language Association, 1936), p. 55 and pp. 48-71 and passim. See also Kathleen M. Lynch, "Conventions of Platonic Drama in the Heroic Plays of Orrery and Dryden," *PMLA* 44 (1929): 456-71; Cecil Victor Deane, *Dramatic Theory and the Rhymed Heroic Play* (London: Oxford Univ. Press, 1931); A. E. Parsons, "The English Heroic Play," *Modern Language Review* 33 (1938): 1-14; and Eugene M. Waith, "Dryden and the Tradition of Serious Drama," in *John Dryden,* ed. Earl Miner (London: Bell, 1972), pp. 58-89, especially pp. 60-68.

2 John Dryden, "Of Heroic Plays: An Essay," in *Of Dramatic Poesy and Other Critical Essays,* ed. George Watson (London: Dent, 1962), vol. 1, pp. 157-58, and "To Roger, Earl of Orrery, Prefixed to *The Rival Ladies,*" in *Of Dramatic Poesy,* vol. 1, p. 9.

3 *The Siege of Rhodes, A Critical Edition,* ed. Ann-Mari Hedbäck, Acta Universitatis Upsaliensis, Studia Anglistica Upsaliensia, 14 (Uppsala: Universitatis Upsaliensis, 1973), Pt. I, Act V. Subsequent references will be noted in the text.

4 Eric Rothstein, *Restoration Tragedy: Form and the Process of Change* (Madison: Univ. of Wisconsin Press, 1967), pp. 127-30; Waith, *Ideas of Greatness: Heroic Drama in England* (London: Routledge and Kegan Paul, 1971), pp. 194-203.

5 *Macbeth,* 1663. For the argument in favor of this date, see Christopher Spencer, *Davenant's "Macbeth" from the Yale Manuscript: An Edition, with a Discussion of the Relation of Davenant's Text to Shakespeare's* (New Haven: Yale Univ. Press, 1961), pp. 1-16.

6 *The Dramatic Works of Roger Boyle, Earl of Orrery,* ed. William Smith Clark, II (Cambridge: Harvard Univ. Press, 1937), vol. 1, III.iii.395-420. Subsequent references to Orrery's plays will be to this edition and will be noted in the text.

7 One of the problems that Hume identifies in the classification of heroic drama is precisely this one of the "prosperous ending" (*The Development of English Drama,* p. 192). The formal definition of the heroic action that I have attempted to develop in this chapter, however, clearly shows how and why heroic plays with fortunate conclusions and heroic plays with unfortunate conclusions are related. Hume's emphasis on "heroic characterization" as the "key element" (p. 194) does not. The issue of the "villain-centred" play (pp. 193 and 199-202), which Hume also raises, is similar, and similarly resolved.

8 B. J. Pendlebury, *Dryden's Heroic Plays: A Study of the Origins* (London: Selwyn and Blount, 1923); Deane, *Dramatic Theory and the Rhymed Heroic Play,* pp. 5-15 and passim; Parsons, "The English Heroic Play"; Reuben Arthur Brower, "Dryden's Epic Manner and Virgil," *PMLA* 55 (1940): 119-38; John Harrington Smith and Dougald MacMillan, Commentary to *The Works of John Dryden,* vol. 8, ed. Smith, MacMillan, Vinton A. Dearing, Samuel H. Monk, and Earl Miner (Berkeley and Los Angeles: Univ. of California Press, 1962), pp. 284-87.

9 I have adopted Waith's term, from *The Herculean Hero in Marlowe, Chapman, Shakespeare and Dryden* (New York: Columbia Univ. Press, 1962), because it includes all the implications of extravagance, near-divinity, egotism, defiance, and subversive individualism absent from the definition of the Orrerian hero. See Dryden, "Of Heroic Plays," pp. 163-66.

10 This observation is substantiated by literary historians, who describe Orrery's drama as a product of the French classical tradition and Dryden's, in contrast, either as the heir of a separate, Homeric tradition, as a reaction to French

classicism, or as a product of the native English tradition. See Allardyce Nicoll, "The Origin and Types of the Heroic Tragedy," *Anglia* 44 (1920): 325-36; Deane, *Dramatic Theory and the Rhymed Heroic Play*, pp. 17-27, 188-203, 207-13; and Parsons, "The English Heroic Play." Corneille's judgmental standard, like Orrery's and unlike Dryden's, is typically defined as a coherent whole. See, for instance, *Le Cid*, in *Théâtre choisi de Corneille*, ed. Maurice Rat (Paris: Éditions Garnier Frères, 1961), III.iv.886-96.

11   The play was originally published by Robert Howard. For primary attribution to Dryden, see Nicoll, *A History of English Drama 1660-1900*, vol. 1: *Restoration Drama 1660-1700*, 4th ed. (Cambridge: Cambridge Univ. Press, 1952), p. 110; J. H. Smith and MacMillan, Commentary to *The Works of John Dryden*, vol. 8, pp. 283ff.; Waith, "Dryden and the Tradition of Serious Drama," p. 69, n. 2; and George McFadden, *Dryden: The Public Writer 1660-1685* (Princeton: Princeton Univ. Press, 1978), pp. 72-79. Howard's biographer, Harold James Oliver (*Sir Robert Howard [1626-1698]: A Critical Biography* [Durham, N.C.: Duke Univ. Press, 1963], pp. 63-67), represents the opposing position.

12   *The Works of John Dryden*, vol. 8, ed. J. H. Smith and MacMillan, I.i.92-95. Subsequent references to *The Indian Queen* will be noted in the text.

13   For example, Jean Gagen, "Love and Honor in Dryden's Heroic Plays," *PMLA* 77 (1962): 208-20; and Anne T. Barbeau, *The Intellectual Design of John Dryden's Heroic Plays* (New Haven: Yale Univ. Press, 1970), pp. 74-76.

14   Waith, *The Herculean Hero*, pp. 178-81. Dryden himself suggests that Maximin "was designed by me to set off the character of S. Catherine" ("Preface to *Tyrannic Love*," in *Of Dramatic Poesy*, vol. 1, p. 139).

15   Ozmyn and Benzayda, like Acacis and Orazia in *The Indian Queen*, are Orrerian characters, deliberately conceived to conform to a French standard of virtue (Dryden, "Of Heroic Plays," p. 165).

16   *The Works of John Dryden*, vol. 11, ed. Loftis, David Stuart Rodes, Dearing, George R. Guffey, Alan Roper, and H. T. Swedenberg, Jr. (Berkeley and Los Angeles: Univ. of California Press, 1978), Pt. I: I.i.206. Subsequent references to *The Conquest of Granada* will be noted in the text.

17   Dryden defends his hero's extravagant defiance and irregular behavior as part of his admirable, epic character ("Of Heroic Plays," pp. 163-66, and dedication to *The Conquest of Granada*, p. 6). Contemporary comments on the play show that Dryden succeeded in his design of representing Almanzor as socially and politically threatening. For a summary of the pamphlet attacks on Dryden and his heroic protagonists, see Arthur C. Kirsch, *Dryden's Heroic Drama* (Princeton: Princeton Univ. Press, 1965), pp. 35-46.

18   John Winterbottom, "The Development of the Hero in Dryden's Tragedies," *Journal of English and Germanic Philology* 52 (1953): 161-73; Gagen, "Love and Honor in Dryden's Heroic Plays"; George R. Wasserman, *John Dryden* (New York: Twayne, 1964), pp. 86-87; and Barbeau, *The Intellectual Design of John Dryden's Heroic Plays*, pp. 114-17. Rothstein (*Restoration Tragedy*, pp. 56-57, n. 7) also takes exception to this assertion of moral movement in the heroic play, arguing convincingly that the heroic technique necessarily produces a morally static character.

19   For a full discussion of the arbitrariness of the play's conclusion, see Alan S. Fisher, "Daring to be Absurd: The Paradoxes of *The Conquest of Granada*," *Studies in Philology* 73 (1976): 414-39.

20   Waith also emphasizes the influence of the heroine in providing the final means of incorporating the hero into society (*The Herculean Hero*, pp. 159-68). My argument, however, gives equal weight to fortuitous circumstance.

21   "The first rule . . . is to make the moral of the work . . . as namely Homer's

(which I have copied in my *Conquest of Granada*) was that union preserves a commonwealth, and discord destroys it" (Dryden, "The Grounds of Criticism in Tragedy," in *Of Dramatic Poesy*, vol. 1, p. 248).

22 For discussions of the public-private analogy in this and Dryden's other plays, see Kirsch, *Dryden's Heroic Drama*, pp. 110-11; and Michael W. Alssid, "The Design of Dryden's *Aureng-Zebe*," *Journal of English and Germanic Philology* 64 (1965): 452-69, and "The Perfect Conquest: A Study of Theme, Structure and Characters in Dryden's *The Indian Emperor*," *Studies in Philology* 59 (1962): 539-59.

23 D. W. Jefferson, "Aspects of Dryden's Imagery," *Essays in Criticism* 4 (1954): 20-41, and "'All, all of a piece throughout': Thoughts on Dryden's Dramatic Poetry," in *Restoration Theatre*, ed. John Russell Brown and Bernard Harris, Stratford-Upon-Avon Studies vol. 6 (London: Edward Arnold, 1965), pp. 159-76; Bruce King, *Dryden's Major Plays* (London: Oliver and Boyd, 1966), p. 2; and Robert S. Newman, "Irony and the Problem of Tone in Dryden's *Aureng-Zebe*," *Studies in English Literature, 1500-1900* 10 (1970): 439-58. These views, I believe, are linked to the belief that Dryden was a sceptical fideist, advanced most notably by Louis I. Bredvold in *The Intellectual Milieu of John Dryden* (Ann Arbor: Univ. of Michigan Press, 1934). For a convincing critique of that position, see Harth, *Contexts of Dryden's Thought* (Chicago: Univ. of Chicago Press, 1968), ch. 1.

24 J. Douglas Canfield makes a similar point, though from a very different perspective, in his discussion of the heroic play's "attempt to reinscribe [an ancient chivalric code] across the pages of a disintegrating cultural scripture." See "The Significance of the Rhymed Heroic Play," *Eighteenth-Century Studies* 13 (1979): 49-62, especially p. 50.

25 For a summary of Dryden's political loyalties in these crucial years, see McFadden, *Dryden: The Public Writer*, especially pp. 59-65 and 88-94. For further background, see David Ogg, *England in the Reign of Charles II*, 2nd ed. (Oxford: Clarendon Press, 1956), vol. 1, pp. 141-47; Christopher Hill, *The Century of Revolution 1603-1714* (Edinburgh: Thomas Nelson and Sons, 1961), pp. 223-32; and Clayton Roberts, *The Growth of Responsible Government in Stuart England* (Cambridge: Cambridge Univ. Press, 1966), pp. 155-96.

26 *Aureng-Zebe*, ed. Frederick M. Link (Lincoln: Univ. of Nebraska Press, 1971), IV.ii.192. Subsequent references will be noted in the text.

27 Kirsch, *Dryden's Heroic Drama*, pp. 118-28; and Waith, "Dryden and the Tradition of Serious Drama," pp. 78-81. Leslie Howard Martin's claim that the play merely embodies the *précieuse* elements of the French heroic tradition, which had not been imported to England, ignores the precedent of Orrery's drama as well as the distinct differences in tone and effect between the French Platonic mode and English pathos ("The Consistency of Dryden's *Aureng-Zebe*," *Studies in Philology* 70 [1973]: 306-28). Waith accounts both for the precedent in the romance tradition and for the significant shift toward pathetic tragedy.

28 In *The Black Prince* (V.iv), when Plantaginet is first reconciled (offstage) with the Prince, Orrery actually chooses to omit the representation of the initial pathos of such a scene, though it is included in the plot.

29 *Gloriana*, V.ii; *Mithridates*, IV.i; and *Constantine*, III.ii, in *The Works of Nathaniel Lee*, 2 vols., ed. Thomas B. Stroup and Arthur L. Cooke (New Brunswick, N.J.: Scarecrow Press, 1954-55). Subsequent references to Lee's plays (except *The Rival Queens* and *Lucius Junius Brutus*) will be to this edition and will be noted in the text.

30 Nicoll, "Origin and Types of the Heroic Tragedy."

31 Waith, *Ideas of Greatness*, pp. 255-57.
32 In *Sophonisba*, Scipio and Massina. In *Gloriana*, Caesario, Augustus, and Julia.
33 For example, Anne Righter, "Heroic Tragedy," in *Restoration Theatre*, ed.
    Brown and Harris, pp. 135-58; and John Traugott, "The Rake's Progress from
    Court to Comedy: A Study in Comic Form," *Studies in English Literature,
    1500-1900* 6 (1966): 381-407. This view is traceable to the stereotype of the
    period advanced early in this century, most notably by Bonamy Dobrée, who
    claimed that, while the comedy represents a realistic depiction of the manners
    of the time (*Restoration Comedy 1660-1720* [London: Oxford Univ. Press,
    1924], pp. 26-30), the serious drama provides an ideal that the epic-hungry but
    disillusioned Restoration could only attain in art (*Restoration Tragedy 1660-
    1720* [London: Oxford Univ. Press, 1929], ch. 1). Thus, he argues in his later
    book that the serious drama is "the reverse of most of the comedy of the pe-
    riod" (p. 22). My argument in this chapter and the next suggests that these
    critics correctly notice particular differences among the plays, but that their
    methodology prevents them from seeing the fundamental formal similarities
    that I have attempted to document. For a different sort of answer to the
    schizophrenic school, see Kirsch, *Dryden's Heroic Drama*, p. 35.

Chapter Two

1 *Fiction and the Shape of Belief*, p. 26 and ch. 1 passim.
2 The notion that the comedy of manners is moral or satiric is, of course, not
   new. See Ben Ross Schneider, Jr., *The Ethos of Restoration Comedy* (Urbana:
   Univ. of Illinois Press, 1971); Charles O. McDonald, "Restoration Comedy as
   Drama of Satire: An Investigation into Seventeenth Century Aesthetics,"
   Studies in Philology 61 (1964): 522-44; and P. F. Vernon, "Marriage of Convenience and the Moral Code of Restoration Comedy," *Essays in Criticism*
   12 (1962): 370-87. I am attempting in this chapter to provide a technical
   formal definition of that morality, without simply dismissing the numerous
   critics who find these plays to be amoral or immoral.
3 For full documentation of Dryden's debt to Tuke, and other contemporary
   romantic drama, see Ned Bliss Allen, *The Sources of John Dryden's Comedies*,
   Univ. of Michigan Publications, Language and Literature, vol. 16 (Ann Arbor:
   Univ. of Michigan Press, 1935), ch. 2; and J. H. Smith and MacMillan, Commentary to *The Works of John Dryden*, vol. 8, p. 267.
4 It is on this basis that these plays are frequently classified as Fletcherian tragicomedy. See Smith and MacMillan, Commentary to *The Works of John Dryden*,
   vol. 8, p. 265. Subsequent references to *The Rival Ladies* will be to this edition
   and will be noted in the text.
5 For the argument in favor of these dates for *Marriage A-la-Mode* and *All Mistaken*, see Hume, "The Date of Dryden's *Marriage A-la-Mode*," *Harvard Library Bulletin* 21 (1973): 161-66; and "Dryden, James Howard, and the Date
   of *All Mistaken*," *Philological Quarterly* 51 (1972): 422-29.
6 For further discussion of the problem of divided tragicomedy, see my "The
   Divided Plot: Tragicomic Form in the Restoration," *ELH* 47 (1980): 67-79.
7 Traugott, "The Rake's Progress"; and Norman Holland, *The First Modern Comedies: The Significance of Etherege, Wycherley and Congreve* (Cambridge:
   Harvard Univ. Press, 1959), pp. 18-19. Holland takes this argument further,
   contending that the evolution begins with the near-parodic heroic drama
   itself. The main problem here is chronological, since the truly extravagant
   heroic drama, as we have seen, is a comparatively late phenomenon, almost
   contemporaneous with the fully developed comedy of manners.

8 *The Works of John Dryden*, vol. 8, ed. J. H. Smith and MacMillan, I.ii.106-07 and III.ii.132-34. Subsequent references will be noted in the text.
9 For an insightful description of this play's criticism of some of the standard prerogatives of the aristocracy—its unlimited and irresponsible access to tradesmen's wives, its tendency to survive on credit, and its renowned bribability—see Smith and MacMillan's Commentary to *The Works of John Dryden*, vol. 8, p. 239.
10 Emmett L. Avery and Scouten, Critical Introduction to *The London Stage, 1660-1800*, Pt. I: *1660-1700*, ed. William Van Lennep (Carbondale, Ill.: Southern Illinois Univ. Press, 1965), p. cxxiii; Hume, *The Development of English Drama*, p. 257.
11 Commentary to *The Works of John Dryden*, vol. 10, ed. Maximillian E. Novak and Guffey (Berkeley and Los Angeles: Univ. of California Press, 1970), pp. 443-44, n. 29.
12 Dedication to *Mr. Limberham*, in *Dryden: The Dramatic Works*, ed. Montague Summers (London: Nonesuch Press, 1931-32), vol. 4, p. 271. Subsequent references to this play will be to this edition and will be noted in the text.
13 Van R. Baker, in "Heroic Posturing Satirized: Dryden's *Mr. Limberham*," *Papers on Language and Literature* 8 (1972): 370-79, provides a considerable amount of specific evidence for seeing Woodall as an object of satire.
14 See Allen, *The Sources of John Dryden's Comedies*, who bases his argument upon the fact that it was presented at Dorset Garden (pp. 194-99). The differentiation of the theaters by class, however, is an unreliable gauge; *The Man of Mode* was also produced at Dorset Garden. For a discussion of the diversity of the audience in both theaters, see Avery and Scouten, Critical Introduction to *The London Stage, 1660-1800*, Pt. I, pp. clxii-clxxi; Loftis, "The Audience," in *The Revels History*, pp. 13-25; and P. Holland, *The Ornament of Action*, pp. 1-18.
15 Frank Harper Moore, *The Nobler Pleasure: Dryden's Comedy in Theory and Practice* (Chapel Hill: Univ. of North Carolina Press, 1963), pp. 142-43.
16 For a description of this plot's affinities with Jonson, Middleton, and Shirley, see K. M. Lynch, *The Social Mode of Restoration Comedy*, Univ. of Michigan Publications, Language and Literature, vol. 3 (New York: Macmillan, 1926), p. 143.
17 *The Gay Couple in Restoration Comedy* (Cambridge: Harvard Univ. Press, 1948), pp. 58-61 and passim.
18 *She Would If She Could*, ed. Charlene M. Taylor (Lincoln: Univ. of Nebraska Press, 1971), V.i.567-71. Subsequent references will be noted in the text.
19 For a summary of the intellectual and philosophical origins of seventeenth-century libertinism, see Thomas H. Fujimura, *The Restoration Comedy of Wit* (Princeton: Princeton Univ. Press, 1952), ch. 3; and especially Dale Underwood, *Etherege and the Seventeenth-Century Comedy of Manners* (New Haven: Yale Univ. Press, 1957), chs. 1 and 2.
20 Ogg, *England in the Reign of Charles II*, vol. 1, pp. 138-39; Perez Zagorin, "The Social Interpretation of the English Revolution," *The Journal of Economic History* 19 (1959): 376-401, esp. 388-89 and 401; Hill, *The Century of Revolution*, pp. 193, 200-01, and 273-74; G. E. Mingay, *English Landed Society in the Eighteenth Century* (London: Routledge and Kegan Paul, 1963), pp. 11-13 and 105-07; Barrington Moore, Jr., *Social Origins of Dictatorship and Democracy: Lord and Peasant in the Making of the Modern World* (Boston: Beacon, 1966), ch. 1, esp. pp. 19-20; H. J. Habakkuk, "England," in *The European Nobility in the Eighteenth Century: Studies of the Nobilities of the Major European States in the Pre-Reform Era*, ed. Albert Goodwin (1953;

rpt. New York: Harper and Row, 1967), pp. 1-21, esp. pp. 15-16; Lawrence Stone, "Social Mobility in England, 1500-1700," in *Seventeenth-Century England: Society in an Age of Revolution*, ed. Paul S. Seaver (New York: New Viewpoints, 1976), pp. 26-70, esp. pp. 61-62; and J. R. Jones, *Country and Court: England, 1658-1714* (Cambridge: Harvard Univ. Press, 1978), pp. 71-94 passim.

21 John Harold Wilson, *The Court Wits of the Restoration: An Introduction* (Princeton: Princeton Univ. Press, 1948); Hill, *The World Turned Upside Down: Radical Ideas During the English Revolution* (London: Temple Smith, 1972), passim, especially pp. 98, 117, 150, 168, 262, 274, and 289, and *The Century of Revolution*, pp. 240-41; Ogg, *England in the Reign of Charles II*, vol. 1, p. 218; George H. Sabine, Introduction to *The Works of Gerrard Winstanley* (1941; rpt. New York: Russell and Russell, 1965); A. L. Morton, *The World of the Ranters: Religious Radicalism in the English Revolution* (London: Lawrence and Wishart, 1970); and E. P. Thompson, "Dissenters and Cranks: Resources of 'Anti-Hegemony'?" (address delivered at the Third Annual Irvine Seminar on Social History and Theory, March 1980). I am especially indebted to Hill, who ends his description of left-wing Puritan ideology and activity in *The World Turned Upside Down* with a brief suggestion of the connection between aristocratic libertinism and Ranter beliefs (pp. 331-36).

22 *The Complete Poems of John Wilmot, Earl of Rochester*, ed. David M. Vieth (New Haven: Yale Univ. Press, 1968), pp. 60-61 ("A Satyr on Charles II"), 94-101 ("A Satyr against Reason and Mankind"), and 150-51 ("A Translation from Seneca's 'Troades,' Act II, Chorus").

23 Jeremy Collier, *A Short View of the Immorality and Profaneness of the English Stage* (1698; rpt. New York: Garland, 1972), pp. 173-76.

24 Ian Donaldson, *The World Upside-Down: Comedy from Jonson to Fielding* (Oxford: Clarendon Press, 1970), pp. 8-10.

25 This view was first advanced as part of the initial defense and reassessment of Restoration comedy by critics like John Palmer, *The Comedy of Manners* (London: G. Bell and Sons, 1913); and Dobrée, *Restoration Comedy*. More recently, it has been reproduced by the critics who argue against any consistent satiric interpretation of the drama. For example, Fujimura, *Restoration Comedy of Wit*; Gerald Weales, Introduction to his edition of *The Complete Plays of William Wycherley* (New York: New York Univ. Press, 1966); and Virginia Ogden Birdsall, *Wild Civility: The English Comic Spirit on the Restoration Stage* (Bloomington: Indiana Univ. Press, 1970).

26 McDonald, "Restoration Comedy as Drama of Satire"; Schneider, *The Ethos of Restoration Comedy*, passim; and Vernon, "Marriage of Convenience." The most recent and most balanced essay in this vein is Hume's "The Myth of the Rake in 'Restoration' Comedy," *Studies in the Literary Imagination* 10 (1977): 25-55. This article confronts the implications of the position perhaps more directly than any other: Hume questions not only the significance assigned to libertinism, but also the relevance of social history to the study of literature. The most suggestive and helpful recent statement which acknowledges and attempts to account for the presence of libertinism in this drama is that of Novak in "Margery Pinchwife's 'London Disease': Restoration Comedy and the Libertine Offensive of the 1670's," *Studies in the Literary Imagination* 10 (1977): 1-23.

27 *The Man of Mode*, ed. W. Bliss Carnochan (Lincoln: Univ. of Nebraska Press, 1966), I.90-93. Subsequent references will be noted in the text.

28 Underwood, *Etherege and the Seventeenth-Century Comedy of Manners*, p. 85;

N. Holland, *The First Modern Comedies*, p. 88; and Carnochan, Introduction to *The Man of Mode*, p. xvii.

29 For example, Palmer, *The Comedy of Manners*, pp. 81-91; Henry Ten Eyck Perry, *The Comic Spirit in Restoration Drama: Studies in the Comedy of Ether-ege, Wycherley, Congreve, Vanbrugh, and Farquhar* (New Haven: Yale Univ. Press, 1925), pp. 16-33; Wilson, *The Court Wits of the Restoration*, pp. 163-65; J. H. Smith, *The Gay Couple*, pp. 88-92; Fujimura, *Restoration Comedy of Wit*, pp. 104-14; Birdsall, *Wild Civility*, pp. 91-98; and Harriett Hawkins, *Likenesses of Truth in Elizabethan and Restoration Drama* (Oxford: Clarendon Press, 1972), pp. 80-97.

30 For example, Vernon, "Marriage of Convenience"; McDonald, "Restoration Comedy as Drama of Satire"; and Schneider, *The Ethos of Restoration Comedy*, pp. 142-43 and passim.

31 Underwood, *Etherege and the Seventeenth-Century Comedy of Manners*, pp. 91-93; N. Holland, *The First Modern Comedies*, pp. 94-95; and Jocelyn Powell, "George Etherege and the Form of a Comedy," in *Restoration Theatre*, ed. Brown and Harris, pp. 43-70.

32 See Loftis, *The Spanish Plays of Neoclassical England* (New Haven: Yale Univ. Press, 1973), ch. 4, for a full discussion of Wycherley's use of Spanish drama in these early plays. Loftis too finds it significant that, despite the influence of Calderón, Wycherley emphasizes character and conversation in *The Gentleman Dancing Master* rather than plot.

33 *The Country Wife*, ed. Fujimura (Lincoln: Univ. of Nebraska Press, 1965), III.ii.115-21. Subsequent references will be noted in the text.

34 See I.i.138-41 and 433-39, III.ii.61-64, IV.iii.237-40, V.ii.11-13, and V.iv. 129-32 and 135-43.

35 Zimbardo, *Wycherley's Drama*, pp. 161-63.

36 For example, Palmer, *The Comedy of Manners*, pp. 128-34; J. H. Smith, *The Gay Couple*, pp. 86-89; Fujimura, *Restoration Comedy of Wit*, pp. 139-46; Birdsall, *Wild Civility*, pp. 135-36 and 154-56; and Wallace Jackson, "*The Country Wife*: The Premises of Love and Lust," *The South Atlantic Quarterly* 72 (1973): 540-46.

37 Fujimura, *Restoration Comedy of Wit*, p. 144; and Birdsall, *Wild Civility*, pp. 139-40.

38 Dobrée, *Restoration Comedy*, pp. 93-102; N. Holland, *The First Modern Comedies*, p. 80; McDonald, "Restoration Comedy as Drama of Satire"; Zimbardo, *Wycherley's Drama*, pp. 155-56; and Righter, "William Wycherley," *Restoration Theatre*, ed. Brown and Harris, pp. 71-91.

39 Among recent critics, this interpretation originates with Perry, *The Comic Spirit in Restoration Drama*, pp. 42-49; and is taken up in turn by Kenneth Muir, *The Comedy of Manners* (London: Hutchinson, 1970), pp. 72-78; and Vernon, "Marriage of Convenience."

40 *The Plain Dealer*, ed. Leo Hughes (Lincoln: Univ. of Nebraska Press, 1967), "The Persons," ll. 7-8. Subsequent references will be noted in the text.

41 In one of the most useful studies of this play, A. M. Friedson ("Wycherley and Molière: Satirical Point of View in *The Plain Dealer*," *Modern Philology* 64 [1967]: 189-97) shows that Wycherley's deviations from *Le Misanthrope* are generally calculated to establish and strengthen our sympathy with Manly.

42 Birdsall, *Wild Civility*, pp. 175-76.

43 Palmer, *The Comedy of Manners*, pp. 134-40; Perry, *The Comic Spirit in Restoration Drama*, pp. 49-55; and J. H. Smith, *The Gay Couple*, pp. 93-94.

44 Dobrée, *Restoration Comedy*, pp. 87-93; K. M. Lynch, *The Social Mode of*

Restoration Comedy, pp. 172–73; Fujimura, *Restoration Comedy of Wit,* pp. 146–55; N. Holland, *The First Modern Comedies,* pp. 98–99; Righter, "William Wycherley"; and Zimbardo, *Wycherley's Drama,* pp. 77–90.

45 Hill, *Century of Revolution,* p. 224.

46 See, for example, N. Holland, *The First Modern Comedies,* p. 101; Righter, "William Wycherley"; and Weales, Introduction to *The Complete Plays of William Wycherley.*

47 For Behn's social and political views, which include radical criticisms of contemporary society as well as a strong allegiance to monarchy, see Maureen Duffy, *The Passionate Shepherdess: Aphra Behn 1640–89* (London: Jonathan Cape, 1977); and especially George Woodcock, *The Incomparable Aphra* (London: T. V. Boardman, 1948).

48 The play is based upon Thomas Killigrew's Spanish-influenced closet drama, *Thomaso, or, The Wanderer* (1654), as well as several subsidiary Spanish sources. See Loftis, *The Spanish Plays of Neoclassical England,* pp. 82–83, 133–34, and 139–43.

49 *The Rover,* ed. Link (Lincoln: Univ. of Nebraska Press, 1967), II.ii.11–15. Subsequent references will be noted in the text.

50 The contention that the comedy of manners is amoral originates in this century with Palmer, whose pioneering "manners" argument is based upon a partial misunderstanding of Lamb's famous essay, "On the Artificial Comedy of the Last Century"; see Walter E. Houghton, Jr., "Lamb's Criticism of Restoration Comedy," *ELH* 10 (1943): 61–72. Despite apparent critical revolutions, which have assimilated naturalism, game theory, authorial self-consciousness, comic wish fulfillment, or sexual fantasy to this reading, the amoral or escapist interpretation remains dominant. See Underwood, *Etherege and the Seventeenth-Century Comedy of Manners;* N. Holland, *The First Modern Comedies;* Traugott, "The Rake's Progress"; Weales, Introduction to *The Complete Plays of William Wycherley,* pp. xi–xx; Birdsall, *Wild Civility;* and Jackson, "*The Country Wife:* The Premises of Love and Lust."

Chapter Three

1 See Rothstein's suggestive analysis of the nature of pathetic tragedy. His description of the affective form of this drama and of its lack of "self-sufficiency" (*Restoration Tragedy,* p. 122) anticipates mine. His conclusions about the evolution of the drama in this period, however, differ fundamentally from my own, since he denies the significance of the historical context or the ideological content of the form (pp. 45–47).

2 Rothstein, *Restoration Tragedy,* p. 96. An admirably appropriate coinage.

3 *The Rival Queens,* ed. Vernon (Lincoln: Univ. of Nebraska Press, 1970), II.95. Subsequent references will be noted in the text.

4 Statira is also described as a child (II.351–54), and pathetic children appear throughout this drama. For the significance of this motif, see Arthur Sherbo, *English Sentimental Drama* (East Lansing, Michigan: Michigan State Univ. Press, 1957), pp. 53–59; Leech, "Restoration Tragedy: A Reconsideration," *Durham University Journal* 11 (1950): 106–15; and Rothstein, *Restoration Tragedy,* p. 153.

5 See Waith's suggestive discussion of the transference of magnanimity from the heroic protagonist to the pitying audience of the pathetic play in "Tears of Magnanimity in Otway and Racine," in *French and English Drama of the Seventeenth Century,* by Waith and Judd D. Hubert (Los Angeles: William Andrews Clark Memorial Library, UCLA, 1972), pp. 1–22.

6   Vernon, Introduction to *The Rival Queens,* pp. xxiv-xxv; and Waith, *Ideas of Greatness,* pp. 239-40.

7   Vernon, Introduction to *The Rival Queens,* p. xxiii; and Hume, *The Development of English Drama,* p. 205.

8   George N. Clark, *The Later Stuarts 1660-1714,* 2nd ed. (Oxford: Clarendon Press, 1955), pp. 56-57; Hill, *The Century of Revolution,* pp. 230-32; and Ogg, *England in the Reign of Charles II,* esp. vol. 1, pp. 204-18 and 314-21, and vol. 2, pp. 450-72 and 485.

9   Loftis, Introduction to his edition of *Lucius Junius Brutus* (Lincoln: Univ. of Nebraska Press, 1967), pp. xiii-xix, and *The Politics of Drama in Augustan England* (Oxford: Clarendon Press, 1963), pp. 15-17.

10 *Lucius Junius Brutus,* ed. Loftis, II.179-81 and V.ii.42-67 and 197-210. Subsequent references will be noted in the text.

11 In echoing Almanzor's characteristic "daring," this passage reveals Lee's transformation of Herculean defiance into loyal service to a republican state. See Waith's description of the fate of the Herculean hero after the emergence of the bourgeois ideal of civic responsibility in the eighteenth century (*The Herculean Hero,* pp. 200-01).

12 *All for Love,* ed. Vieth (Lincoln: Univ. of Nebraska Press, 1972), III.13-16. Subsequent references will be noted in the text.

13 R. J. Kaufman, "On the Poetics of Terminal Tragedy: Dryden's *All for Love,*" in *Dryden: A Collection of Critical Essays,* ed. Bernard Nicholas Schilling (Englewood Cliffs, N.J.: Prentice-Hall, 1963), pp. 86-94, originally published as the Introduction to *All for Love* (San Francisco: Chandler, 1962).

14 For a full development of the theme of nostalgia, see Frank J. Kearful, "'Tis Past Recovery': Tragic Consciousness in *All for Love,*" *Modern Language Quarterly* 34 (1973): 227-46.

15 Dryden felt the pathos of the pleading children scene to be an affective error, detracting sympathy from Cleopatra. See Preface to *All for Love,* pp. 13-14.

16 The use of minor characters to motivate the action is evidence of Dryden's debt to French classical tragedy at this point in his career, and especially to Racine, whose recently published *Phèdre* obviously influenced *All for Love.* Notably, both Dryden and Racine seek to justify their affective forms on the same, ultimately irrelevant, moral grounds (Dryden: preface to *All for Love,* p. 12; Racine: préface to Phèdre, in *Théâtre complet de Racine,* ed. Rat [Paris: Editions Garnier Frères, 1960], pp. 541-42). Though Dryden criticizes the French manner in his preface (pp. 15-16), the form of *All for Love* can be seen as an attempt at the reconciliation of Shakespearean impulse and French neoclassical structure.

17 For an additional perspective on this depoliticization, see Novak, "Criticism, Adaptation, Politics, and the Shakespearean Model of Dryden's *All for Love,*" in *Studies in Eighteenth-Century Culture,* vol. 7, ed. Runte, pp. 375-87.

18 For an account of the license taken with character by other pathetic dramatists, see Leech, "Restoration Tragedy," who notes that "Dryden would never do things like this" (p. 112).

19 Rothstein, *Restoration Tragedy,* p. 103.

20 Geoffrey Marshall, "The Coherence of *The Orphan,*" *Texas Studies in Literature and Language* 11 (1969): 931-43.

21 *The Orphan,* ed. Aline Mackenzie Taylor (Lincoln: Univ. of Nebraska Press, 1976), I.8-26. Subsequent references will be noted in the text.

22 See, for instance, *Venice Preserved,* ed. Malcolm Kelsall (Lincoln: Univ. of Nebraska Press, 1969), IV.i.87-94. Subsequent references to *Venice Preserved*

will be noted in the text. See also *Lucius Junius Brutus,* I.1-17 and 44-50, and
   III.iii.22-30 and 32-39.
23 See I.223; III.273-77 and 488-89; and IV.105-06 and 390.
24 See, for instance, Marshall, "The Coherence of *The Orphan*"; A. M. Taylor,
   Next to Shakespeare: Otway's "Venice Preserv'd" and "The Orphan" (Durham,
   N.C.: Duke Univ. Press, 1950), pp. 13-36; and Rothstein, *Restoration Tragedy,* pp. 100-01.
25 For further discussion of the violence and brutality of the play, especially in
   the subplot, see Derek W. Hughes, "A New Look at *Venice Preserved,*" *Studies
   in English Literature, 1500-1900* 11 (1971): 437-57; William H. McBurney,
   "Otway's Tragic Muse Debauched: Sensuality in *Venice Preserv'd,*" *Journal of
   English and Germanic Philology* 58 (1959): 380-99; and Rothstein, *Restoration Tragedy,* pp. 106-08.
26 Useful descriptions of the role of the dagger include McBurney, "Otway's
   Tragic Muse Debauched"; and Kelsall, Introduction to *Venice Preserved,*
   p. xviii.
27 David R. Hauser, "Otway Preserved: Theme and Form in *Venice Preserv'd,*"
   Studies in Philology 55 (1958): 481-93; Marshall, *Restoration Serious Drama*
   (Norman: Univ. of Oklahoma Press, 1975), p. 88; and Rothstein, *Restoration
   Tragedy,* pp. 103-09.
28 Hill, *The Century of Revolution,* p. 301.
29 A. M. Taylor, *Next to Shakespeare,* pp. 56-59.
30 G. N. Clark, *The Later Stuarts,* pp. 92-95; Ogg, *England in the Reign of Charles
   II,* vol. 2, pp. 455-59, 576-79, 591-619, and ch. 27, passim; and Hill, *The
   Century of Revolution,* pp. 200-54.
31 For further discussion of Otway's disturbing cynicism, see Stroup, "Otway's
   Bitter Pessimism," *Studies in Philology,* extra series (1967), *Essays in English
   Literature of the Classical Period Presented to Dougald MacMillan,* ed. Daniel
   W. Patterson and Albrecht B. Strauss, pp. 54-75; Kelsall, Introduction to
   Venice Preserved, p. xiv; and McBurney, "Otway's Tragic Muse Debauched."
32 For this repeated motif, see *The Unhappy Favourite: or the Earl of Essex*
   (London: for Richard Bentley and Mary Magnes, 1682), III.i, p. 29 and IV.i,
   p. 55; and *Vertue Betray'd: or, Anna Bullen* (London: for R. Bentley and
   M. Magnes, 1682), I.i, p. 9. Subsequent references to *Vertue Betray'd* will be
   noted in the text.
33 Rothstein, *Restoration Tragedy,* pp. 96-97.
34 Rothstein, *Restoration Tragedy,* pp. 97-98; Hume, *The Development of
   English Drama,* p. 217; Waith, *Ideas of Greatness,* pp. 267-69.
35 *The Fatal Marriage: or, the Innocent Adultery* (London: Jacob Tonson, 1694),
   I.iii, p. 12.
36 For discussions of the social and economic position of women in the period,
   see Alice Clark, *The Working Life of Women in the Seventeenth Century* (London: George Routledge, 1919); Robert Palfrey Utter and Gwendolyn Bridges
   Needham, *Pamela's Daughters* (New York: Macmillan, 1936), ch. 2; Ian Watt,
   The Rise of the Novel: Studies in Defoe, Richardson and Fielding (London:
   Chatto and Windus, 1957), pp. 138-51; Marlene LeGates, "The Cult of Womanhood in Eighteenth-Century Thought," *Eighteenth-Century Studies* 10 (1976):
   21-39; and Stone, *The Family, Sex and Marriage in England 1500-1800* (New
   York: Harper and Row, 1977), pp. 195-205, 270-88, and 325-404.
37 On the role of women in this generic transition, see my "The Defenseless
   Woman and the Development of English Drama," forthcoming in *Studies in
   English Literature, 1500-1900* (1982).
38 For additional perspectives upon the continuities of Restoration and eighteenth-

century literary and intellectual history, see Waith, "Tears of Magnanimity in Otway and Racine"; and Crane, "Suggestions Toward a Genealogy of the 'Man of Feeling,'" *ELH* 1 (1934): 205-30. Significantly, Donald Greene's attempted refutation of Crane in "Latitudinarianism and Sensibility: The Genealogy of the 'Man of Feeling' Reconsidered," *Modern Philology* 75 (1977): 159-83, takes no account of this affective trend in the drama.

39 See especially Nahum Tate's *History of King Lear* (1681), Dryden's *Troilus and Cressida* (1679), and Otway's *History and Fall of Caius Marius* (1679).

Chapter Four

1 For the details of Shadwell's position as defined in his dispute with Dryden, see R. Jack Smith, "Shadwell's Impact upon John Dryden," *The Review of English Studies* 20 (1944): 29-44.

2 *The Sullen Lovers,* in *The Complete Works of Thomas Shadwell,* ed. Summers (1927; rpt. New York: Benjamin Blom, 1968), vol. 1, p. 11.

3 "To the Reader," *The Royal Shepherdess,* in *The Complete Works of Thomas Shadwell,* ed. Summers, vol. 1, p. 100.

4 Prologue to *The Squire of Alsatia,* in *The Complete Works of Thomas Shadwell,* ed. Summers, vol. 4, p. 204.

5 Loftis, *The Spanish Plays of Neoclassical England,* pp. 131-32 and 172-77.

6 For a description of *Epsom-Wells* as an anomaly in Shadwell's canon, see J. H. Smith, *The Gay Couple,* p. 120.

7 See, for instance, Alssid, *Thomas Shadwell* (New York: Twayne, 1967), pp. 137-46.

8 Hume, in *The Development of English Drama,* pp. 78-86, effectively dismisses the notion that Belfond junior is the object of Shadwell's deliberate irony. Instead, he argues that the play's disquieting elements are signs of an unconscious contradiction in the author's ideology.

9 Ronald Berman, "The Values of Shadwell's *Squire of Alsatia,*" *ELH* 39 (1972): 375-86.

10 Shadwell, *The Volunteers,* in *The Complete Works of Thomas Shadwell,* ed. Summers, vol. 5: I.ii, pp. 171-73. Subsequent references will be noted in the text.

11 K. M. Lynch, "Thomas D'Urfey's Contribution to Sentimental Comedy," *Philological Quarterly* 9 (1930): 249-59.

12 Durfey, *The Richmond Heiress: or, A Woman Once in the Right* (London: Samuel Briscoe, 1693), V.v, p. 64.

13 *The Wives Excuse: or, Cuckolds Make Themselves,* ed. Ralph R. Thornton (Wynnewood, Pa. : Livingston, 1973), IV.i.1971-72. This critical edition is marred by printing errors, but since it is readily available, all references will be to it and will be noted in the text.

14 For a recent discussion and commendation of Southerne's psychological insight, see Anthony Kaufman, " 'This hard condition of a woman's fate': Southerne's *The Wives' Excuse,*" *Modern Language Quarterly* 34 (1973): 36-47.

15 Epilogue to *Love's Last Shift,* in *Colley Cibber: Three Sentimental Comedies,* ed. Maureen Sullivan (New Haven: Yale Univ. Press, 1973), p. 84, l. 16. Subsequent references to Cibber's plays will be to this edition and will be noted in the text.

16 For other discussions of Cibber's mixed appeal, see Sherbo, *English Sentimental Drama,* pp. 103-05; Paul E. Parnell, "Equivocation in Cibber's *Love's Last Shift,*" *Studies in Philology* 57 (1960): 519-34; and Alan Roper, "Language and Action in *The Way of the World, Love's Last Shift,* and *The Relapse,*"

ELH 40 (1973): 44-69. In response to this position, B. R. S. Fone has attempted, I believe without success, to prove that the play is thoroughly sentimental from start to finish. See *"Love's Last Shift* and Sentimental Comedy," *Restoration and 18th Century Theatre Research* 9, No. 1 (1970): 11-23.

17 *The Relapse,* ed. Curt A. Zimansky (Lincoln: Univ. of Nebraska Press, 1970), I.iii.13-16 and I.ii.54-62. Subsequent references will be noted in the text.

18 For a full analysis of Vanbrugh's dependence upon Restoration convention, see Gerald M. Berkowitz, "Sir John Vanbrugh and the Conventions of Restoration Comedy," *Genre* 6 (1973): 346-61.

19 See Roper, "Language and Action in *The Way of the World, Love's Last Shift,* and *The Relapse,*" for a more detailed description of the collision of the language of wit and the language of virtue in this play.

20 See Lincoln B. Faller's "Between Jest and Earnest: The Comedy of Sir John Vanbrugh," *Modern Philology* 72 (1974): 17-29, for a detailed description of the psychological complexity represented in that play.

21 Dedication to *The Double-Dealer,* in *The Complete Plays of William Congreve,* ed. Herbert Davis (Chicago: Univ. of Chicago Press, 1967), p. 120. Subsequent references to Congreve's plays will be to this edition and will be noted in the text.

22 See I.i.321, II.i.312, IV.i.52-62, IV.ii.123-24 and 153, and V.i.153 and 264-66.

23 For a useful detailed discussion of the formal subordination of Mellefont to Maskwell, see Corman, "'The Mixed Way of Comedy': Congreve's *The Double Dealer,*" *Modern Philology* 71 (1974): 356-65.

24 Critics who have commented on the significance of Congreve's use of soliloquy include Palmer, *The Comedy of Manners,* pp. 154-56; Leech, "Congreve and the Century's End," *Philological Quarterly* 41 (1962): 275-93; W. H. Van Voris, *The Cultivated Stance: The Designs of Congreve's Plays* (Dublin: Dolmen Press, 1965), pp. 64-70; Muir, *The Comedy of Manners,* p. 104; and Novak, *William Congreve* (New York: Twayne, 1971), p. 104.

25 On the unusual seriousness of the play, see N. Holland, *The First Modern Comedies,* p. 160; Novak, "Love, Scandal, and the Moral Milieu of Congreve's Comedies," in *Congreve Consider'd,* by Aubrey Williams and Novak (Los Angeles: William Andrews Clark Memorial Library, UCLA, 1971), pp. 23-50; and William Myers, "Plot and Meaning in Congreve's Comedies," in *William Congreve,* ed. Brian Morris (London: Ernest Benn, 1972), pp. 73-92.

26 Novak, "Love, Scandal, and the Moral Milieu of Congreve's Comedies."

27 N. Holland, *The First Modern Comedies,* pp. 187-90; Donaldson, *The World Upside-Down,* pp. 125-31; Novak, *William Congreve,* pp. 148-49; and Hawkins, *Likenesses of Truth in Elizabethan and Restoration Drama,* pp. 119-23.

28 K. M. Lynch, *The Social Mode of Restoration Comedy,* pp. 201-03.

29 This trope begins its career early in the century with Palmer's characterization of *The Way of the World* as a "pageant" (p. 191) and Perry's emphasis on the play's superficiality (pp. 70-73). More recent critics have elaborated the metaphor, N. Holland (*The First Modern Comedies,* p. 197) and Van Voris (*The Cultivated Stance,* pp. 130-31, 146-48, and 151) by describing the self-referentiality of Congreve's dramatic artifice and H. Teyssandier in "Congreve's *Way of the World*: Decorum and Morality," *English Studies* 52 (1971): 124-31, by discovering an aesthetic ideal in the social decorums of the drama.

30 Gagen, "Congreve's Mirabell and the Ideal of the Gentleman," *PMLA* 79 (1964): 422-27.

31 McDonald, "Restoration Comedy as Drama of Satire."

32 For discussions of the ideology of Congreve's comedy, see Loftis, *Comedy and Society from Congreve to Fielding* (Stanford: Stanford Univ. Press, 1959), pp. 43-44; Van Voris, *The Cultivated Stance*, pp. 125-32, 139, and 149-50; Novak, "Love, Scandal, and the Moral Milieu of Congreve's Comedies"; and Myers, "Plot and Meaning in Congreve's Comedies."

33 Rothstein, *George Farquhar* (New York: Twayne, 1967), p. 167.

34 *Love and a Bottle*, in *The Complete Works of George Farquhar*, ed. Charles Stonehill (Bloomsbury: Nonesuch Press, 1930), vol. 1: V.iii, p. 73. Subsequent references to Farquhar's plays, except for *The Beaux' Stratagem*, will be to this edition and will be noted in the text.

35 On this mixture of forms, see Palmer, *The Comedy of Manners*, pp. 258-60; and Rothstein, *George Farquhar*, pp. 30-39.

36 For the important influence of this play on the new comic mode, see Shirley Strum Kenny, "Theatrical Warfare, 1695-1710," *Theatre Notebook* 27, No. 4 (1973): 130-45.

37 See J. H. Smith, *The Gay Couple*, p. 183, for further discussion of the mixture of risqué and sentimental in her character.

38 Rothstein, *George Farquhar*, pp. 61-62 and 70-71; and Hume, *The Development of English Drama*, p. 465.

39 Nicoll thought that Farquhar's professions of morality in the preface were probably satirical (*A History of English Drama 1660-1900*, vol. 2: *Early Eighteenth Century Drama*, 3rd ed. [Cambridge: Cambridge Univ. Press, 1952], p. 148). Rothstein, on the contrary, argues that the play is genuinely moral (*George Farquhar*, pp. 61-71). And Hume emphasizes the originality of the comedy and the complex irony of the preface (*The Development of English Drama*, pp. 464-65).

40 Peter Holland's interesting interpretation of the casting of *The Twin-Rivals* as a complex challenge to Restoration dramatic convention supplies another perspective on the transitional form of the play (*The Ornament of Action*, pp. 86-98).

41 Ernest Bernbaum, *The Drama of Sensibility: A Sketch of the History of English Sentimental Comedy and Domestic Tragedy 1696-1780* (Boston: Ginn, 1915), pp. 102-03; and Hume, *The Development of English Drama*, p. 466.

42 "Restoration Comedy as Drama of Satire."

43 On Farquhar's sympathy for the country, see Loftis, *Comedy and Society*, pp. 72-74; and Hume, *The Development of English Drama*, p. 466.

44 On the serious social and legal implications of Farquhar's treatment of divorce, see Martin A. Larson, "The Influence of Milton's Divine Tracts on Farquhar's *Beaux' Stratagem*," *PMLA* 39 (1924): 174-78; Gellert Spencer Alleman, *Matrimonial Law and the Materials of Restoration Comedy* (Wallingford, Pa.: n. pub., 1942), pp. 106-12; and Stone, *The Family, Sex and Marriage*, p. 327.

45 See *The Beaux' Stratagem*, ed. Michael Cordner (London: Ernest Benn, 1976), IV.i.418-44 and V.ii.51-61.

Chapter Five

1 Obviously the issue has great significance from an extrageneric perspective, and in fact the scholarship on sentimentalism establishes parameters for the description of its appearance in literature. See Crane, "Suggestions Toward a Genealogy of the 'Man of Feeling'"; Ernest Tuveson, "The Origins of the 'Moral Sense,'" *Huntington Library Quarterly* 11 (1947-48): 241-59; A. O. Aldridge, "The Pleasures of Pity," *ELH* 16 (1949): 76-87; Bredvold, *The Natural History of Sensibility* (Detroit: Wayne State Univ. Press, 1962); and Greene,

"Latitudinarianism and Sensibility: The Genealogy of the 'Man of Feeling' Reconsidered."

2 For a brief overview of the debate see: F. W. Bateson, *English Comic Drama, 1700-1750* (Oxford: Clarendon Press, 1929), ch. 1; DeWitt C. Croissant, "Studies in the Work of Colley Cibber," *Bulletin of the University of Kansas, Humanistic Studies* 1, No. 1 (1912), and "Early Sentimental Comedy," *Essays in Dramatic Literature: The Parrott Presentation Volume*, ed. Hardin Craig (Princeton: Princeton Univ. Press, 1935), pp. 47-71; Bernbaum, *The Drama of Sensibility*, pp. 2-10; Nicoll, vol. 1, pp. 263-64; K. M. Lynch, "Thomas D'Urfey's Contribution to Sentimental Comedy"; Joseph Wood Krutch, *Comedy and Conscience after the Restoration* (1924; rev. ed. New York: Columbia Univ. Press, 1949), pp. 228-58; J. H. Smith, "Shadwell, the Ladies, and the Change in Comedy," *Modern Philology* 46 (1948): 22-33, and *The Gay Couple*, pp. 131-34; Sherbo, *English Sentimental Drama*, ch. 1 and passim; Loftis, *Comedy and Society*, pp. 127-32; and Parnell, "The Sentimental Mask," *PMLA* 78 (1963): 529-35.

3 Goldsmith's comments on sentimental drama are particularly illuminating in this regard. He describes the collapse of generic distinctions as one of the most pernicious characteristics of the form. See *An Essay on the Theatre; or, A Comparison Between Laughing and Sentimental Comedy* (1772).

4 For relevant historical overviews, see J. H. Plumb, *England in the Eighteenth Century* (Harmondsworth: Penguin, 1950), especially pp. 11-33; and Hill, *The Century of Revolution*, Pt. IV.

5 Nicholas Rowe, *The Ambitious Step-Mother*, 2nd ed. (London: for R. Wellington and Thomas Osborne, 1702), sig. A3^r. Subsequent references to the prefatory material of this play will be to this edition and will be noted in the text.

6 For Rowe's use of the female lead, see Malcolm Goldstein, "Pathos and Personality in the Tragedies of Nicholas Rowe," in *English Writers of the Eighteenth Century*, ed. John H. Middendorf (New York: Columbia Univ. Press, 1971), pp. 172-85.

7 *The Fair Penitent*, ed. Goldstein (Lincoln: Univ. of Nebraska Press, 1969), p. 5, ll. 15-18. Subsequent references to this play will be to this edition and will be noted in the text.

8 Massinger and Field's *The Fatal Dowry*. See J. R. Sutherland, "Life of Nicholas Rowe," in *Three Plays*, by Nicholas Rowe, ed. Sutherland (London: Scholartis Press, 1929), pp. 25-27.

9 "The Nature of Tragedy in Rowe's *The Fair Penitent*," *Papers on Language and Literature* 2 (1966): 351-60.

10 For the problematic relationship between Rowe's and Marlowe's versions of the story, see Donald B. Clark, "The Source and Characterization of Nicholas Rowe's *Tamerlane*," *Modern Language Notes* 65 (1950): 145-52.

11 Rowe, *Tamerlane*, in *Three Plays*, ed. Sutherland, II.ii, p. 85. Subsequent references will be noted in the text.

12 Rowe acknowledges his allusion to William in his dedication, p. 53. See also Loftis, *The Politics of Drama*, pp. 31-34; and Willard Thorp, "A Key to Rowe's *Tamerlane*," *Journal of English and Germanic Philology* 39 (1940):124-27.

13 *The Tragedy of the Lady Jane Gray* (London: for Bernard Lintott, 1715), III.i, pp. 33-37.

14 Alfred Schwarz, "An Example of Eighteenth Century Pathetic Tragedy: Rowe's *Jane Shore*," *Modern Language Quarterly* 22 (1961): 236-47; and Harry William Pedicord, Introduction to his edition of *The Tragedy of Jane Shore* (Lincoln: Univ. of Nebraska Press, 1974), pp. xv-xvi and App. B.

15 *Jane Shore*, ed. Pedicord, p. 9. Subsequent references to this play will be to this edition and will be noted in the text.

16 For further analysis of the mitigation of Jane's guilt, see Canfield, *Nicholas Rowe and Christian Tragedy* (Gainesville: Univ. Presses of Florida, 1977), pp. 149-50.

17 *Nicholas Rowe and Christian Tragedy.*

18 Alexander Pope, Prologue to *Cato*, by Joseph Addison, in *British Dramatists from Dryden to Sheridan*, ed. George H. Nettleton and Arthur E. Case (Boston: Houghton Mifflin, 1939), p. 479, ll. 1-6. Subsequent references to this play will be to this edition and will be noted in the text.

19 Donaldson, "Cato in Tears: Stoical Guises of the Man of Feeling," in *Studies in the Eighteenth Century*, vol. 2, ed. R. F. Brissenden (Toronto: Univ. of Toronto Press, 1973), pp. 377-95.

20 Loftis, *The Politics of Drama*, pp. 57-61.

21 Preface to *The Fatal Extravagance* (London: for T. Jauncy, n.d. [1721]), sig. A4^r-a2^v. Though Mitchell claims to have written the play here, Hill is the most likely author; see Bernbaum, *The Drama of Sensibility*, p. 129; and Nicoll, *A History of English Drama*, vol. 2: *Early Eighteenth Century Drama*, p. 119.

22 Dedication to *The London Merchant*, by George Lillo, ed. McBurney (Lincoln: Univ. of Nebraska Press, 1965), p. 3, ll. 19-20. Subsequent references to this play will be to this edition and will be noted in the text.

23 Prologue to *Caelia: or, the Perjur'd Lover* (London: for J. Watts, 1733), sig. A3^{r-v}.

24 Henry Fielding, Prologue to *Fatal Curiosity*, by George Lillo, ed. McBurney (Lincoln: Univ. of Nebraska Press, 1966), p. 3, ll. 9-14. Subsequent references to this play will be to this edition and will be noted in the text.

25 *The Gamester*, with an introduction by Charles H. Peake (1756; rpt. n.p.: Augustan Reprint Society, 1948), p. 417.

26 For nationalism and imperialism, see I.i.31-43 and III.i.1-28; for "tradesmen's bills," see I.i.55-59; for the reception of the bourgeoisie at court, see V.ix.21-24; and for the rest, see the exchange between Thorowgood and Maria in I.ii.

27 Michael M. Cohen, "Providence and Constraint in Two Lillo Tragedies," *English Studies* 52 (1971): 231-36; and Herbert L. Carson, "The Play that Would Not Die: George Lillo's *The London Merchant*," *Quarterly Journal of Speech* 49 (1963): 287-94.

28 "The Ballad of George Barnwell," The Second Part, ll. 65-78 and 85-92, reprinted in McBurney's edition of *The London Merchant*, pp. 86-96. See also Bernbaum, *The Drama of Sensibility*, pp. 153-55.

29 Bernbaum, *The Drama of Sensibility*, pp. 153-55.

30 George Bush Rodman, "Sentimentalism in Lillo's *The London Merchant*," *ELH* 12 (1945): 45-61. The most recent statement of this antisentimental interpretation is Stephen L. Trainor, Jr.'s claim for Lillo's Calvinism in "Tears Abounding: *The London Merchant* as Puritan Tragedy," *Studies in English Literature, 1500-1900* 18 (1978): 509-21.

31 Raymond D. Havens, "The Sentimentalism of *The London Merchant*," *ELH* 12 (1945): 183-87.

32 McBurney, Introduction to *The London Merchant*, pp. xxi-xxv. One recent critic who notes the contradiction in Lillo's method is Cohen, who explains it as a problem in writing a tragedy that assumes the omnipotence of a benevolent God ("Providence and Constraint in Two Lillo Tragedies").

33 A familiar seventeenth-century criminal history. See McBurney's edition of *Fatal Curiosity*, App. B, pp. 55-58, and Introduction, p. xii.

34 For further discussion of the dissociation of character and destiny in the period, see Bernbaum, *The Drama of Sensibility*, pp. 110–14, 136, and 173.

35 This earlier play has its source in the protobourgeois *Yorkshire Tragedy* (Mitchell, Preface to *The Fatal Extravagance*, sig. a2^r; Bernbaum, *The Drama of Sensibility*, p. 130; and Nicoll, *A History of English Drama*, vol. 2: *Early Eighteenth Century Drama*, p. 119), and is also indebted to Trotter's *Fatal Friendship* (1698; Peake, Introduction to *The Gamester*, p. 2). It was originally written in one act, but in 1726 expanded to five (Bernbaum, *The Drama of Sensibility*, p. 129; Nicoll, *A History of English Drama*, vol. 2: *Early Eighteenth Century Drama*, p. 336).

36 Like Lillo, Hill too alters his source in order to ensure the essential innocence of the protagonist. See Bernbaum, *The Drama of Sensibility*, pp. 130–31; and Sherbo, *English Sentimental Drama*, pp. 26–27.

37 For further discussion, see John Wilson Bowyer, *The Celebrated Mrs. Centlivre* (Durham, N.C.: Duke Univ. Press, 1952), pp. 172–76.

38 See also, for instance, Charles Shadwell's *The Fair Quaker of Deal; or, The Humours of the Navy* (1710) or Charles Johnson's *The Wife's Relief; or, The Husband's Cure* (1711).

39 Bernbaum, *The Drama of Sensibility*, p. 101; Sherbo, *English Sentimental Drama*, pp. 81–83 and 105–06; and Kenny, "Richard Steele and the 'Pattern of Genteel Comedy,'" *Modern Philology* 70 (1972): 22–37.

40 *The Funeral*, in *The Plays of Richard Steele*, ed. Kenny (Oxford: Clarendon Press, 1971), V.iv.83–97. Subsequent references to all of Steele's plays will be to this edition and will be noted in the text.

41 Bernbaum, *The Drama of Sensibility*, pp. 88–89; Kenny, "Richard Steele and the 'Pattern of Genteel Comedy,'" and "Humane Comedy," *Modern Philology* 75 (1977): 29–43; and Hume, *The Development of English Drama*, pp. 439–40.

42 On the symptomatic incongruity of the Newgate scene, see Kenny, "Richard Steele and the 'Pattern of Genteel Comedy.'"

43 Steele's use of his source corresponds to the formal shift in the play. He follows *Le Menteur* (Corneille, 1642) quite closely through the first four acts, and abandons it completely in Act V (*The Plays of Richard Steele*, ed. Kenny, pp. 103–04).

44 Loftis, *Steele at Drury Lane* (Berkeley and Los Angeles: Univ. of California Press, 1952), pp. 183–93.

45 Steele, like many mid-eighteenth-century critics, misread Terence as a sentimental dramatist, specifically mistranslating a comic line from *Heautontimorumenos* (*The Spectator*, ed. Donald F. Bond [Oxford: Clarendon Press, 1965], vol. 4, pp. 280–93 [No. 502, 6 October 1712]). See Bernbaum, *The Drama of Sensibility*, pp. 16–21.

46 On the ideology of both plays, see Loftis, *The Politics of Drama*, p. 125.

47 See II.iii.90–96 for his generosity toward the talented but poor; II.iii.128–44 for his preference for thinking over eating, his opposition to excessive expenditures on horses, and his dislike of dogs, cards, dice, drinking companions, and loose women; V.iii.100 for his plain manner of dress; Preface, p. 299, ll. 17–19 and IV.i.201–18 for dueling; and passim for the rest.

48 For an enlightening discussion of the relation between the damaging inconsistencies in this comedy and Fielding's didactic latitudinarian morality, see Michael Irwin, *Henry Fielding: The Tentative Realist* (Oxford: Clarendon Press, 1967), pp. 27–29.

49 This play was performed late. For its placement between *Rape upon Rape* and *The Modern Husband* in Fielding's career, see L. P. Goggin, "Development of Techniques in Fielding's Comedies," *PMLA* 67 (1952): 769–81.

50 See ibid.
51 For Fielding's increasing technical skills in the standard comedy, see Winfield H. Rogers, "Fielding's Early Aesthetic and Technique," *Studies in Philology* 40 (1943): 529-51; and Goggin, "Development of Techniques in Fielding's Comedies."
52 For further discussion of Fielding's problems with good nature, see Jack D. Durant, "The 'Art of Thriving' in Fielding's Comedies," in *A Provision of Human Nature: Essays on Fielding and Others in Honor of Miriam Austin Locke*, ed. Donald Kay (University, Alabama: Univ. of Alabama Press, 1977), pp. 25-35.
53 Prologue to *The Modern Husband* (Dublin: S. Powell for G. Risk and others, 1732), sig. A3^{r-v}. Subsequent references to this play will be to this edition and will be noted in the text.
54 For a recent acknowledgement of the special nature of this play, see Loftis, "The Social and Literary Context," in *The Revels History*, pp. 72-73.
55 Leo Hughes, *A Century of English Farce* (Princeton: Princeton Univ. Press, 1956), pp. 73-93.
56 Nicoll, *A History of English Drama*, vol. 2: *Early Eighteenth Century Drama*, pp. 216-17.
57 For the inventiveness and superiority of Fielding's burlesque, see W. R. Irwin, "Satire and Comedy in the Works of Henry Fielding," *ELH* 13 (1946): 168-88; J. Paul Hunter, *Occasional Form: Henry Fielding and the Chains of Circumstance* (Baltimore: Johns Hopkins Univ. Press, 1975), ch. 3; and Jean B. Kern, "Fielding's Dramatic Satire," *Philological Quarterly* 54 (1975): 239-57.
58 For an argument emphasizing the importance of the Licensing Act, see Loftis, *The Politics of Drama*, pp. 150-53.
59 This is the most commonly held thesis in regard to the decline of the drama, and it has taken a variety of forms. Krutch, *Comedy and Conscience after the Restoration*, pp. 248-58; Sherbo, *English Sentimental Drama*, p. vii; and Muir, *The Comedy of Manners*, pp. 154-55, blame the death of drama on sentimentalism. Dobrée, *Restoration Tragedy*, pp. 157-61; J. H. Smith, *The Gay Couple*, pp. 225-30; and Birdsall, *Wild Civility*, pp. 250-52, accuse the middle class or the "reforming impulse." MacMillan, "The Rise of Social Comedy in the Eighteenth Century," *Philological Quarterly* 41 (1962): 330-38, specifically cites the failure of the tragedy to reflect contemporary society. And Eugene Hnatko, "The Failure of Eighteenth-Century Tragedy," *Studies in English Literature, 1500-1900* 11 (1971): 459-68, claims the problem is the adherence to poetic justice. For useful alternative interpretations closer to and supportive of my own, see John W. Draper, "The Theory of the Comic in Eighteenth-Century England," *Journal of English and Germanic Philology* 37 (1938): 207-23; James J. Lynch, *Box, Pit, and Gallery: Stage and Society in Johnson's London* (Berkeley and Los Angeles: Univ. of California Press, 1953), pp. 175-76; McBurney, Introduction to *The London Merchant*, p. xxv; M. Irwin, *Henry Fielding: The Tentative Realist*, pp. 38-40; and Hunter, Afterword to *Occasional Form*.

Chapter Six

1 Watt, *The Rise of the Novel*.
2 Tillyard, *The Epic Strain in the English Novel* (London: Chatto and Windus, 1958), pp. 197-98.
3 Spearman, *The Novel and Society* (London: Routledge and Kegan Paul, 1966), ch. 2.

4   Alter, *Fielding and the Nature of the Novel* (Cambridge: Harvard Univ. Press, 1968) and *Partial Magic: The Novel as a Self-Conscious Genre* (Berkeley and Los Angeles: Univ. of California Press, 1975).
5   For the treatment of romance, the French novella, epistolary fiction, novels of manners, domestic history, and related works, see Charlotte E. Morgan, *The Rise of the Novel of Manners: A Study of English Prose Fiction Between 1600 and 1740* (New York: Columbia Univ. Press, 1911); Arthur Jerrold Tieje, "A Peculiar Phase of the Theory of Realism in Pre-Richardsonian Fiction," *PMLA* 28 (1913): 213-52; Helen Sard Hughes, "English Epistolary Fiction Before *Pamela*," in *The Manly Anniversary Studies in Language and Literature* (Chicago: Univ. of Chicago Press, 1923), pp. 156-69; Ernest A. Baker, *The History of the English Novel*, vol. 3: *The Later Romances and the Establishment of Realism* (London: H. F. and G. Witherby, 1929), pp. 11-37 and 79-129; B. G. MacCarthy, *Women Writers: Their Contribution to the English Novel, 1621-1744* (Cork: Cork Univ. Press, 1944); Robert Adams Day, *Told in Letters: Epistolary Fiction Before Richardson* (Ann Arbor: Univ. of Michigan Press, 1966); Charles C. Mish, "English Short Fiction in the Seventeenth Century," *Studies in Short Fiction* 6 (1969): 233-330; and Margaret Anne Doody, *A Natural Passion: A Study of the Novels of Samuel Richardson* (Oxford: Clarendon Press, 1974), ch. 2.
6   For the description of the popular tradition in the seventeenth and eighteenth centuries, see John J. Richetti, *Popular Fiction Before Richardson: Narrative Patterns, 1700-1739* (Oxford: Clarendon Press, 1969); Mish, "English Short Fiction in the Seventeenth Century"; and George A. Starr, *Defoe and Spiritual Autobiography* (Princeton: Princeton Univ. Press, 1965).
7   For accounts of the antiromantic, satiric, picaresque, or Spanish tradition, see E. A. Baker, *The History of the English Novel*, vol. 3: *The Later Romances and the Establishment of Realism*, pp. 38-49; Martin C. Battestin, *The Moral Basis of Fielding's Art: A Study of "Joseph Andrews"* (Middletown, Conn.: Wesleyan Univ. Press, 1959), pp. 85-87; Mish, "English Short Fiction in the Seventeenth Century"; Novak, "Some Notes Toward a History of Fictional Forms: From Aphra Behn to Daniel Defoe," *Novel* 6 (1973): 120-33; and Hunter, *Occasional Form*, pp. 15-19. It is tempting to argue that the line of influence passes from Spanish to English realism: Richardson is Cervantes's heir by way of the early importation of the Spanish-influenced French romantic *nouvelle*; Fielding is Cervantes's heir more directly, by way of the self-conscious and antiromantic narrative of *Don Quixote.* Thus Richardson and Fielding, romantic and antiromantic, arise from the same source and together establish the genre in England.
8   See Bernbaum, *The Drama of Sensibility*, pp. 112-14 and passim; Ira Konigsberg, *Samuel Richardson and the Dramatic Novel* (Lexington: Univ. of Kentucky Press, 1968), ch. 2 and passim; and Richetti, *Popular Fiction Before Richardson*, ch. 5 and passim.
9   See Day, *Told in Letters*, ch. 4.
10 Mish, "English Short Fiction in the Seventeenth Century," p. 330.
11 Day, *Told in Letters*, pp. 210-11. For a similar assessment of Richardson's originality, see Richetti, *Popular Fiction Before Richardson*, pp. 262-65.
12 Rader, "Defoe, Richardson, Joyce," pp. 38-47.
13 See Loftis, *Comedy and Society*, p. 137.
14 Rader, "Defoe, Richardson, Joyce," pp. 34-35.
15 For a very full and convincing documentation of the novel's comic intention, see Doody, *A Natural Passion*, ch. 3. Sacks, however, finds *Pamela* to be a "serious" and not a comic action (*Fiction and the Shape of Belief*, pp. 22-23).

16 Rader, "Defoe, Richardson, Joyce," p. 35.
17 Watt, *The Rise of the Novel*, pp. 208-09 and 288-91.
18 Rader, "Defoe, Richardson, Joyce," p. 68, n. 6.
19 For other discussions of this parallel, see: Bernbaum, *The Drama of Sensibility*, p. 165; Nicoll, *A History of English Drama*, vol. 2: *Early Eighteenth Century Drama*, p. 122; Alan Dugald McKillop, *Samuel Richardson: Printer and Novelist* (Chapel Hill: Univ. of North Carolina Press, 1936), p. 144; Loftis, *Comedy and Society*, p. 137; George Sherburn, "Samuel Richardson's Novels and the Theatre: A Theory Sketched," *Philological Quarterly* 41 (1962): 325-29; and especially Konigsberg, *Samuel Richardson and the Dramatic Novel*, pp. 40-45. The most recent studies of Richardson, however, do not mention the similarity, either to affirm or deny it. See Doody, *A Natural Passion*; and Mark Kinkead-Weekes, *Samuel Richardson: Dramatic Novelist* (Ithaca, N.Y.: Cornell Univ. Press, 1973). T. C. Duncan Eaves and Ben D. Kimpel, *Samuel Richardson: A Biography* (Oxford: Clarendon Press, 1971), dismiss the issue in a phrase (p. 235).
20 For a different view of Congreve's significance, which sees him not as a dead end but rather as a link between drama and novel, see Loftis, *The Politics of Drama*, pp. 152-53; and Donaldson, *The World Upside-Down*, pp. 122-23.
21 Battestin, *The Moral Basis of Fielding's Art*, chs. 3 and 6; and Rader, "Idea and Structure in Fielding's Novels," Ph. D. Diss., Univ. of Indiana, 1957.
22 For a contrasting view, which sees it as a coherent "episodic action," see Sacks, *Fiction and the Shape of Belief*, pp. 24-25.
23 For the relation between Tom's moral virtue and Fielding's view of contemporary society, see M. Irwin, *Henry Fielding: The Tentative Realist*, pp. 111-12.
24 Crane, "The Concept of Plot and the Plot of *Tom Jones*."
25 Robert V. Wess, "The Probable and the Marvelous in *Tom Jones*," *Modern Philology* 68 (1970): 32-45.
26 Wayne C. Booth, *The Rhetoric of Fiction* (Chicago: Univ. of Chicago Press, 1961), p. 217.
27 See, for example, Sherbo, *English Sentimental Drama*, ch. 3.
28 Peter Holland's recent examination of the casting and staging of Restoration comedy in *The Ornament of Action*, for instance, though very different in scope and conclusion from this essay, documents a recurrent tension between satiric convention and sentimental or bourgeois values in the plays of the 1690s that closely matches my description of the formal incoherence of transitional comedy. In his analysis of the casting in particular, Holland discovers "a reexamination of the methods of contemporary comedy" (p. 148), an "exhaustion of a mode of drama" (p. 150), "a drift away from conventional satire" (p. 153), and "an attack on the conventional forms of comedy" (p. 157).

INDEX